ADVENTURE
IN
POLITICS

ALSO BY DONALD YOUNG

AMERICAN ROULETTE
The History and Dilemma of
the Vice Presidency

ADVENTURE IN POLITICS:

THE MEMOIRS OF PHILIP LaFOLLETTE

EDITED BY
DONALD YOUNG

HOLT, RINEHART AND WINSTON

NEW YORK   CHICAGO   SAN FRANCISCO

GRATEFUL ACKNOWLEDGMENT IS MADE TO THE FOLLOWING:
SUNPAPERS FOR EXCERPTS FROM THE SUN.
THE MACMILLAN COMPANY FOR EXCERPTS FROM ROBERT M. LaFOLLETTE:
JUNE 14, 1855–JUNE 18, 1925 BY BELLE CASE LaFOLLETTE.
COPYRIGHT 1953 BY FOLA LaFOLLETTE.

CONTENTS

Eight pages of black and white photos follow page 140.

FOREWORD

Few families in American public life have rivaled the LaFollettes of Wisconsin in intellectual brilliance, uncompromising integrity, and in success at the voting booth. And few families have experienced so much travail. Robert LaFollette, Sr., was designated in 1957 by the United States Senate as one of five outstanding men who had ever served in that body—only thirty-nine years after LaFollette's colleagues had nearly succeeded in expelling him from the Senate on a charge of treason. Before entering the Senate, "Old Bob," as governor of Wisconsin, had built the foundation for the Progressive Era by winning adoption of a body of reform legislation unsurpassed in state government throughout American history. His sons, Bob, Jr., and Phil, carried the Progressive legacy through another generation, achieved great distinction, and then saw their aspirations end in frustration and tragedy.

Phil and Bob, Jr., were among the last of the classical Middle Western Progressive insurgents. The LaFollette brothers and the political leaders who stood with them saw their careers and some of the causes for which they fought damaged during the New Deal period and then obliterated by World War II and the conservative reaction that followed. Nationally, the dominant wing of the Democratic party subsequently continued along the paths laid down in the thirties—concentration of power in the central government at the expense of the states, and commitment to internationalism in foreign affairs. The Republican party—certainly the midwestern division—settled for the smug comforts of a more affluent Main Street. And the third party movements and rumors of third party movements that had swept the prairies like angry dust storms for three quarters of a century seemingly vanished from the political landscape without a trace.

By the end of the 1960's, however, political orthodoxies were increasingly being called into question again. The remote and heavily bureaucratized federal government seemed less able than in the past to satisfy the demands of a volatile population. Furthermore, the United States was encountering grave difficulties in achieving its diplomatic and military objectives overseas.

Therefore, the publication at this time of the memoirs of Philip LaFollette is fortunate, not because he addressed himself directly to the issues of today—he died in 1965—but because he has recounted the part that he and his family played in the fight for vigorous and creative state government and because he recalls the abuse to which the members of his family were subjected for voicing dissent against wars that they believed were instigated by the arms manufacturers and by undemocratic foreign "allies."

Phil's family found in politics and public service a commitment, a livelihood, and a way of life, and his memoirs are at once a moving personal story and a dramatic chronicle of men and events.

In the last third of the nineteenth century, American farmers found themselves in a difficult economic situation for several complicated reasons that included the collapse of a frenzied western land boom, overproduction as a result of improved machinery, and the increased worldwide competition for markets caused by a revolution in transportation. Agrarian discontent was first of all directed at the railroads, on which the farmer had to rely to get his produce to market and which were owned by several eastern capitalists who dictated the freight rates. The control of money and credit by a few more easterners, excessive charges by grain elevator operators, plus a tariff designed to favor manufacturers, also angered the farmers.

The government of the United States was then the patron of the moneyed interests, but new men writing new laws could create new bases of economic power. Men of the frontier turned somewhat reluctantly and yet resolutely, said Frederick Jackson Turner, "from the ideal of individualism to the ideal of social control through regulation by law." This ideal gave rise to the Populist Movement of the 1890's. However, Populists proved vulnerable to charges of radicalism and anarchism; they viewed issues and solutions in simplistic terms, and their rural orientation did not attract significant urban support. But from 1900 on, the sense of dissatisfaction with things as they were came to be shared widely by small businessmen, professional people, and intellectuals. With respect to these groups, Richard Hofstadter has written, "One of the primary tests of the mood of a society at any given time is whether the comfortable people tend to identify, psychologically, with the power and achievements of the very successful or with the needs and sufferings of the under-privileged." The comfortable people disapproved of the new class of scandalously rich railroad and financial magnates, and they also disdained the corrupt and cynical bosses who manipulated public affairs through stuffed ballot boxes, rigged conventions, and bribed legislators. The middle class response was, of course, due in part to a decline in its own status in the community as a result of the rise of the exploiters. But its response was remarkably altruistic, and its thrust toward social and political reform catalyzed the Progressive Era.

The Progressive Movement was characterized by a commitment to bring equality and human dignity to all people and by a resolve to achieve its objectives within the existing social and political framework rather than through social upheaval and revolution. Progressives were willing to study the issues carefully to find solutions that would serve the greatest public good rather than the particular advantage of any person or group. And they effected a ground swell at the political grass roots that extended in due course to the state capitals and finally to the seat of the federal government.

Lord Bryce, British ambassador to the United States early in this century, observed that the American state can serve as a laboratory where experiments that succeed may benefit the nation at large, while those that fail will cause harm only within the boundaries of a single state. Wisconsin, more than any other state, has served as a laboratory for political and social reform. The political scientists who concocted their Progressive reforms in this midwestern laboratory were initially mobilized and energized by Bob LaFollette, Sr. His wife, Belle Case LaFollette, wrote after his death, "In his early manhood the conviction was deeply implanted, to become the very fiber of his political thought, that our government was being subverted from its true purpose by the great corporate interests and that the people were thereby being robbed of their birthright."

Under the elder LaFollette and the other Progressive governors of his generation, Wisconsin established the direct primary, the taxation of railroads on the basis of the value of their property, a railroad commission to regulate rates, a workmen's compensation law, the income tax and other reforms designed to distribute the tax burden more equitably, a pure-food law, restrictions on child labor, a corrupt practices act, teachers' pensions, a civil service law, and other reforms. Other states moved fitfully along the same lines, but the Wisconsin effort was distinguished by the practicality and comprehensiveness of the program as a whole and by the efficiency and honesty with which it was administered.

In waging the protracted and often bitter fight for this program, LaFollette, Sr., and his associates enlisted the support of the University of Wisconsin. Philip LaFollette describes at length in these pages the intimate relationship between the campus and the capitol—a relationship that inspired one political opponent to ask, "Do we want a State University or a University State?" It is sufficient to say here that this relationship was the principal feature of what is called the "Wisconsin Idea."

But the famous Idea was primarily a blueprint for action. The LaFollettes were activists, not theoreticians. During his own governorship Philip LaFollette grew impatient with what he viewed as the preoccupation of some New Dealers with abstractions. He told an interviewer, "I'm not against ideas. I do my share of theorizing. Theory, of course, is necessary, but theories, discussion, resolutions are empty, futile, provocative of wasteful dissension if they do not soon lead to practical, constructive action. The important, the practical thing about the Wisconsin Idea has been—and still is—that it produced the Progressive movement, which has been—and is—dedicated to action, to doing things for the people, making for progress, not on some distant tomorrow but now, as soon as humanly possible. . . . It is no accident that nearly every forward-looking, concrete achievement in public affairs during the past thirty years has had its origins in action in Wisconsin."

Bob LaFollette the elder was short in physical stature, although his dynamic appearance, abetted by his pompadour-style hair, made him seem larger than he was. On the stump, he could hold an audience for hours, overwhelming them with facts and figures, the logic of his arguments, and his sharp political—though rarely personal—attacks on his opponents. LaFollette's strength derived from his statewide army of political volunteers and from the deep mutual affection that bound him and his constituents. Wis-

consin progressivism was not monolithic, and some of his lieutenants were alienated by his moral rigidity, his unwillingness to
compromise, and his tempestuous nature. But these personal characteristics were, paradoxically, sources of his political strength
as well.

LaFollette's wife was his loyal partner throughout his political
career. A crusader no less than her husband, Belle Case LaFollette
fought for woman's suffrage, disarmament, consumer protection,
reform in women's dress, and the abolition of discrimination
against Negroes in the District of Columbia.

Robert and Belle Case LaFollette had four children. Fola, the
oldest, was an actress and the wife of George Middleton, the
playwright. Mary was the youngest. Bob, Jr., was the older son,
and his character was shaped by his deep devotion to his parents
as well as by chronic and debilitating illnesses. While in his early
twenties Bob, Jr., nearly succumbed to a general body infection
that denied him a college degree and left him an invalid for years.
Major and minor ailments recurred frequently throughout his
life and eventually included heart trouble. He became cautious
and reserved. One Wisconsin newspaperman recalls young Bob
as "a truly *gentle* man."

For the last six years of his father's life, Bob, Jr., was his
secretary and confidant. On the campaign trail, he would sit
inside the automobile with the local politicians and engage in political "shop talk" while his father or younger brother harangued
the crowd. Although popular socially, he was introspective and
anxious ("I still have ⅖ of a degree of temperature today," he
wrote his family in 1925) and did not seem marked for great
success. Mrs. Philip LaFollette, in her unpublished memoirs, recalls that in the early 1920's "one of the main topics of family
discussion . . . was 'What is Bobby going to do?,' as his many
abilities were obvious but he had not found the desired avenue.
Each time he was about to strike out on his own road, however,
some crisis . . . seemed to make it impossible for him to leave
his father at that particular moment."

After his father died, Bob, Jr., was thrust somewhat reluctantly
into a senatorial election at the age of thirty. He became the
youngest senator since Henry Clay, and it was in the Senate that
his promise was fulfilled brilliantly. Unlike his father, Bob became a senator's senator, ready to compromise at the crucial
moment, a master of parliamentary procedure, a young man who

manifested respect for his elders and who during twenty-one years in the Senate came to command great respect and affection himself.

He became a champion of labor, heading a subcommittee to investigate violations of the rights of free speech and assembly and the right of labor to organize and bargain collectively. Long before Franklin Roosevelt was elected, Bob sought to get funds for relief and public works to the states. A Senate authority on taxes, he was instrumental in securing a sharply graduated tax structure. He supported the Good Neighbor Policy, reciprocal trade agreements, and United States membership in the United Nations (but not in the League of Nations). He initially opposed United States entry into World War II. His last great achievement was the Congressional Reorganization Act of 1946, which streamlined the committee system and greatly improved the efficiency of the legislative branch.

When in 1955, Philip LaFollette presented his own papers to the State Historical Society, a writer for the *Wisconsin Magazine of History* observed that he had been "part of the Wisconsin political scene since his birth in 1897." From the time Phil was three years old his father served in high public office, and the younger son held his father in awe and deep respect from earliest childhood. Phil inherited his father's superior mind, his inner fire and impetuosity, his skill as an orator and political organizer, and his size—he weighed only 124 pounds when first elected governor at the age of thirty-three. He was the son of a great and beloved man, he was impatient, imperious, ambitious, and aggressive, and his career was a beneficiary and a victim of all these factors. While a student at the university Phil endured with the rest of his family the hysteria that came with World War I. The burning in effigy of his father was but one humiliation meted out by the people of Madison to the family that had been so devoted to the city and its welfare.

Phil's political values were the same as his father's, and one can do no better in characterizing the son than quote from his father's autobiography: "I believe that half a loaf is fatal whenever it is accepted at the sacrifice of the basic principle sought to be attained. Half a loaf, as a rule, dulls the appetite, and destroys the keenness of interest in attaining the full loaf. A halfway measure never fairly tests the principle and may utterly discredit

it. It is certain to weaken, disappoint, and dissipate public interest. Concession and compromise are almost always necessary
in legislation, but they call for the most thorough and complete
mastery of the principles involved, in order to fix the limit beyond which not one hair's breadth can be yielded."

Philip LaFollette held a law degree and practiced law from
time to time, but he aimed at public office, and the aim was high.
Not one to run from a fight, he always pushed harder and harder,
against ever more formidable odds—his ultimate goal was the
Presidency—until he was so overwhelmingly defeated that his
public career was ended when he was forty-one. His fortunes as
governor rose or fell with his degree of success in getting his
program through a skeptical and fractious legislature. His pro-
nouncements could be unexceptionable; in addressing Harvard
business students he observed that Wisconsin "is in the best sense
conservative, in that Wisconsin aims to conserve and preserve
our best American traditions. We have at times been ahead of the
rest of the country in recognizing the need for common action.
But the form of that action has always preserved individual
opportunity and responsibility."

This statement might be reassuring to political leaders holding
traditional views. Yet LaFollette came to the governorship during
the Great Depression—and everything in his upbringing and
temperament compelled him to seek bold new methods of attaining unemployment relief and other measures that would create
wealth and distribute it more equitably. Inaugurated in 1931, he
had to act two years before Franklin Roosevelt became President. Later in these pages, the governor describes his program,
including unemployment compensation and other labor legislation, reorganization of state government, rural electrification and
public ownership of utilities, and public works. One need add
here only that his capacity to grasp economic concepts beyond
the reach of other men and his desire to act at once on any question led to great difficulties with the legislative branch.

David Lilienthal, a LaFollette appointee and later chairman of
the United States Atomic Energy Commission, has a high regard
for LaFollette's ability to attract able young men to public service and has pointed out that "Many of the best things that were
part of the New Deal . . . came out of the minds and imagina-
tions of the men and women who were around Phil in Madison
in 1931–1933." Lilienthal regards LaFollette as one of the ablest
administrators he has ever known in government.

During the 1930's, Phil became increasingly controversial and radical. In 1934 he and his brother led their Progressive flock out of the Republican party, which had been the family's uneasy home for fifty years. Not surprisingly, the LaFollettes and their supporters chose the name "Progressive Party" for their new political vehicle. At that time, with a look sideways at the New Deal Democrats, Phil said, "We are not liberals. Liberalism is nothing but a sort of milk and water tolerance." He accepted the appellation "radical" in the sense "that radicalism implies that you mean business."

During his third term as governor Phil became somewhat disillusioned with the democratic process, notably the interminable struggles with the legislature. He favored a plan by which executive and legislative roles would be reversed, with the governor empowered to create laws that would stand unless vetoed by the legislature. "I've lived with the legislature for three terms and it is discouraging," he said in 1937. He visited Germany three times during the 1930's and of course found the cruelties of the Nazi regime reprehensible. And yet he also found something to approve in Germany. Max Lerner, after interviewing LaFollette in 1938, wrote, "He thinks that it is easy to underestimate Hitler's positive achievements, and admires the energy he has shown in reorganizing an anarchic economy. Even more is he impressed by what Mustapha Kemal has done in Turkey in evoking a new economic energy and a new nationalism. . . . Phil insists that the nationalist pattern is a deep and slumbering force in American life, with enormous power for evoking middle-class and mass support."

In 1938, Governor LaFollette announced the founding of the National Progressives of America, a movement that he hoped would lead to a new political party. Its formation was tied to the expectation that the Democratic party would fall back into conservative hands after President Roosevelt's presumed retirement. But it was Governor LaFollette who retired from public life—involuntarily—after losing his bid for reelection in 1938. Then, in a flurry of speeches and articles, Phil supported efforts to keep the United States out of World War II. But after Pearl Harbor was bombed, LaFollette volunteered his services, as he had in World War I.

Like his father, Phil had an intelligent and politically astute wife who helped fight his battles. After marrying into the family, Isabel Bacon LaFollette attained an understanding no outsider could possess. In her own unpublished memoirs she records that the LaFollettes "always remained a closed corporation to the outside world. I came to appreciate that this developed from the terrific pounding they had taken from the opposition, especially during the first World War, on account of Senator LaFollette's political views. While we Bacon girls had always engaged in internecine battle when so disposed and let the fur fly where it might, the LaFollettes when I came to know them were, although deeply devoted, very restrained, and treated each other with the utmost seriousness. I remember once casually remarking to Bob, Jr., that Glenn Roberts, Phil's assistant district attorney and later his law partner, thought Phil was perfect. Instantly Bob shot back, 'Well, he is!' Not being of the 'blood royal'. . . I couldn't help being amused."

Phil and Bob did not always see eye to eye. Bob, serving in Washington, developed a different perspective on public affairs. He was less ready to criticize the New Deal, whose domestic policies he generally supported, and he enjoyed a good personal relationship with FDR. He did not share Phil's enthusiasm for the third-party movements of 1934 and 1938. He relied on Phil to look after their political organization in Wisconsin and was displeased when his brother entered the army during World War II. Phil, for his part, felt that Bob was not hitting hard enough at the issues during his later years in the Senate. That both were mentioned as presidential possibilities did not, however, lead to rivalry. Phil had presidential ambitions, but Bob had no interest in the office.

During all the years that the LaFollettes figured prominently in Wisconsin politics, the state Democratic party was weak and conservative. Since World War II it has taken on a vigorous liberal cast, and many of its present leaders were nourished on LaFollette progressivism. Bronson Cutting LaFollette, son of Bob, Jr., was elected state attorney general in 1964 at the age of twenty-eight. He was reelected in 1966 and was the unsuccessful Democratic candidate for governor in 1968.

Philip LaFollette considered public life a high calling, and he hoped that his memoirs would be read widely by young people who might be moved to follow in his footsteps. Because he died before the memoirs were in final order, I have ventured to make editorial revisions in several forms. First of all, the manuscript has been somewhat compressed through the elimination of material of marginal interest to the general reader, and some of the remaining material has been rearranged for clarity and continuity. Furthermore, I have found it advisable to add certain factual data to assist the reader not intimately familiar with this period of Wisconsin history. These data appear in italics. Italics are also used to introduce documents that were not part of LaFollette's manuscript, as well as some reminiscences of Mrs. Philip LaFollette. All documents so introduced are in the Philip Fox La-Follette papers in the State Historical Society of Wisconsin. I do not feel that their inclusion is inconsistent with the purpose of the book. The author's death broadens somewhat the range of material that is now suitable for publication, and his inclusion of these documents in his papers suggests his intention that they be considered for publication after his death. I believe that they add to the understanding of the governor and his family.

I have not presumed to debate the governor in his own book. Many people will, of course, not share his assessment of the political scene in all particulars. My own brief summary of his character, personality, and career has been based on majority viewpoints of contemporaries and scholars, and it suggests the framework within which a rounded evaluation of LaFollette's career can be made.

The publication of this book could not have been possible without the dedication and cooperation of Mrs. Isabel Bacon LaFollette. I also wish to acknowledge the assistance of the following persons who shared their recollections with me or who read all or part of the manuscript at some stage and offered helpful comments, or who did both:

Gordon Sinykin and Glenn Roberts, former law partners of Governor LaFollette; David E. Lilienthal, chairman of the board of the Development and Resources Corporation; Elizabeth Brandeis, Paul W. Glad, Harold Groves, Merle Curti, Paul A. Raushenbush, Walter Brandeis Raushenbush, and E. M. Coffman of the University of Wisconsin; Harold C. Deutsch of the University of Minnesota; the late John M. Gaus of Harvard University; Arthur J. Altmeyer, former United States commissioner for social security; Jack K. Kyle, former chairman of the state central committee of the Wisconsin Progressive party; Fred E. Risser and Stanley W. Slagg, former members of the Wisconsin state legislature; Morris Rubin, editor of *The Progressive;* John Wyngaard, manager of the Madison News Bureau; and William Haygood, editor of the *Wisconsin Magazine of History.* I also wish to acknowledge the assistance of Leslie H. Fishel, Jr., former director of the State Historical Society of Wisconsin, and the members of his staff, including Mrs. Margaret Hafstad, Miss Josephine Harper, and Paul Vanderbilt.

A bibliographical note and a note on sources follow the main text.

—Donald Young

ADVENTURE
IN
POLITICS

1

GROWING UP

WHAT MILLIONS COULD BUY THAT LIFE TODAY?

I was born in Madison, Wisconsin, on May 8, 1897, the third child and second son of Robert Marion and Belle Case LaFollette. The date of my birth and the fact that I was the younger son were controlling influences on my public career. Public affairs and politics dominated the life of the family into which I was born. One of my earliest recollections—when I was about 3½ years old—is of my maternal grandmother coming into the room where I was looking at a picture book and sucking my thumb. She said, "Phil, your father has just been elected governor of Wisconsin, and we can't have the governor's son sucking his thumb."

With few exceptions, this is a firsthand story—an account of people and events as it was given to me to see, hear, and understand.

My great-great-grandfather LaFollette came to this country with his father and two brothers about 1745. They were French Huguenots who came to New Jersey from the valley of the Loire in France. It is a family tradition that during the provincial wars at the end of the twelfth century an ancestor, known for his headlong bravery, was surnamed "Le Follet"—The Reckless. This was the family name until the brothers, who admired General LaFayette, under whom they may have served at Yorktown, changed the spelling to its present form. In the family Bible of Joseph LaFollette (my father's great-grandfather) the births of the first four children are entered under Le Follet, and those born later under La Follette.

After the Revolution, Joseph and his second wife moved from New Jersey to Virginia and then over the Cumberland Pass. He bought farmland near Hodgenville, Kentucky. The farm where my grandfather was born adjoined that of the Lincolns. Trouble over land titles led them (as well as the Lincolns) to leave Hodgenville and go to Indiana and then (in the case of my grandfather) to Dane County, Wisconsin.

My paternal grandmother was born in 1817 in Indiana. Her paternal grandfather came from northern Ireland. He was a revolutionary soldier who came to Indiana from North Carolina in 1809. The Fergusons (my paternal grandmother's maiden name) were, of course, Scots.

My mother's family took the northern route to the West from Vermont to Ohio, stopping off for a time in Elyria before coming to Wisconsin. My maternal grandfather Case had an English name, but his forebears bore good Scot names such as Cahoon and Moore. And his wife, Mary Nesbit, was pure Scot. So, in spite of our French name, our predominant strain is Scot and English.

Mother's family were pioneer farmers. She was raised on a farm near Baraboo, Wisconsin. She walked two miles each way to school. She was eager to learn and was never late or absent, from grade school through high school. Her family, by skimping and saving, paid for her modest needs while she was in college so she could devote herself to study. Mother graduated at the head of her class, but she was not a grind. People who knew her in her younger days reported her as being gay, high-spirited, and having the most contagious laugh they ever heard.

My paternal grandfather died when my father was a baby, and Dad had to work his way through college as well as help support his sister and mother. His scholastic record was undistinguished. As a lawyer and a public servant, he would prove that he had the intellect, the capacity for prodigious work, and the meticulous respect for facts that are the foundations for scholarship in any field.

While an undergraduate, Dad did win the Interstate Oratorical Contest, which meant more then than being captain of a championship football team today. And it gave him a lot of favorable publicity, which he put to good advantage in 1880. In that year, when he was twenty-five, he successfully bucked Colonel E. W. Keyes, the local Republican boss, to be elected district attorney of Dane County. Four decades later I would be elected to the same office and start on my road to the governorship of Wisconsin.

In 1884, at the age of twenty-nine, Dad was elected as a Republican to the United States House of Representatives. He served three terms before being defeated in 1890, when the foreign-born population—angered by a new state law requiring that English be taught in all schools—voted the Republicans out of office. He went back to his law practice. Until he himself later broke the tradition, it was assumed in Wisconsin that if you were licked in politics it was for keeps.

In the last three decades of the nineteenth century, Wisconsin's political life was controlled by the Republican party (the 1890 election excepted), which in turn was controlled by the lumber barons and the railroads. The big boss in the nineties was a millionaire lumberman, United States Senator Philetus Sawyer. He had been a bondsman for several former state treasurers. When the Democrats came into power in 1891 they started suits to recover interest on state funds that the former treasurers had put into their pockets. The suits were to be tried before Circuit Judge Robert G. Siebecker, who was my father's brother-in-law. Senator Sawyer sent for my father and tried to hand him a large roll of bills. Sawyer insisted later that he was offering a retainer and that he did not know that my father and Judge Siebecker were related. When my father told Judge Siebecker what had happened, the latter declined to try the case.

Before long the story was out, and its impact on state politics was tremendous. For the next fifty years the Wisconsin Republican party would be divided into two warring camps—the Conservatives (or Stalwarts) and the Progressives. There would be no truces, no mercy, no quarter given or asked. Few political wars have been so intense, so bitter, so absorbing.

In my father's generation many men spelled honor with a capital H. Dad was instinctively a Progressive in his economic and political thinking. He grew up in poor circumstances and understood the lot of those at the bottom of the ladder. And he hated tyranny and special privileges for the mighty. That insult to his honor by Sawyer put iron into father's soul: he vowed to smash Sawyer's wicked, boss-ridden Republican machine no matter what or how long it took.

In 1894, Dad induced an able man of Norwegian descent, Nils P. Haugen, to become a candidate for the Republican nomination for governor. Though Haugen did not have a chance in the boss-ruled convention system, his candidacy is important as the first Progressive challenge to Conservative rule in Wisconsin. Haugen's defeat prompted my father to fight for the enactment of legislation establishing the primary election and the secret ballot.

He conducted a grass roots campaign to accomplish these reforms. He spoke during and between elections and at every crossroad and hamlet in the state. By 1900 he had built a following of devoted people. The opposition collapsed, and my father was elected governor. The Stalwarts accepted the principle that "if you can't lick 'em, join 'em." But it was only a token surrender. They had wrongly assumed that Bob LaFollette's platform pledges to the people were "campaign oratory."

For my father, a platform was a contract made by a candidate with the voters who elected him to public office. Yet it took him two more elections to the governorship (1902 and 1904) and intense, bitter fighting before he finally got a majority in both houses of the Legislature to carry out his pledges.

The Legislature of 1905 completed the enactment into law of every pledge he had made to the voters of Wisconsin. It also elected him to the United States Senate. But he did not resign the governorship to take his seat in the Senate until January,

1906, so as to be certain that the new legislation was working smoothly.

The city of Madison was carved out of virgin forest of maples, elms, and oaks. The territorial legislators yielded to the persuasion of land speculators and, by a small margin of votes obtained by dubious methods, chose the uninhabited site of Madison as the future state capital. Few capitals sit in more beautiful surroundings. The city occupies land embracing the northern pair of a chain of four lakes. The Capitol building stands in a ten-acre park on a mile-wide isthmus between the two larger lakes.

Significantly, the University of Wisconsin is just a mile from the Capitol, on the shore of Lake Mendota. These two institutions have been in view of each other for more than a century. I doubt that any state university has had more influence on a state and the life of its people.

In my childhood and youth Madison was a small town of about twenty-five thousand. The Capitol at one end of State Street and the university at the other dominated the life of the city. Most professional people and many in business had graduated from the university. There were people of wealth in Madison, but the social and intellectual climate was set by the influence of the university.

The first settlers in Wisconsin came from New England and Upstate New York. They were followed by immigrants from Germany, Norway, Ireland, and later from Italy and Poland, but Madison remained distinctly Yankee in tone. The names of the streets reflect these early influences—Washington, Webster, Doty, Hamilton, Pinckney, Gilman, Gorham, Fairchild, and, of course, Main, State, and King.

Mother and Dad both graduated from the University of Wisconsin with the class of 1879. They were married in 1881, and two years later my older sister, Fola, was born. Twelve years then elapsed before the birth of Bob—a long wait for a son and heir. Bob was the apple of his father's eye.

Then I came along, and Mary followed in two years. Mother told me that with her first sight of me she had said to herself:

"This is *my* boy." She, her mother, and my wife have been the molding influences in my life. I have always been intense, mischievous, happy, imaginative, and endowed with energy.

As a child and in my youth, my father did not dislike me, but I worried him. He was often irritated with me—and in spite of himself he could not help showing it. My restless energy seemed to be galloping off, unbridled, in all directions at once. Ironically, in basic temperament, my brother Bob was like Mother, while I was more like Dad.

Mother, Grandma, and my wife—with that rare intuition of teachers—understood how to handle me: They gave me all the rope I wanted, in the belief that I would find self-discipline or break my neck.

When I was born, our home was a frame house set back from the street with a spacious, well-kept lawn. At the rear was a beautiful view of Lake Monona. My father's law partner and brother-in-law owned the adjoining property. Across the street was the barn for horses and a Jersey cow, with a trusty hired man to do the chores. My father had been born in this county (Dane), and Mother was raised in Sauk County, immediately to the north. They both loved horses, and we three younger children, Bob, Mary, and I, were taught to ride early. I started to ride when I was about three, and on my fifth birthday Mother let me ride her Kentucky Saddler alone. That was a red letter day for me: I was growing up.

In 1899, Dad was sick with what we would call today nervous indigestion caused by the terrific demands he had made on his physical and nervous systems. So I stayed with my maternal grandparents on their farm near Baraboo for nearly a year, and most of the summers thereafter until my grandmother died in 1904. I suppose some people would say that she spoiled me. Perhaps she did, but I thrived on it and got certain values that have gone with me through life.

Today everyone talks about security. But because of my grandparents' thrift and the economics of their day, their home had a greater feeling of security than almost anyone can know today. When the cold wind blew out of the North in fall and winter, the house Grandpa and his father and brother had built was warm and comfortable. The woodshed was piled to the roof. In the cellar were jars of vegetables, crocks filled with salted meats, plenty of eggs, chickens, and milk. Except for chore time (mine, collecting the eggs), we lived in the kitchen, where the range gave off warmth and comfort exceeded only by the love of my doting grandparents. Come bedtime, Grandma tucked me into bed at the head of the stairs under the eaves, with heated sandstones at my feet.

Then, on Saturday, the buggy, or sleigh, was hitched up behind Charlie—all three horses were Grandma's, bought with her butter and egg money—and we drove to Baraboo to Mr. Peck's grocery store, where Grandma traded and sold her produce. On Sunday, time for chicken and biscuits, Grandma gave me lessons in anatomy and physiology as she carved up the fowl. And there was the privilege of riding Charlie bareback up and down the dusty country road. I remember one day when Leonard, a Case cousin, was plowing with the two big draft horses and using Charlie as a third. Grandma came out on the porch, saw the situation, and ordered Charlie released for riding purposes. Leonard swore under his breath but unhitched the horse, and I had my usual ride. What millions could buy that life today?

When my father was elected governor in 1900, we left our home on Lake Monona and moved to the Executive Residence (Mother did not like the word *mansion*) on Lake Mendota. I was to live there longer than any other governor—five years during my father's terms and six years more during my own.

The Executive Residence was a stately, sandstone house built by a millionaire lumberman in 1854 and eventually bought by the state as the governor's residence. You entered a central hall, with a library on the left and a beautifully proportioned drawing room on the right. A dining room across the width of the house could be entered at the end of the hall or through either the library or the drawing room. When we lived there in the thirties, my wife often remarked that this arrangement made it possible to entertain twice as many people at receptions as most houses of its size because guests could move from the hall to the drawing room to the dining room to the library and out the side entrance of the library.

There were four good-sized bedrooms and one small bedroom and a bath on the main second floor, and three bedrooms and a bath on a slightly lower level at the rear.

A large, lovely lawn extended down to the lakeshore. We had a stable for the horses and a room for the state-employed coachman. We had three horses of our own and a fourth on loan from a friend. It all seemed magnificent to us children, and on anybody's terms, it was comfortable and dignified.

The Executive Residence was on what was known locally as Big Bug Hill. Our former home was on the opposite side of town, called the Bloody Fourth. These names aptly described their social status. The Executive Residence was in a neighborhood overwhelmingly Conservative Republican and bitterly opposed to my father. Our neighbors looked on him and his politics as a personal challenge to them and the particular niches they occupied in the economic and political system in which they had thrived for so many decades. Although it was the custom for their ladies to call on the governor's wife, few called on my mother.

In spite of the intensity of political animosities during the five years my father was governor, we had an extremely happy childhood. Our neighbors and their children never carried their political feelings to our generation. Indeed, the older people had good-natured fun out of me. The first four years was the period when my father was battling his program through the Legislature. The adoption of a primary election law was a key item in his program. At the home of the Conservative Republican chief justice I was on occasion asked to mount the railing on his front porch to speak in favor of the primary election, regulation of the railroads, and other issues. Though I was only about seven years old, I had heard a great deal of talk at home about what was going on at the Capitol, so I was able to hold the attention of my audience, which often broke into uproarious laughter.

During my father's governorship he often brought his political friends and associates home to dinner. Current political problems and issues were daily fare for Bob and me all through our childhood and youth. Naturally, it would be silly even to suggest that we had any understanding of all that was going on in the political world. But we were constantly absorbing more and more as the years passed.

Our neighbors often pumped me for inside information about formal social affairs. I remember particularly when I was asked how Mother arranged the seating of the guests at formal dinners. Of course I knew the answer: "She seats first a dull one and then a bright one, and so on around the table." That one went around town in a hurry. And thereafter, guests at our table would good-naturedly wonder who was who.

Mother also told the story of one reception when she noted that as the ladies entered the drawing room they all seemed to be suppressing chuckles. During a slight lull in the arrival of guests she looked around the corner into the hall and out toward the front door. There she saw Bob sitting on a chair, with his feet on the railing of the front porch and with a piece of rope in his hand, which was attached to the screen door. As guests approached, he would courteously pull the door open for them while still sitting in his chair.

Nineteen four was the university's jubilee year, and there were many social affairs from which Bob and I were excluded. However, by this time, we had discovered a register under the rug in our bedroom and over the dining room. By opening the register, heat from downstairs could float up to warm the bedroom. It had not been used for years. After we discovered the register, Bob and I had refrained from opening it until some very special dinner. Our chance came at the jubilee celebration, during a formal white-tie-and-tails affair for some of the most important university guests. Everything was going splendidly at the dinner. We rolled up the rug and very carefully opened the register and looked down into the dining room. To our horror there was a large black spot right in the middle of the white tablecloth: the accumulated dust and dirt of a decade in the register had been dumped on the table. Bob and I thought we were surely in for it now. We were wrong. Mother and

Father treated it as a joke, and we went scot-free for that one.

During the university jubilee I got an important lesson in character. Charles R. Van Hise had been a classmate of Father and Mother at the university, and he and his wife were intimate friends in our household. For years these couples exchanged Sunday night suppers. Van Hise was world-famous for his work in geology. He was a man of wide and deep ranges of interest in many fields. He was not a good speaker and was devoid of the superficial "front" of the Madison Avenue type of public relations. He was a scholar and shared with Father and Mother the deep conviction expressed by President John Bascom when they were students—that the university and its graduates owed a lasting obligation to the state and its people.

After my father became governor, he made his appointments to the university regents with an eye to the selection of Van Hise as president when a vacancy occurred. It did occur. Van Hise was selected but over the strenuous objection of Colonel William F. Vilas. Colonel Vilas had served in President Cleveland's cabinet and in the United States Senate. He was also a millionaire. And he was an influential regent and devoted to the university. Colonel Vilas opposed Van Hise because he felt that he lacked those social and public platform qualities needed in a university president. Vilas even threatened to resign from the board of regents, but Dad dissuaded him.

Van Hise had been president for a year before the jubilee, during which time he had made a very favorable impression. One Sunday morning the doorbell rang. I opened the door, and there stood the stately figure of Colonel Vilas. He said, "Is your father at home?" "Yes, sir," I replied. Then he said, "Is it convenient for me to see him?" I said, "Yes, sir," and I showed him into the library, where Dad was working. Dad stood up and shook hands with Colonel Vilas. This is what I then heard:

Father: "Good morning, Colonel. It's nice to see you. Won't you sit down?"

Vilas: "No, thank you, Governor. I shall stay only a moment. I merely came to tell you that you were right about Van Hise and I was wrong. Good morning."

And he left. I have never forgotten it to this day. Telling the truth and admitting one's errors clear a beclouded atmosphere like nothing else. And doing so usually baffles one's opponents.

We children must have felt the stress and strain of public life and the intense feeling pro and con about our father and the program that he was fighting for in the five years he was governor. But because we lived in that atmosphere from birth, perhaps we accepted it as normal. In any event, as I have said, we had a happy childhood. We had horses to ride. There was wonderful swimming. In winter we iced Pinckney Street hill. We could start at the top and gain enough speed to carry us three blocks and then make two turns to the left that carried us another three blocks, from which we had only two blocks to walk to our starting point. There were plenty of kids our age in the general neighborhood who provided healthy, normal companionship.

There were no nursery schools then, but Mother had a fine German teacher who came a few times a week. I acquired an adequate German accent—the kind which, if I am in Berlin, is taken as coming from Hamburg, perhaps, and vice versa. Mother tried to have us learn to play the piano, but it did not work. We were sent to dancing school, which all boys my age detested.

I went to first grade in a public school. For some reason, Mother sent Bob and me, for second and third grades, to the Wisconsin Academy (called by some contemporaries "Fools' Retreat"). The academy came into existence before my father's college days, and he attended it to cram for the university. When Bob and I went there it was conducted by two spinsters. They were excellent teachers, and the elder was a disciplinarian who ran the school with an iron hand.

In 1904 my older sister, Fola, graduated from the University of Wisconsin, after having been honored with membership in Phi Beta Kappa. She subsequently went to New York City to begin a career as an actress, and in 1911 she married the playwright George Middleton.

My father had been reelected in 1902. In 1904, Wisconsin was to hold what proved to be the last legal statewide nominating convention. Progressives controlled the state Republican party machinery, but it was clear the Old Guard Republicans were going to make a desperate effort to control that convention, even if they had to use force.

The convention was to be held in the university gymnasium. The hall was on the second floor. The Progressive forces took due precautions. We had learned that our opponents had imported a gang of rough lumberjacks to rush the doors. When the doors were opened on the first day, most people were astonished at what they saw. Barbed wire had been put up on the staircase so that people had to climb the steps single file. At the head of the stairs and on the floor of the convention hall, members of the University of Wisconsin football squad were serving as sergeants at arms. When the first contingent of jacks got to the top, a few footballers sent them reeling backward with good hooks to the jaw. Peace reigned. We won a smashing victory at the convention, and in November, Dad was easily reelected governor.

With his program written into law in 1905, Dad resigned the governorship in January, 1906, to take his seat in the United States Senate, to which he had been elected by the 1905 Legislature. Mother and Father decided to leave Bob, Jr., Mary, and me in Wisconsin until they had found a place in which to live in Washington. So we were left at the Hillside Home School at Spring Green, Wisconsin. This school was owned and headed by two maiden ladies, sisters of Jenkin Lloyd Jones, the clergyman and reformer, and aunts of Frank Lloyd Wright, the architect. They were always addressed as Aunt Nell and Aunt Jen.

In the fall of 1905, Mother and Father had ridden horseback over the countryside around Madison looking for a desirable farm. They had decided that when we left the Executive Residence we would move to a farm. The place they liked above all was a sixty-acre farm 3½ miles from the Capitol Square, with twelve hundred feet of Lake Mendota shoreline. The price, thirty thousand dollars, seemed awfully high. Nevertheless, when I came home from school one afternoon, Mother was on the phone. She hung up with a wonderful smile and said, "Daddy has just signed the papers, and we have bought Maple Bluff Farm."

The months at Spring Green crawled as we waited impatiently to get to our new home. The day finally came. We rode back to Madison in the caboose of a freight train, and Mother met us at the station and we drove to the farm. My, were we happy after all those months of separation!

Our farm was a "working" farm. We had a dairy herd and eleven acres of orchard, and in 1906 we got the surprise of our lives. In those days congressional sessions were not protracted. That meant that Dad had a summer full of lecture engagements. When he came home at the end of his tour he had earned, for us, a lot of money. He felt flush and took Bob and me to a small city forty miles from Madison and bought eight Shetland pony mares and a stallion. Arrangements were made to have them shipped to Madison.

Bob, Mary, and I met the train at the freight yards of the Milwaukee Road. We three kids were in seventh heaven as we rode and led our string home to Maple Bluff Farm. Dad had some stationery printed for us: "LaFollette Brothers' Shetland Pony Farm." We were in business. But all the family became so attached to each pony that it was hard to sell even the colts as they came along, and I am afraid it was not a very profitable operation. However, it did teach Bob and me to do chores and to meet the daily obligations that are a part of growing up on a farm.

Bob liked the ponies, but Mary and I were devoted to them. I trained them to drive single, tandem, and four abreast. On one occasion when Ringling Brothers' circus came to Madison, I took along one of the hired men, gave him one of Dad's old silk hats to wear, and we went to the starting point of the parade. Somehow I wangled a position in the parade just ahead of the calliope. As we circled the Capitol Park we apparently attracted considerable attention. For days afterward we were the talk of the town.

One year we rented a tent, put up seats, and put on a real pony show and charged admission. It was a good show and made a great hit. I think that after our expenses were paid, we had made something like twenty-five dollars.

The big event of the year for me was the county fair. Our ponies were purebreds, and they snagged most of the prizes. One year it was decided to have a pony race. That was my meat. I was in the lead as we came down the home stretch when suddenly something frightened Jessie and she stopped abruptly. I jumped off, grabbed her bridle, and led her over the line. The rules were not strict, and I was declared the winner.

Despite such exciting and happy activities Bob, Jr., and Phil apparently felt very lonely when their parents became preoccupied with public affairs. In 1906, after his mother had left Madison to join Senator LaFollette in Washington, nine-year-old Phil dictated a letter to one of his father's employees:

Dear Daddy:

I am feeling fine. I hope you are well. It is a beautiful day. Mother has gone to see you,—she is gone now. . . . The ponies are fine. I think Princess is with foal. Tony and I came in today to get some paint for Mr. Nelson. I am just dying to go to Washington, not to leave the ponies, not to leave the place, not to leave where I love to stay, but because I will see you not one day, not fifteen minutes, not an hour, but about six months,—and then you are gone. I hope it will not disappoint you to tell you that I do not want any new house, because I want you more at home with us than you are. How it did surprise Robert to find out that mama had gone. He called up Miss Jacobs, told her he wanted to talk to Mrs. LaFollette, and he pretty near fainted when he heard that she had gone.

Your boy

2

POLITICAL HIGH SCHOOL

... EVERY TWO YEARS FOR THE NEXT FORTY YEARS

While Bob and I were beginning to learn something about farm life, we were also getting some stiff political lessons. Nineteen six would see the first test of the primary election law in Wisconsin. When Dad resigned the governorship, Lieutenant Governor James O. Davidson took his place. Dad firmly believed Davidson's pledge that he would not be a candidate for governor and just wanted the honor of serving one year.

Davidson did not have much education, and his training had been confined to the operation of a grocery store in a rural area in southwestern Wisconsin. My father was apprehensive that the Conservatives might gain control and endanger the program that he and other Progressives had worked so hard to enact into law.

My father's choice for governor in 1906 was Irvine L. Lenroot from Superior. He had been Speaker of the Assembly and had great ability. (Later he served in the United States House of Representatives and, from 1918 to 1927, in the United States Senate.) Lenroot was of Swedish descent, whereas Davidson was a Norwegian. There are many more Norwegian than Swedish voters in Wisconsin, and the Norwegians took great pride in having one of their own as governor.

Davidson decided to run for a term of his own. During the short time that he had been in office Davidson had accomplished little, but he had committed no blunders and people liked him personally. Perhaps the controlling influence in the election was that my father had gone to Washington. He had been the undisputed leader of the Progressives since 1896. In ten years of intense political fighting, he necessarily left injured feelings and resentments. And some persons may have felt relief at not having that dominating character so close at hand.

On primary election night we were to receive the returns at Maple Bluff Farm. Bob and I went into town to pick up Dad. As we were driving home, the owner of a grocery store hailed us. He seemed delighted, because he was of Norwegian descent, to give us the results from the first precinct reporting: It was two to one for Davidson.

That night was gloomy and black in the dining room at the farm. It was my first lesson in seeing election figures put on tablets, in comparing the vote of each precinct with that of the previous election, and in picking up a trend and forecasting the results. Bob and I would do that together every two years for the next forty years. We had now both graduated from political grammar school and were in political high school.

Davidson won, 110,000 to 61,000. He had the support of the Conservatives, but my father's apprehension proved unwarranted. On public issues Davidson remained a Progressive. He was re-elected in 1908. He left the Capitol with the Progressive program intact on the statute books.

The election of 1906 was my first experience with defeat. It began to teach me that politics is hazardous and should rarely be undertaken by those who do not recognize it as such, and who do not have the toughness to accept it and take with a smile the often unjustified criticism and even personal abuse that go with it.

In 1906, Mother and Father decided that she and we children would stay on at Maple Bluff Farm during the short session of Congress, with Dad to come home for Christmas. Bob went to school in Madison, traveling the 3½ miles on horseback. Mother had taught high school at Spring Green before her marriage, so she decided to teach Mary and me at home.

The winter of 1906–7 was bitterly cold even for Wisconsin. Mary and I were busy with our chores, which included keeping the firewood stacked for ready use. In her biography of Dad, Mother tells of this incident: "Phil and Mary had Topsy hitched to their hand sled, working hard bringing wood from the woodshed to the kitchen wood box, and Mary was heard to say to Phil with great earnestness, 'Really, I don't see any use of having lessons; there is so much work to do on the farm, we'll never have any time to read and write.' "

My younger sister and I have always been particularly close. In the drives in the pony cart to and from Madison I let my imagination have a free rein and told her tales of what I was going to do for Mother and her. One of my favorites was getting a closed carriage with a prancing pair of horses, and foot warmers because Mother felt the cold so badly in her feet. Eventually Dad and I went to an auction and bought an old carriage for twenty-five dollars. But by that time, automobiles were coming in, and I think I took Mother for only one ride, and the carriage just stood in the shed until some junkman hauled it away.

Mother and Dad loved fine books, and we had a good library. At my age, Dumas and Stevenson were of far greater interest than the classics. That winter mother gave me a *Child's History of England*. It opened new horizons. I found that history and biography were more exciting than most adventure stories.

In the fall of 1907, after a strenuous lecture season, Dad took a few old friends and Bob, Jr., on a bear hunt to Colorado. I was only ten years old and was left behind. To console me, Dad gave me an especially fine double harness for the ponies. It was a bitter disappointment not to go with Dad and Bob, but when the harness arrived I felt better.

The school year of 1907–8 began the uneven and erratic primary and high school life that we three youngsters would have for the next seven years. We would begin a school term in Madison and stay until Christmas, then pick up and move to Washington and try to fit into schools there. Mother and Father had to choose between that method of schooling or being separated from their children. You may ask: Why not boarding schools? For one thing, none of us had liked the Hillside Home School at Spring Green, and for another thing it would have been too expensive.

With the press so overwhelmingly against him, my father felt that he must have a paper of his own. He took on the problems of publishing *LaFollette's Weekly Magazine* in 1909. Except for two or three years, the magazine had to be subsidized. Friends and supporters helped, but the bulk of the deficit had to be made up by Dad's lecture fees. An unprofitable paper drinks money. So, despite a sizable income, we did not have an excess.

Even so, financial problems were not the main reason we went to Washington. The controlling factor was the need to be together.

In December, 1907, we started to Washington. There were seven of us—Mother; Bob; Mary; the two young girls from neighboring farms whom we called "help," as was the farm custom in the Midwest; a retired teacher, Emma Gattiker, who would help care for the children; and me. It was an expensive tribe to move. We had the choice of two to a berth and eating in the dining car, or taking our food and having a drawing room and berths. It was a hard choice, but the drawing room won.

Mother had rented a house on California Street in Washington. It was built like a thin cigar box on end, fine for a small family of three or four, but for eight, cramped and uncomfortable.

In those days the President was easily accessible, and on New Year's Day, 1908, President Theodore Roosevelt held a reception at the White House. We all went—eight in a four-seated, closed carriage. Bob and I tried unsuccessfully to draw the curtains to hide our unseemly crowdedness from the public eye. When we reached our destination, person after person stepped out until a policeman walked around to the other side to make sure that a line had not been formed by persons using the carriage as a passageway to the White House. As we passed down the receiving line all this was forgotten. The President greeted us with an enormous smile, gleaming teeth, and "Oh, the dear children!" in a voice one could have heard for hundreds of feet.

Alice Wood, a Washington schoolteacher, recalled, in 1966, her encounters with young Philip LaFollette:

One day my class-room door opened and there breezed into the room with utter informality and absence of self-consciousness, a stocky blue-eyed, red-cheeked boy in short trousers, who looked pleasantly around and without approaching the desk or lowering his voice, addressed me as one human being to another, "Is this where I belong? I can't seem to find out where I belong."

"I certainly hope so!" I thought, as I approached him to conduct the interview in a proper schoolroom manner with lowered voices. It was Philip LaFollette, who, as his mother said later, went out in friendship to all the world. He did later conform to most outward procedure, but essentially our relation was always as one human being to another. We became the best of friends and I was often in the most delightful of homes.

Nothing was outside the pale of his interest, and we discussed matters of state or my hats, which indeed he sometimes helped me choose, with equal ardor. . . .

On one occasion a theme subject had been assigned on some such topic as The Advantages of Democratic Government. Phil asked me if he had to favor it for all people, and I told him to treat it as he pleased. Fola told me later that as he prepared to discuss the unreadiness of some nations for democratic government, he said, "Isn't she liberal?". . .

"Young Bob" as he was so long called, was also a graduate of Western High School, and was a most interesting student, not leading in academic standing but always fascinating as a personality and following the tradition of his father's love for the drama in the school dramatic club. Life in this home was so rich that it was not surprising that the school activities took second place. They met at their table notables from all over the world and were up on politics and world affairs at an early age.

Mary, the youngest daughter, looked like a lovely blonde doll. Her interest was in art and not in the conventional academic course. She was prone to "play hooky" when the grind became too boring, and Phil became her very strict guardian. She bore it unresentfully, but my feminist soul resented it for her!

In December, 1908, we moved to 1864 Wyoming Avenue, into a much larger house. Dad's study, his secretary's office, and a large kitchen were on the ground floor. On the second floor were a drawing room, back parlor, and dining room. On the third floor there were four bedrooms and a bath; and on the fourth only one large bedroom and a bath, because this story was but one-third the length of the others. It was a spacious, comfortable house, and we all enjoyed it.

Dad liked to read aloud to the family and close friends. We had a large, majestic armchair that we called "the throne." When he was not too burdened with work, we would have an evening of reading, with Dad on the throne. One evening it would be Edward Bulwer-Lytton's *Richelieu*. On other occasions it would be *Hamlet* or some other dramatic play or story. But our real choice was Herminie Templeton Kavanagh's *Darby O'Gill and the Good People*. This is a collection of stories about Darby and his adventures with the Irish fairies who inhabit the mountain Sleive-na-mon. They come out at night to take Darby on exciting adventures.

Dad had considered becoming an actor as a young man, and he had great dramatic gifts. He could read Robert Burns with a perfect Scotch accent and *Darby* with an equally good Irish brogue. These evenings provided virtually the only entertainment Mother and Father had. They did not like the whirl of either official or Washington society. And more important, Dad did not have the time. He usually worked until ten at night or later, and on Sundays too. He was effective on the platform and in the Senate because he had mastered his subject and because he had an extraordinary ability to simplify complicated facts and make clear how they affected the daily lives and the pocketbooks of his audience.

It was not unusual for him, on the platform, to speak for three or four hours on the tariff or railroad rates and hold an audience spellbound. And in the Senate he might talk for hours until, from his point of view, every item of importance on a given question had been put into the record. Louis D. Brandeis, later a justice of the United States Supreme Court and himself a master of facts, once said that my father knew more about American railroads than any other man.

Mother, however, did not approve of these long speeches and bought him a Swiss alarm watch. She instructed him to set it for a two-hour speech and to stop speaking when it went off. The first time it went off Dad said to his audience: "My wife gave that to me and told me to quit when the alarm went off." Loud cries came from the audience: "Shut 'er off. Go on."—which he did.

From the time that we moved into the Wyoming Avenue house in 1908, Dad took Bob and me—we were then thirteen and eleven—into his complete confidence. In politics and in public affairs he had no secrets from us. We opened and read his mail that came to the house, and when we called for him to drive him home at the end of the day we pored over the mail that came to his office. Many important conferences were held in his study at home. Because these were usually at night, Bob and I were silent witnesses to all that went on. At first some of his Progressive callers looked askance at us because the subject was thought to be too confidential to trust to young boys. But Dad would assure them we were to be trusted. In fact, we never leaked anything that we had heard or read. Perhaps the fact that our schoolmates for a number of years had no interest whatever in public affairs made it easier to avoid disclosing anything that we had learned.

We came to know intimately men like George Norris of Nebraska (Uncle George); William Borah of Idaho; Moses Clapp of Minnesota (Uncle Mose); Albert Cummins of Iowa; Jonathan Bourne, Jr., of Oregon; A. J. Gronna of North Dakota; Joseph Bristow of Kansas; Jonathan Dolliver of Iowa; and others in the Senate and House. These men made up the Progressive Republican bloc in the Senate. The hard core were my father, Norris, Bourne, Gronna, Bristow, and Dolliver. Those six saw eye to eye on most important issues.

Senator Albert Beveridge of Indiana was a man of great ability, but he once remarked to Mother: "I just do not have courage like Bob's." And Borah played more or less a lone hand. My father used to describe him as a man "who shook his lionlike mane, drew his sword, called for a charge on the enemy's breastworks, and stopped in his tracks before he got there."

As early as 1908, Bob and I, by courtesy or sufferance, had access to the floor of the Senate. Mother recalled an incident that illustrates how closely we followed what was going on. Dad was leading the fight against the Aldrich-Vreeland currency bill to authorize banks to use state, municipal, and railroad bonds as backing for the issuance of United States currency. He had prepared an attack on the bill—particularly its weak spot, the railroad bond provision—and had given notice that he would speak in the Senate on March 17, 1908.

Mother, several close friends, and Bob were in the Senate gallery early that day, while Dad worked on his speech at home. After the usual preliminaries, Senator Nelson Aldrich rose and casually offered some amendments to the bill. One was to strike out the provision relating to the railroad bonds. This maneuver would have undercut the keynote of Dad's attacking speech, while leaving the way open for Aldrich to restore the railroad provision later.

Mother could hardly believe her ears. She turned to ask my brother if she had heard correctly. She wrote later, "I noticed that Bob, Jr., had left the gallery. He was soon back again. 'I got Daddy on the telephone before he had left the house and told him what had happened,' he whispered. The quick wit of his thirteen-year-old son, who had rushed out to warn his father before anyone else recognized the significance of Aldrich's announcement, gave Bob [our father] a chance at the very beginning of his speech to counter the shrewd last-minute move of the Senator from Rhode Island."

Another incident, a little ahead of my story, illustrates Bob's and my deep interest in public affairs. While Bob was a freshman at the University of Wisconsin he wrote Dad, "Things are going all right here but I *miss* home   I miss you each one. I dont think I will ever be contented except at home   I miss politics and the big men that come to the house. I got more out of one conference with Mr. Brandeis and John Commons than I will ever get out of a year's work in geology."

In 1908 my father was a candidate for the Republican nomination for President. He knew he did not have a chance against William Howard Taft, the Secretary of War, who had Theodore Roosevelt's complete backing. But he saw it as an opportunity to get the Progressives' program before the nation as well as to keep the Progressive machinery in Wisconsin in good shape.

All but one of Dad's slate of Wisconsin delegates to the Republican convention were elected. Mother took Bob and me to the convention in Chicago that June. The packed hall was steaming hot, and the din was so bad that the chairman's gavel seemed to be pounding most of the time.

Having control of the Wisconsin delegation, we had a representative on the platform committee, which enabled us to present a minority report. Our platform included direct election of senators, control of the trusts, and prohibition of injunctions in labor disputes. It was rejected amid hoots and howls of disapproval. Just twenty years later Bob, in making the minority report at the Kansas City convention, could report that almost all the planks proposed by Progressives since that 1908 platform had been enacted into law.

The Chicago convention had been exciting, but it was good to get back to Maple Bluff Farm. Dad had decided to support Taft, and when Taft opened his campaign in Madison, Dad introduced him to the audience. But we had nothing personally at stake in the election of 1908. Governor Davidson's smashing victory in 1906 made certain his reelection in 1908. So politics that summer and fall were, for us, comparatively quiet.

Bob and I were responsible for the care of the ponies, and we worked in our cherry orchard. We got the same pay as the other pickers—mostly kids our age or a bit older. We sold some cherries through a large (for Madison) grocery store, but most of them Bob and I peddled from back door to back door. We became friends with many a housewife. Years later I was often stopped on the street by a smiling lady who would say: "You may not remember me, but you and Bob sold cherries to me."

One special feature of the orchard operation was Mother's proposition that I could pick up to ten bushels of apples and sell them in town and keep the proceeds for myself. I had noted one day that summer the glaring posters announcing the coming of a play at the Fuller Opera House. A picture of a beautiful heroine was featured. I stared at it every time I got to town. I must see her in the flesh. I picked six bushels of apples and got a dollar a bushel—six silver dollars. So I hurried to the ticket office. To my anguish the manager of the theater told me all the seats were sold. Then he said, "Wait a minute. There is one box still open." "How much?" I asked. "Two dollars each for its four seats." Being two dollars short, I hustled home, picked two more bushels, sold them, and the next day I got my four tickets. I now invited my guests—our two hired girls and the same hired man who had accompanied me in the Ringling Brothers' parade. The appointed day came. It was the matinee, and the two girls sat in the two front seats, and Tony and I sat in the other two. I cannot remember a thing about the play, but to this day I remember how beautiful the leading lady was and that I fell head over heels in love with her. I recovered shortly—I was eleven years old.

Nineteen ten was an important year to us because my father would be up for reelection. Although Wisconsin had adopted the primary election in 1905, this did not apply to the United States Senate. The United States Constitution still provided for the election of senators by the state legislatures. The Seventeenth Amendment, ratified in 1913, would provide for their election by direct vote of the people.

Thus, Dad's campaign in 1910 would center on the election of Progressive Republican legislators who would vote for him. As for the governorship, Davidson had decided to retire after having been elected for two two-year terms. We had a strong state ticket headed by the candidate for governor, Francis E. Mc-

Govern, who had effectively fought municipal corruption while district attorney of Milwaukee County. He was a seasoned campaigner and a man of real ability.

Although the Legislature of 1911 would elect the United States senator, Wisconsin's primary provided for a senatorial preference vote. Dad was having trouble with his gallbladder that summer and did not make a single speech in the primary campaign—on his doctor's orders. But nationally known Progressives, including Senators Borah, Bristow, Clapp, and Cummins, former Secretary of the Interior James R. Garfield, Judge Ben Lindsey, Congressman (later Senator) George W. Norris, Gifford Pinchot, and others came to Wisconsin, at their own expense, to help in the campaign. Dad received an overwhelming endorsement, defeating his Stalwart opponent by more than three to one. McGovern and the rest of the Progressive slate won but not by so large a majority.

In the general election in November, McGovern won by a three-to-two margin, and a Progressive majority was elected in both houses of the Legislature. This assured my father's reelection to the Senate.

Early in 1911, under Dad's leadership, the Progressives in the Senate and House, aided by other leaders across the country, formed the National Progressive Republican League, an organization to promote the Progressive program in Congress and to lay the foundation for Dad's candidacy for the Republican nomination for President in 1912.

Former President Theodore Roosevelt had formally committed himself (much to his later regret) against a third term. As President Taft's administration became more and more conservative my father loomed larger on the political horizon as the obvious candidate of the Progressive Republicans in 1912. I do not propose to repeat here in detail the events of the 1912 campaign, about which so much has been written. I think it will be sufficient for me to summarize the highlights of that picture as I saw it then and as I now see it in retrospect.

When Colonel Roosevelt returned from his African hunting trip in 1910, he did not think Taft could be beaten for renomination. (He was later to find his estimate correct. The bloc of delegates from the southern states would be completely controlled by the Republican machine, in turn controlled by Taft. This bloc, together with the machine control in some northern states, would give the Taft forces enough delegates to run the show as they pleased.) During 1911, support for my father increased. Colonel Roosevelt sent messages of encouragement to Dad but made no irrevocable commitment to Dad's candidacy. My father gathered his principal backers and told them that if he entered the race he would stay in it until the end—that he would not be a stalking horse for Roosevelt. He stuck to his word.

But Roosevelt began to be more and more an unannounced candidate himself. Finally, he threw his hat into the ring. Dad adhered to his original pledge when he announced his candidacy, and he refused to withdraw. But Roosevelt's candidacy eliminated whatever chance Dad might have had.

In the Wisconsin primary in April, 1912, Dad's slate of delegates won by two to one. The delegation was headed by Governor McGovern. Dad also carried North Dakota over both Roosevelt and Taft. The Roosevelt forces at once began to work on McGovern to be their candidate for temporary chairman of the convention. This was a move on their part to make it appear that Roosevelt was a Progressive of the Wisconsin variety. Dad would have none of it and vigorously opposed any such action that would suggest a Roosevelt-LaFollette "deal." Nonetheless, McGovern was the Roosevelt candidate for temporary chairman but was defeated. The rift between McGovern and the LaFollette Progressives later widened, but Dad endorsed him for reelection in 1912 for the simple reason that McGovern had made a fine record, and that must be the test in our kind of politics.

Of course, Roosevelt's defeat by Taft and his subsequent third-party campaign split the Republican vote, and Woodrow Wilson was elected. Wilson had made a Progressive record as governor of New Jersey, and during the campaign he had said, "I take my cap off to Bob LaFollette." We all looked forward to Wilson's inauguration, though with some reserve.

Mother did not care for "society," but she always read the society columns in the Washington papers. She said you could get important leads to political affairs by watching "who went where." The human side of Washington social life interested me. According to tradition (largely ended by World War I), the wives of juniors were expected to call on the wives of seniors in officialdom. During the social season specified days in the week were allotted for receiving. A senator's wife was expected to pay a first call on the wives of the Supreme Court justices, ambassadors, cabinet members, and senators senior to her husband, and to leave calling cards at the White House and at the residence of the Vice-President.

I liked to go along for the ride when Mother hired a carriage for these occasions. One day she said, "Why don't you come in with me at this call?" That started it. Occasionally the husband would be home, and I would visit with him, too. This I did from about the ages of eleven to fourteen. I thus acquired a speaking acquaintance with quite a few ladies of the official world. I was particularly fascinated with the diplomatic corps, and for a few years I thought I would like to go into the diplomatic service. But when I sought the advice of John Barrett, director-general of the Pan American Union, he asked me if I would have a substantial private income. I told him that I would not, and he said, "Unless you can marry a wealthy lady, such a career is out for you."

About 1911 we bought our first automobile, a seven-passenger Lewis touring car made in Racine, Wisconsin. It would look to you like an ark, but to Bob and me it looked like an up-to-date Cadillac. Bob and I could get it for a dance now and then, but its primary function was to make traveling easier for Dad and Mother. Either Bob or I, or both, drove it to the Senate Office to pick up Dad at the close of the day, or to take Mother for her calls or shopping.

In 1911, I entered Western High School in Washington. There I began to learn to study under some superb teachers, especially in German, mathematics, and English. I still treasure a beautifully bound book of Schiller's with the inscription "Zu Meinem besten Schüler. [To My best Scholar.] /s/ Emma M. von Seyfried."

Algebra did not appeal to me, and I failed at the end of the school year. It was June, and I was hungry to get to Maple

Bluff Farm, but Mother insisted that I remain in Washington for tutoring. I had no choice. For several weeks I stayed on in Washington's sweltering heat and finally passed the examination. Then I got the first train I could catch back home.

Although algebra was a chore, I enjoyed geometry. For me there was logic in the latter and a jumble of figures in the former. I liked languages, but I was fascinated with history. And I was now old enough to enjoy parties and to be interested in girls.

In the fall of 1913 we moved to 3320 Sixteenth Street, a large house built by a successful owner of a bakery. It was ideal for entertaining and, for Bob, Mary, and me, a place where we could, on occasion, hold dances. Our affairs were not elaborate—a three-piece orchestra, punch (nonalcoholic), cake, and cookies, and plenty of dancing in the large hallway and the four rooms that led off it. We had room for as many as thirty or forty couples, mostly from Western High. There was no darkening of lights, or beer or liquor, and no necking (at the dances). We all had a normal interest in sex, but any outward manifestation of such interest had to be carried out with great discretion. I do not think my generation, as far as the "facts of life" were concerned, differed essentially from those that preceded it or have followed it. The difference was that mine did not recover from the influence of the Victorian Age until after World War I.

On March 4, 1913, Woodrow Wilson was inaugurated as President. Dad was, as I recall, cautiously hopeful that the President would carry forward his enlightened program called the New Freedom. Dad would do, during Wilson's terms, as he had done all his public life—support the right, as he was given to see the right, and oppose the wrong, as it was given him to see the wrong. In any event, his personal relations with the White House would be friendly until World War I loomed.

This more cordial relationship enhanced my own social life. When the Wilsons put Mother and Dad in the "blue card" category, I was the one who took the advantages, so-called, that it conferred. The blue cards were for the cabinet, ranking members of the Senate and House, and perhaps a few others. They were not numbered and had no identifying name on them but were enclosed with invitations to White House receptions. They entitled you to enter the south entrance and go to the reception rooms without having to stand in line like those who came to the east entrance. Moreover, you could wander at will behind the "rope." This was the heavy cord behind the Presidential receiving line. So, having been presented to the President and Mrs. Wilson and the cabinet wives, I could walk from room to room visiting with the official elite. I took full advantage of my parents' blue card, chatted with those I knew, and introduced myself freely to those I didn't know.

Before embarking on this blue card enterprise, I had acquired —off the rack—a dress suit for twenty-five dollars, which was perfectly adequate for these occasions and other social affairs. Bachelors are always in some demand, and no one asked for a birth certificate to testify as to my age. I liked to dance and was usually available if asked. I must not leave the impression that I was in great demand, but still it was rather amazing that a young fellow of sixteen or seventeen would be asked at all. On only two occasions was the matter of my age raised:

At a dinner party at the Chevy Chase Club given, I think, by General William ("Billy") Mitchell, Miss Margaret Wilson (the president's oldest daughter) was seated on the general's right and I next to her. When the champagne was passed, he suddenly leaned over and asked me how old I was. When I told him, he said, with a smile but with military firmness, "Much too young for this stuff. Please turn your glass upside down."

On another occasion, when Dad and Mother were giving a formal dinner, Lady Barlow, a distinguished guest from England, having heard me participating freely in the conversation, suddenly turned toward me and said: "Philip, just how old are you?" I replied, "Seventeen." "My word," said she, "you *are* previous."

3

AUGUST 4, 1914

. . . I WAS WITNESSING A WORLD EVENT . . .

After school closed in June, 1914, I traveled to England for the first time. When my beloved Grandma Case died in 1904 she left fifteen hundred dollars in savings—three hundred dollars for each of her five grandchildren. These savings had built up over the years from the sale of the butter and eggs from the Case farm near Baraboo.

Mother put our inheritances in savings accounts. Sometime around 1912 a substantial part of Bob's went to satisfy his strong mechanical bent—a Harley-Davidson motorcycle. Mine was to be the basis of a trip to England. That summer David Thompson, whose late wife had been a classmate of my parents, and his sister were planning a trip to England. Mother thought it would be a fine opportunity for me to see England. She was going on a lecture tour that summer, speaking for woman's suffrage. She said she would add to my grandmother's legacy out of her lecture fees. So passage was engaged on the S.S. *Philadelphia.*

"Uncle David" Thompson and his sister were both born in England but were naturalized American citizens. The fourth person in our party was dad's personal secretary, Nellie Dunn, who began work in his law office in her early teens, went to the governor's office, and lived with us in Washington for a number of years. She was almost like a sister.

From the time we embarked at New York until we reached our English port, Uncle David's and his sister's English accents grew more pronounced. Worse still for Nellie and me, they became unbearable for us as more English than the English. And our presence made it more and more difficult for them to maintain their Britishness undefiled. So, by mutual agreement, it was decided that Nellie and I would go our own way in England.

We planned a walking tour and we walked most of the time, taking third class on a train only when the hop was a bit too much. We walked through the Shakespeare country, saw the castles (my eyes bulged most at Warwick), and the great cathedrals of York and, above all, Durham. We stayed at a whitewashed stone cottage at Ambleside. Most people could not make us out, but our obvious age difference—she in her late twenties and I seventeen—gave us the benefit of the doubt, and everyone was very nice, indeed. An older man and his daughter were especially thoughtful. The gentleman became particularly interested in me and talked with me about preparation for a young man's future. He wrote a weekly letter to me for several years about books to read and how to cultivate a taste for literature. When he died a few years afterward, his daughter sent me his gold topaz signet, which I still have on my watch chain.

After visiting Wales, we arrived in London at the end of July, 1914. Until then the world crisis that had begun in late July had meant little to us. Once in London, the news vendors' sandwich boards with their glaring red headlines made us aware that Europe was on the brink of war. We stayed at a temperance hotel where no liquor was sold, because the hotel was inexpensive. I had some letters of introduction from "Uncle Louis" Brandeis and from Charles R. Crane, a multimillionaire supporter and friend of my father, and one of those "Secretary of State letters" handed out at the request of members of Congress. Those addressed to Mr. and Mrs. Sidney Webb, the economists, and Ramsay MacDonald, leader of the Labour party, I sent by mail. Promptly I received an invitation to tea at the Webbs'. I went at the appointed hour, to find myself among eight or ten guests. The only one I recognized was H. G. Wells. Everyone was cordial, but I was fully conscious in that gathering that I was only a high school senior and prudently kept my silence and listened to their talk of war and what awful damage it would cause to Europe and the world. It was not the identical intellectual atmosphere I knew in our home, but I needed no "interpreter," and I think I grasped the fact that I was witnessing a world event of vast magnitude.

Mr. Crane's letter went to T. P. O'Connor, popularly known as Tay Pay and as "father" of the House of Commons because of his long service. On August 4, 1914, a day that would end with Britain at war with Germany, I went to the House of Commons. Long lines of people waited for the remote chance to get into the public gallery. The House of Commons was then, and is now —as rebuilt after World War II—a comparatively small, rectangular chamber with the Speaker on his high-backed chair at one end and rows of leather-covered benches facing each other, with the prime minister and the cabinet seated on the Speaker's right and His Majesty's loyal opposition on the left.

It did not seem likely that I would have the slightest chance to get in, but I walked to the head of the line and handed my letter to a guard. To my surprise, Mr. O'Connor came into the lobby shortly and came up to me with a warm handshake, a twinkle in his eye, and a cordial smile. He said, "It's a bit crowded today, but I shall see the Speaker and we'll see what can be done."

In a moment he came back with a card that, to my amazement and immense excitement, gave me a seat in the front row of the "distinguished strangers" gallery. There I heard Sir Edward Grey, the foreign secretary; Herbert Asquith, the Prime Minister; Winston Churchill, the first lord of the admiralty; David Lloyd George, the chancellor of the exchequer; and others. But these four were, for me, the most impressive. The most forceful opposition to Britain's entering the war came from Ramsay MacDonald, leader of the Labour party. The attacks on MacDonald, in particular, were a foretaste of what my father would face in 1917. Of this, of course, I had no glimmer.

Mr. MacDonald later came around to my hotel and took the

time to tell this young man at length why he opposed Britain's entry into the war. He foretold with amazing accuracy not only the terrific cost in lives and destruction but what the war would do to the whole political, economic, and social structure of Europe and the world. "It will never be the same again," he said as he left. The next time I would see him, years later, he would be Prime Minister of Great Britain.

With the outbreak of war, Nellie and I shared with most American tourists a desire to get home. We had to make new arrangements for our return, and this entailed a week's wait in Liverpool. The hotel there was third rate and at that, for us, enormously expensive. This extra burden on our funds, plus increased return fares for poorer quarters, forced me to wire Dad for money, but the American Express in Liverpool had no word for me. I was down to my last sovereign after paying for one night's lodging. We had tea and biscuits for breakfast. I remember we got ten cups of tea out of the pot by adding hot water. That tea broke into the sovereign, so I marched off to the American consul armed with that letter from the Secretary of State. The consul, a charming gentleman named Horace Lee Washington, was most obliging but had great difficulty in comprehending that I was almost flat broke and needed cash *now*. Once he grasped the situation, he opened his purse and advanced a few pounds for my immediate needs and got from some member of his staff the address of a small but good boardinghouse owned by a charming spinster with cats. Once there, we waited out our week of delay quite content. I headed for home loaded with the memories of a wonderful trip and filled with all that I had seen and heard. I knew, of course, that the experiences I had in London were due solely to my father's name and his position in American public life. But that did not detract from them at all.

While in London I had bought a heavy woolen suit. It cost something like twenty dollars, but with some imagination one could believe that it was of English make. I had also bought a monocle for something like fifty cents. When we got home, the family gathered around to hear all about our trip. I had on my new suit and the monocle, and I spoke with a clipped English accent. Everyone thought it very funny except Mary. She burst into tears and ran out of the room wailing, "Oh, Phil has changed. He isn't Phil anymore." The monocle and the accent disappeared, and Mary could laugh again.

In 1906 the Old Guard Republicans had to give my father, as a Republican, some committee assignments. So he was made chairman of the obsolete Committee to Investigate the Conditions of the Potomac River Front, and was given an office in the sub-basement of the Capitol. To this office came—in December, 1909—Andrew Furuseth, president of the International Seamen's Union. Andy, as we always knew him, was a tall, raw-boned Norwegian with a weather-beaten face lined, Dad said, as if it had been "clawed by an eagle." He had a beaked nose, and fearless eyes. Andy never married. He had gone to sea as a lad and out of his meager pay he had bought books—history books— and absorbed them into the warp and woof of his being. "Andy," Dad used to say, "knows more history—ancient, medieval, and modern—and can apply it more pointedly to our times than any man I have ever known."

Andy had come to Washington years before Dad was first elected to the Senate. He lived on the same wage paid the janitor in the union headquarters in San Francisco. He had tramped the corridors of the Capitol, calling on any member of Congress who would listen to his plea. He was seeking to free seamen from what was, for practical purposes, slavery. Once signed on a ship, a seaman was a chattel. No matter how brutal the captain, no matter how unseaworthy the vessel, he could not escape his articles, or contract, even in a safe port but could be hunted down and returned to his ship. Later, when a student in law school, I was to study and be shocked at two Supreme Court decisions interpreting the Thirteenth and Fourteenth amendments to the United States Constitution. The antislavery amendment did not apply to seamen but the due process and equal protection guaranteed to "persons" under the Fourteenth Amendment also protected corporations.

Andy Furuseth knew that if one great Western nation freed seamen, other nations would have to follow suit. So he picked the United States as his battleground. Until his appeal to Dad, he had never found a congressional leader strong enough to become the champion of the seamen. In 1910 and 1911, Dad introduced legislation to give seamen on any ship using our ports the same rights as any other human being protected by the American flag.

The fight Dad led from 1910 to 1915 was intimately personal in our family. For years Andy was our guest for Sunday breakfast. He always wore the same double-breasted blue suit. And he ate so heartily that I often wondered if that was the only square meal he had during the week. In fair weather on these Sunday mornings, Andy and I sat on our front porch while he talked about world history, modern world trends, philosophy—in a word, about all he had learned from life, people, and books. He introduced me to William Romaine Paterson's *The Nemesis of Nations*, which describes the rise and fall of Babylon, Greece, and Rome. The book attributes their doom to slavery, which corrupted the fiber of the slave owners and sapped any incentive in the enslaved to fight invaders.

I once asked him, "Andy, what is courage?"

"Courage," he repeated twice. He hesitated for a minute or so and then said, "If a man understood how short human life is and what little progress we have made in bringing out the good in human beings and how eagerly the evil in us breaks forth; if he understood that the earth is a tiny speck in a limitless universe and that the earth in due time will die like unnumbered planets before us have died; knowing all this, if he has real courage, he'll spit in the face of destiny and go on fighting on the side of the angels."

For more than fifteen years Andy fought on the side of the angels to free the seamen.

The superliner *Titanic* sank in 1912 with a terrible and totally unnecessary loss of life. The ship went under two hours after hitting an iceberg in the Atlantic. The sea was calm, but the *Titanic* carried woefully inadequate lifeboats, and many of the crew could not speak English. Stricter safety measures were included in the Seamen's bill proposed by Dad. The American, and especially the foreign, shipowners fought this legislation to the bitter end. The fight Dad began, inspired by Andy in 1910, resulted in the final passage of the bill by Congress on February 27, 1915.

Now the opposition shifted its fight from Capitol Hill to the State Department and the White House. President Wilson had supported the bill verbally and in writing, but the pressure on him not to sign it, especially from foreign shipping interests, was fierce. The short session of Congress would end automatically at noon on March 4, 1915. Dad asked for an appointment with the President. It was set for March 2. Andy had not been included, but Dad took him along and asked the President to hear him for ten minutes.

Dad told us later that Andy made one of the most eloquent pleas he had ever heard. He got down on his knees and clasped Wilson's knees as, with tears in his eyes, he pleaded for freedom for the men who went down to the sea in ships. Dad said that as Andy talked, both Wilson and he had tears rolling down their cheeks. Dad stayed alone with Wilson for another twenty minutes and then went back to the Senate. The next morning Wilson's secretary, Joseph Tumulty, phoned Dad and told him the President had just phoned him and said, "Tumulty, I have just experienced a great half-hour, the tensest since I came to the White House. That man LaFollette pushed me over tonight on the Seamen's bill." Wilson signed the bill into law. A great fight had been won.

4

AMERICA
AT WAR

. . . THE HOLOCAUST OF
ABUSE AND ASSAULT . . .

Bob entered the University of Wisconsin as a freshman in September, 1913. He was elected president of his class and pledged to Beta Theta Pi fraternity. Two years later I followed suit with Beta. My freshman year I lived and boarded with my Uncle Robert and Aunt "Josie" Siebecker, Dad's sister, at their rented home on Gorham Street.

Dad often told us how Uncle Robert, when a student, carried his trunk on his back nearly two miles from the railroad station to his rooming house to save fifty cents' handling charge. He read and spoke almost perfect German and knew his Goethe, Schiller, Heine, and other classics thoroughly and read them throughout his life. He was a big, robust man with an excellent mind. He boarded with my Grandmother Ferguson and thus came to know Dad and Aunt Josie. He married my aunt and became Dad's law partner. He subsequently served on the Circuit Court and on the state Supreme Court, where, by seniority, he eventually became chief justice.

During my freshman year, while I was living with the Siebeckers, I had the worst and only really serious row I ever had with my father. When the family moved to Washington, Nellie Dunn lived with us as part of the family until she married Fred McKenzie, then managing editor of *LaFollette's Magazine*. On the occasion of her marriage Dad blew off with indignation because two of his trusted workers had got married without letting him know in advance. I spoke up in their defense, and this made him even angrier. We both had our fists clenched as we glared at each other. Happily, Aunt Josie heard the row and shooed me out of the house. I walked the streets for an hour or so and then went to Uncle Robert's office, where I discussed my plan to leave home for good. Uncle Robert calmed me down, and he gave me an insight into his own situation. I began to understand the difficulties he faced in being not only a brother-in-law to a famous man but also a husband whose wife's first love throughout her life was her own brother rather than himself.

There has never been even a whisper that Dad ever had any special interest in any woman other than Mother. But losing two of his important people at the same time—and without his blessing—caused him to lose his temper, especially when challenged by his eighteen-year-old son. In my childhood and youth I had been quick-tempered. To the best of my recollection I never lost control of myself again.

During the fall of 1915, Dad stopped off in Madison to look over the political fences in Wisconsin. It was during such visits that Dad began to look on me not as a youth but as a young man who in certain respects might be more like him than Bob was.

What caught his deep interest was that without any prodding from him I had begun my first basic training in oratory and debating. My first opportunity came with the Freshman Declamatory Oration. The difference between this kind of event and debating is that the oration is memorized and debating requires more preparation. I chose Robert Ingersoll's address at his brother's funeral. I practiced it until it was letter perfect. I had a good speaking voice—totally untrained—and because the competition was not tough I won first place. When I came back to the Siebecker home I found Dad awake in front of the living room fire. He hesitatingly asked how I came out. I told him, and he got out of the chair to give me a bear hug and a kiss, with tears in his eyes. Because he thought in terms of the more vigorous oratorical competition of his day nearly forty years before, he did not realize that I had really not done very much.

Of more importance, I joined one of the three student debating societies. They were beginning to decline, but they were still the best training for debate at the university. They were wholly under the control of their own membership, and there was no faculty supervision or instruction. Once a week the officers selected a topic, and teams were designated by the senior group. The emphasis was on solid preparation—facts—and clarity and force of delivery. Oratory, as compared with mastery of the factual, was frowned on. At the end of the debates, the seniors sailed in with their criticisms—and no holds were barred. It was fortunate that the comments came from students rather than from some faculty member. Fellow debaters spoke with a penetrating freedom no member of the faculty would have thought proper.

Under normal conditions, there was a Joint Debate in the senior year. But the coming of World War I in the spring of 1917 had eliminated a number of seniors, so I had my chance when only a junior. The Joint Debate was serious business. Those who participated were excused from writing a thesis for graduation. The Joint Debate came on January 18, 1918. I was a bit apprehensive that because of my name the judges might be prejudiced against the side I was on. They were not, and we won.

After being on the winning team in the Joint Debate, I was encouraged to try out for intercollegiate debating under the guidance of the Department of Speech. At the first meeting I attended, the professor announced that the subject of the tryout would be so-and-so. Apparently the students were expected to stand up and talk on the chosen subject without any preparation. This might be a good test of one's ingenuity, but it so contrasted with the training I had had from the debating societies that I declined to speak, and at the close of the hour I left, never to return.

The training that I had in public speaking was essentially sound except in one important particular. Until I was in my early thirties I had no training whatever in the use of the voice.

Learning how to breathe and control one's voice is as essential to a speaker as to a singer. But to the untutored like myself, elocution was scorned as the height of artificiality. Without amplifiers, Dad, Bob, myself, and most other public speakers talked themselves hoarse trying to reach large audiences, both in and out of doors. When my wife, Isen, began speaking, she had some expert advice and when I saw how much better her voice stood the strain than mine, I learned enough to improve my staying power a lot. For those who aim at public speaking in any form, the basic rule remains the same: Know how to begin; know what you want to say; know when and how to quit; and finally, learn how to breathe and thus gain voice control.

When I entered the university in 1915 I made a great effort to speak to everyone I knew—and some, perhaps, that I didn't know. After a few weeks I was advised by one of the seniors in the Beta house that I was getting a reputation for being "a politician" because I was too free in mixing and visiting with any and all with whom I came in contact. Then, abruptly, I tried to appear what I was not—reserved with fellow students. It was only a few months later that another senior took me to task for appearing snobbish. I wrestled uncomfortably with that dilemma for a few weeks and decided to be myself again. I learned from this something that experience taught me was vital to anyone in any form of public life: listen to criticism from whatever source, weigh it objectively, accept all or part of it if it seems sound but always adhere to a course you believe right.

Four of us in the Beta Theta Pi fraternity became fast friends. Joe (Joseph R.) Farrington from Hawaii, with whom I roomed for three years, was one of the most lovable men I ever knew. He came from a conservative background. His father was publisher of the *Star-Bulletin* in Honolulu and later governor of the Islands. Joe was later a delegate to the United States Congress and an outstanding leader in the effort to have the Islands admitted to the Union. He would likely have become a United States senator had he not died before Hawaii was admitted.

Another close friend was Miles (Mike) Colean, a gifted writer

—alas, his first novel was his last—keen of mind, and with a charming personality.

And Ralph Sucher, coming from Illinois, was steeped in Lincolniana and had some of the clarity of mind and expression of his hero. He went into journalism—though he had a law degree. He worked for Dad and helped Bob and me, and he married my younger sister, Mary. Tragically, the marriage ended in divorce.

Joe Farrington had an athletic build and was a fine swimmer, but he was not intercollegiate material. The other three of us had no athletic qualifications although, foolishly, I tried out for football. The spirit was willing but the flesh was too meager: I weighed about 120 pounds. However, what we lacked physically, we made up for with enthusiasm—especially for football and basketball. The fraternity house—an old frame building—was on Lake Mendota with its wonderful swimming, skating, and ice-boating, but I must admit I had no great interest for any of those sports. Joe and Ralph shared my interest in politics, and Mike and I relished long verbal and, later, written discussions on philosophy.

The Betas were respected for their athletic prowess and for the fact that many were working to pay for all or part of their education. We had a minimum of "lounge lizards," and dating girls was considered acceptable if kept within reasonable limits; only a handful dated their girls as "regulars." Drinking—except for some very special occasion—was not done, not because of moral scruples but because of the athletic atmosphere in the house and, of course, because it was expensive.

In the fall of 1916, the Presidential contest between Woodrow Wilson and Charles Evans Hughes shared attention in Wisconsin with Dad's campaign for renomination and reelection to the Senate. In August, Dad finally got back to Wisconsin for his campaign. We had acquired a Model T Ford, which Bob and I drove for Dad during the few weeks he was able to speak in Wisconsin. He was easily renominated and reelected, by the then largest plurality in the state's history. Wilson, campaigning on the slogan, "He kept Us out of War," was reelected, though narrowly.

Nineteen seventeen and 1918 were the two most difficult years in the lives of two generations of our family. I suppose I thought up to the end of January, 1917, that Bob and I had lived in difficult times. The political fights in Wisconsin during Bob's and my childhood and youth had been intense and, at times, bitter. But little, if any, of this intensity of political feeling had touched Bob or me in our personal lives. Bob had been elected president of his class as a freshman, and I had made the Wisconsin Union Board without any difficulty. Our father was generally looked on as the university's outstanding alumnus. By 1917, Mother and Father had lived a major part of their adult lives. My parents had been involved in intense political activity for nearly four decades. They had fought uphill all the way against the Old Guard in both the Republican and the Democratic parties. Behind them was an impressive record in both state and national legislation, and this record constituted the hard core of the Progressive Movement in the nation. But all those years of effort, personal sacrifice, and trial of character were only a prelude to the holocaust of abuse and assault that was to be theirs during 1917 and 1918. I completed my sophomore and junior years during this period, but my academic life was completely overshadowed by the violent emotional storm that swept over the country in general, and Wisconsin in particular, in opposition to my father and his stand against America's entry into World War I.

America was still at peace on January 22, 1917, when President Wilson delivered a special message to the Senate. His speech related to terms of peace which the Senate, under the Constitution, would consider if they were a part of a treaty ending World War I. In his message the President called for a "peace without victory." He said that equality for great and small nations, freedom of the seas, and a limitation of armaments were prerequisites to a durable peace. His proposals came close to Dad's position, and Dad led the Senate applause when the President finished. But in another week Germany announced resumption of unrestricted submarine warfare. With this, the President addressed the Congress and announced the severance of our diplomatic relations with Germany. Three weeks later the President asked for authority to arm American merchant vessels. My father opposed this action, believing that it would result in a shooting war without a formal declaration by Congress.

No one can say with any accuracy what the majority of the American people felt in February and March, 1917. We do know that on March 9 the British ambassador, Sir Cecil Spring-Rice, wrote his foreign secretary, Arthur Balfour: "All I can record for certain is that the vast majority of the country desire peace and would do a great deal to secure peace."

And we know that a referendum on the issue was held at the time in Monroe, Wisconsin. This was perhaps the only poll taken on the issue of war or peace at an official election. The vote was: for peace, 954; for war, 95. Monroe's population was largely second- and third-generation Swiss and Yankee. In an unofficial post card poll of twenty thousand representative citizens of Massachusetts, two thirds of those responding opposed war. Congressman Ernest Lundeen of Minnesota sent a war ballot to the poll lists in his district. The results showed nearly eight thousand against war and fewer than eight hundred for it.

It is safe to say that a substantial number of our people felt that it would be a tragic mistake for America to become involved in the war in Europe. In any event, my father and eleven other senators were determined to resist passage of the President's Armed Ship Bill. Because Congress adjourned automatically at noon on March 4, these twelve were able to use parliamentary tactics to block its adoption. The President then issued an angry denunciation: "A little group of willful men, representing no opinion but their own, have rendered the great Government of the United States helpless and contemptible."

The President then authorized the navy to arm and man the guns on American ships without any specific authority from Congress. The German submarines continued to attack American vessels. Wilson called Congress into a special session. On April 2 the President asked for a declaration of war against Germany. In his message he conceded that the arming of merchant ships meant war. He said that armed neutrality "is practically certain to draw us into the war without either the rights or effectiveness of belligerents."

The opposition of the "Willful Twelve" to the Armed Ship Bill had been for the very reason the President himself now conceded: it meant war—and without a declaration for it by Congress. The President's denunciation of the Willful Twelve, however, had unleashed an avalanche of criticism on these senators. The New York *Times* predicted, on March 5, that "the odium of treasonable purpose and achievement" would "rest upon their names forevermore." The New York *World*, under the heading "Delinquents and Dastards," charged "those wretches in the Senate" with having "denied their consciences and courage in order to make a Prussian Holiday," and added: "Shame on them, now and forever." The New York *Herald* predicted that the senators would be fortunate if their names were not bracketed in history with that of Benedict Arnold. At mass meetings, these men were denounced as traitors and burned in effigy, and vicious cartoons depicted them receiving the German Iron Cross. These attacks were but a prelude to what would follow.

On the final vote on the declaration of war, six senators voted No. They were William J. Stone, Democrat, Missouri; James K. Vardaman, Democrat, Mississippi; Asle J. Gronna, Progressive Republican, North Dakota; Harry Lane, Democrat, Oregon; George W. Norris, Progressive Republican, Nebraska; and Robert LaFollette, Progressive Republican, Wisconsin.

Before Dad took his position, he, like his five colleagues, recognized that they were probably committing political suicide and incurring a disgrace that would not be overcome for a generation. Before he went to the Senate floor to take his position against war, he said to George Middleton, Fola's husband: "I may not live to see my own vindication, but you will."

These six men were intelligent and were experienced in politics. They knew what they were doing and what it would cost them. Why did they take this stand? Stone was chairman of the Senate Foreign Relations Committee. He stated his reason with clarity: "I fear that the Congress is about to involve the United States in this European war, and when you do that, my belief is that you will commit the greatest national blunder of history. I shall vote against this mistake, to prevent which, God helping me, I would gladly lay down my life."

In his April 4 speech to the Senate opposing the declaration of war, Dad cited Wilson's assertion that World War I was "for democracy, for the right of those who submit to authority to have a voice in their own government," and then challenged his colleagues to meet the test of democracy themselves by submitting the issue of war or peace to a referendum of American voters. He said: "You . . . dare not do it, for you know that by a vote of more than ten to one the American people as a body would register their declaration against it."

He said that the deep, underlying cause of the war in Europe was economic rivalry: "England would tolerate no commercial rivalry. Germany would not submit to isolation." (Two years later, President Wilson himself would say: "The real reason for that war . . . was that Germany was afraid her commercial rivals were going to get the better of her, and the reason why some nations went into the war against Germany was that they thought that Germany would get the commercial advantage of them.")

Furthermore, Dad contended that we had not in fact been neutral, that our rights had been violated by both sides, and that "[our] failure to treat belligerent nations of Europe alike, the failure to reject the unlawful 'war zones' of both Germany and Great Britain, is wholly accountable for our present dilemma." He maintained that we had two honorable courses—to insist that our neutral rights on the high seas be respected by both Germany and Britain, or to withdraw our commerce from both.

He also referred to the persistent rumors of secret treaties between the Allies and said: "We do not know what is in the minds of those who have made the compact, but we are to subscribe to it. We are irrevocably, by our vote here, to marry ourselves to a nondivorceable proposition veiled from us now. Once enlisted, once in the copartnership, we will be carried through with the purposes, whatever they may be, of which we now know nothing."

On April 4 in the Senate, and on April 6 in the House, Congress voted for the declaration of war, with six senators and fifty congressmen voting No. Basically, those who voted No did so for identically the same reasons President Wilson had so long refused to lead his country into World War I. It was not based on pacifism: my father was neither by temperament nor by conviction a pacifist in any sense. Nor did any of them deny in any way that Germany had grievously violated our rights as neutrals and, in fact, had given us ample grounds for war with her. Fundamentally, they agreed with Wilson's earlier statement that "every reform we have won will be lost if we go into this war."

For those who find it difficult to understand why my father and his associates who opposed our entry into World War I were so viciously attacked, there are, I believe, clear explanations. I speak of them here because they explain the impact on me of the war hysteria while I was a student at the university in Madison.

Before America entered the war, the sentiment in the United States was divided several ways. Some people, from ties of birth and environment, were either pro-British or pro-German. Others were bound to the Allies by economic interests. The remainder, and I believe the great majority of our people, were opposed to our entry into the war because they were convinced that American involvement would make us parties to a peace that would sow the seeds of future wars and unfavorably alter American institutions and her place in the world. I do not claim that they foresaw in detail all the woes that beset the world after 1920. I do assert that they would have less to explain for their convictions than those who led us into the war.

Of these groups the pro-German counted least. The pro-British and those with economic and financial ties to the Allies were powerfully placed and wielded influence far beyond their numbers. The great financial interests—railroads, war contractors, editors and publishers of the great dailies and magazines, leaders of Society (with a capital S), and the intelligentsia—these were the most powerful molders of public opinion and the wielders of American economic power.

Big Businessmen saw that under the cloak of Patriotism they could smash the "troublemakers" of the Progressive Movement. Our entry into the war brought their Allied sympathies into unison with their economic and political interests—both foreign and domestic. They could now fight their domestic enemies—whom they called radicals—with a new and vicious weapon—the cry of Treason!

With the declaration of war, Dad supported legislation to bring the war to a successful conclusion, though he opposed conscription—I think incorrectly—and to finance its cost equitably, especially by taxing war profits. Dad led the fight to "tax the profit out of war." Roll call after roll call on his proposed amendments to tax legislation made even the Conservatives in the Senate squirm as they voted to conscript men but refused to tax war profits—at least as much as most Progressives felt to be fair. Dad told how Senator Boies Penrose, the hardboiled Republican boss from Pennsylvania, leaned over Dad's desk to say: "Baub, if you keep trying to tax these war profits, you're gonna make this war darned unpopular." This fight of Dad's on financing the war added fuel to the already burning dislike—if not hatred—of him by the Conservatives in both parties.

Except for some brief trips to Washington, I was in Madison throughout 1917 and until June, 1918. The hostile feeling against Dad had free reign throughout the country, but it seemed higher in intensity and more venomous in Wisconsin. This was so, perhaps, because it was mixed with deep personal animosities that went back for more than two decades. In Madison, in particular, it cut our family more deeply than elsewhere, for here was home —the place where our grandparents had lived and died, where Mother and Father were born, and where they had raised their children.

Again, as so often before, the daily press in Madison, in the state, and in two neighboring states—Illinois and Minnesota—were bitterly against us. In Madison the *Democrat* had been anti-LaFollette for years. The other Madison daily, the *Wisconsin State Journal*, was edited by Richard Lloyd Jones, who in 1911 had acquired control with the financial aid of supporters and friends of Dad—principally Charles R. Crane of Chicago. With the issue of the Armed Ship Bill and our entry into the war,

Jones turned against my father, and few editors exceeded his wrathful attacks on Dad. So, morning and night we got it from the two local papers. They were ably abetted by the dailies in Milwaukee and elsewhere in the state.

Until September, 1917, Dad could be attacked on little other than his failure to "stand behind the President." These attacks, though violent and often vicious, had no legal or, for that matter, even moral or patriotic foundation. Lincoln, Clay, Webster, and others had defended the right of Congress, even after the declaration of war against Mexico, to a voice in defining the war aims and had defended the right of all citizens to free speech. In Britain the same right to speak was asserted by John Bright during the Crimean War and by David Lloyd George in the Boer War—not to mention William Pitt and Edmund Burke during the American Revolution.

In August, Dad introduced a resolution calling for a statement of our aims in the war. This brought another avalanche of attacks on him from coast to coast. Although those who opposed Dad's position might question its propriety or timing, no one but those blind with animosity could call it treasonable. Wilson himself, five months later, would proclaim his Fourteen Points. Again, as with Dad's arguments against the Armed Ship Bill and the declaration of war, it is astounding how close Wilson and Dad were on essentials.

In September, 1917, Dad spoke before the convention of the farmers' Nonpartisan League in Saint Paul, Minnesota. He had intended to speak on the financing of the war. When he arrived he found that Senator Borah had already addressed the convention on that topic, so Dad decided to speak on the war aims and the right of Congress to participate in their declaration. When he showed a copy of this speech to the leaders of the convention, they objected. The war hysteria made them apprehensive. Dad offered to withdraw from the program but these men, his personal and political friends, begged him not to do so. Finally he agreed to "say a few words."

When he arrived at the auditorium, it was packed, with thousands outside unable to get in. On his entrance Dad received an ovation. The applause for this leader of the Willful Twelve, who had received nothing but rabid denunciation for months, caused the leader of the convention to say: "Go ahead, Bob; make your speech!" But it was too late for that particular speech because the manuscript was in his hotel room. However he later gave the speech in the Senate, and it was recognized as one of his ablest.

So he spoke from notes, spontaneously. Fortunately, three stenographic reporters were present and took down what he said. He discussed the financing of the war and said he had not been in favor of going to war. This statement brought cheers, so he added: "I don't mean to say that we hadn't suffered grievances; we had—at the hands of Germany—serious grievances. . . . They had interfered with the right of American citizens to travel upon the high seas—on ships loaded with munitions for Great Britain." A hostile voice called out: "What about the *Lusitania?*" Dad then asserted that the *Lusitania*, which had been torpedoed by a German submarine in 1915, carried six million rounds of ammunition. He again stated that our rights were violated by Germany, but that he had not believed that these grievances justified our going to war.

That night the Associated Press, through its Saint Paul correspondent on the *Pioneer Press*, sent out the report on his speech. Someone inserted the word *no*, so he was quoted as saying, "We had no grievances against Germany," and that he justified the sinking of the *Lusitania* and that the Morgan and Company loans and the profits of the munitions makers were our only stakes in the war. This Associated Press story was on the front pages of the nation's press by the next day, and a roar of anger came from almost every editorial page in the United States. I say "almost," but so far as I know not a newspaper in the country stopped to think before joining in the denunciation of Bob LaFollette. I say "stopped to think" because anyone who did so would have realized that no one of any competence thought we had "no grievances." But when people, especially in wartime, want to believe something, they do so.

Two days after this Saint Paul speech, the Minnesota Public Safety Commission, headed by Governor Joseph Burnquist, began proceedings to petition the United States Senate to expel Dad

for making a "disloyal and seditious" speech. There was no statement in the speech that was seditious, disloyal, or treasonable—
unless one takes the position that no one can question the wisdom
of a war once it is declared. And such a position is not legally
tenable. Two statements in the speech as *reported* in the press
were subject to challenge—that we "had no grievances against
Germany" and that the *Lusitania* carried six million rounds of
ammunition. As to the first, not only was it false, but he had repeated four times in the speech that America did have grievances
against Germany. As to the second, he was prepared to present
two witnesses who would testify that former Secretary of State
Bryan had so told them and that Bryan had so advised the President. Further, Dudley Field Malone, the collector of the Port of
New York, was prepared to testify that the manifest of the
Lusitania supported Dad's charge.

5

WAR
HYSTERIA

*"WE HAVE LIVED
WITH AN AWFUL FEAR. . . ."*

Unless one has lived through the hysteria that war foments, one cannot understand how otherwise sensible people can lose their balance of reason. Not a single great newspaper—not a single great figure of national stature—wrote or spoke a word of caution demanding that this man LaFollette at least "have his day in court" before he was condemned as a traitor. So it is not surprising that in Wisconsin few defended my father. The state Legislature overwhelmingly passed a resolution condemning him.

William T. Evjue was business manager of the *Wisconsin State Journal* when Richard Lloyd Jones published an editorial in the *Journal* branding Dad a traitor. Evjue, who was also a Progressive member of the state Assembly, angrily quit his job on the *Journal*. With the help of Dad's law partner Alfred T. Rogers and other brave friends, Evjue raised a few thousand dollars to start a new daily paper, the *Capital Times*.

The new paper faced tough sledding. Evjue and others kept it afloat almost literally by "passing the hat" at small schoolhouse meetings and through aid from loyal Progressives. By his extraordinary skill as a journalist and his courage, Evjue made it a newspaper of national standing. From September, 1917, on, we at long last had one daily that told the Progressive story.

Several incidents will give you an insight into the atmosphere that prevailed in Wisconsin in 1917 and 1918.

ITEM: At a patriotic mass meeting in the university gymnasium one of the principal speakers was a history professor—a thin, middle-aged man who would have jumped out of his skin if he had ever heard a shot fired in anger. He screamed in a high-pitched voice at young men who would soon be in the trenches in France: "I do not know about you, but as for me, *I am at war!*"

ITEM: The *Wisconsin State Journal* denounced the Beta house (where I was living) as a "hotbed of sedition and German propaganda."

ITEM: The Board of Directors of the Madison Club expelled my father as a "disloyal citizen."

ITEM: A small group of students, abetted by two faculty members, burned Dad in effigy on the university campus.

ITEM: As a guest for dinner at the Chi Psi house, I sat down only to have those at the table, with angry glances, swiftly leave my host and myself alone.

ITEM: Returning to Madison from the Christmas holidays in Washington, I saw Professor John R. Commons sitting in the same Pullman and spoke to him. I felt his coolness and could not understand, because he had often been an overnight guest in our home. In making conversation, I casually pulled a five-dollar gold piece out of my pocket. He pointed at it as if I had a snake in my hand, saying: "Where did you get *that?*" I replied: "From Dad for Christmas." He snarled: "No patriotic citizen would have gold in his possession in time of war."

But of all the harsh and bitter things said or written, nothing cut so deeply with our family as the round robin circulated among the faculty of the University of Wisconsin in 1918 and signed by four hundred of its members, addressed to the United States Senate and accusing my father of giving aid and comfort to the enemy. It was signed, among others, by President Charles R. Van Hise—Mother and Dad's classmate and intimate friend. For them, this was "Et tu, Brute!"

Aside from the dinner incident, the only animosity shown toward me personally was at a chapter meeting of the Betas after the "hotbed of sedition" editorial in the *Journal*. One member suggested that Joe Farrington, Ralph Sucher, Mike Colean, and I guard our tongues. So Joe and I moved to other quarters. During the war years I never heard the name LaFollette spoken in public places without flinching and bracing myself for some epithet.

On November 9, 1917, Dad filed a suit for libel against the Madison *Democrat* and followed with two others against the *Journal* and the directors of the Madison Club (except Alf Rogers, who had voted No to the charge that Dad was disloyal). Under the practice in Wisconsin, and generally elsewhere in the United States, parties to civil suits are subject to examination by the other party to the action before trial. Such examinations were conducted against Richard Lloyd Jones of the *Journal*, O. D. Brandenburg of the *Democrat*, and the directors of the Madison Club.

Political experience in America has taught that anyone in public life who resorts to libel or slander suits runs a great risk. The law of libel and slander is comparatively lenient in the United States, compared, for example, with Britain, and gives wide latitude for "fair comment." Also, in the nature of our politics, leaders must be prepared to "take it" as well as "dish it out." Resorting to legal action in politics is something akin to a boxer yelping to the referee instead of slugging it out. Lastly, once a complaint is filed, the subject of the complaint is privileged and may be published freely.

Dad's three libel suits proved the exception to the rule. The subject of the libels was the charge of treason—"giving aid and comfort to the enemy," etc. Such a charge is libelous per se if it cannot be proved. Once the suits were filed, it was a danger signal to editors and publishers throughout the country.

Gilbert Roe was born in Dane County, Wisconsin, and had been one of Dad's law partners until Dad was elected governor. Gil then moved to New York, but he remained one of the most beloved and intimate friends of Dad's life. Gil was a first-class lawyer, with courage that matched his brains. He took the laboring oar in these cases in association with another old friend and adviser of Dad's, Charles Crownhart. Gil was also Dad's counsel in the proceedings before the Senate Committee on Privileges and Elections, to which the petitions for his expulsion had been filed.

The adverse examinations of the defendants—especially Richard Lloyd Jones—were dramatic and powerful antidotes to the reckless and vicious attacks they had made on Dad. I sat through the proceedings and occasionally made a suggestion that Gil welcomed, not so much for its worth but because my obvious, though I think controlled, anger added to the witnesses' discomfort. Not a single defendant could offer a scintilla of evidence to justify the charges. It was gratifying to watch them squirm as, in effect, they ate their words. The *Capital Times* carried the verbatim questions and answers as they were taken down by the court reporter. Its circulation was not large, but it went to leading Progressives throughout the state and was manna from Heaven.

In addition to our other troubles during this period, Bob came down with another attack of illness in January, 1918. I say "another" because he had taken sick in his sophomore year in 1915 with a streptococcus infection that had lasted through the summer of that year. Now the second attack of the same infection was to prove worse than the first. Bob was to be in bed in critical condition until late July and would not fully recover for ten months more.

Another complication in this period was our family finances. The salary of a United States senator was then $7,500 a year. Then, as now, nearly every senator and congressman had to maintain two homes—one in Washington and the other in the area he represented. Because Dad had assumed the responsibility of a weekly magazine, he had to borrow money to keep it afloat. To meet these expenses, we had incurred a $14,000 mortgage on Maple Bluff Farm, and, as Dad anticipated, the Madison bank that held it notified him it must be paid. By the middle of June the medical expenses of Bob's illness exceeded $3,500. After an internal fight, the board of directors of the Beaver's Mutual Life

Insurance of Madison, by a vote of three to two, voted to grant a new mortgage loan of $20,000 on the farm. Dad had just about that amount in life insurance, a few shares of stock, and an interest in a zinc mine in southwestern Wisconsin that paid some dividends during the war period.

Another serious blow to our finances was the loss of Dad's earning power on the platform because of the controversy over his war position. During his five years as governor he had supplemented his salary by filling lecture dates, and during the first twelve years in the Senate he had a substantial income from lecturing.

The spring of 1918 brought another disappointment. A special election was held in Wisconsin to fill a vacancy caused by the death of Dad's colleague, Senator Paul Husting. Irvine Lenroot, a former supporter of Dad who now favored the war, was the choice of the Conservative Republicans, and James Thompson of La Crosse was ours. The war hysteria made it impossible to conduct our usual type of campaign. Progressive finances were worse off than ever. Aside from the struggling *Capital Times*, the daily press was unanimously and bitterly against us. In retrospect, Thompson made a remarkable run, losing by only 2,400 votes to Lenroot, who then won out over the Democratic candidate. We had hoped to win, and the result increased, if possible, our dark gloom.

As I have mentioned, petitions had been filed with the Senate Committee on Privileges and Elections asking Dad's expulsion from the Senate. These petitions and the nub of the attacks on Dad had stemmed from the misquotation in his Saint Paul speech that we "had no grievances against Germany" and his statement that the *Lusitania* carried six million rounds of ammunition. It was not until May 21, 1918, that the committee met, and Gil Roe, Dad's counsel, got the opportunity to present formally and publicly the argument for Dad's defense. He did a masterly job because he was an able lawyer and because his cause was immensely right. The transcripts of the speech showed that the wicked "no" had been inserted—and, without doubt, deliberately. Furthermore, both Senator Thomas J. Walsh (hostile to Dad at the time) and Senator James A. Reed publicly conceded that the *Lusitania* carried munitions.

At the time of the committee hearings the Associated Press telegraphed the committee chairman, formally acknowledged its error, and apologized. On October 11, 1917, Dad had formally called the attention of the committee to the misquotation. Yet it was not until seven months later that it was retracted. And the charges were not discussed by the Senate until January, 1919— sixteen months after they were filed. Before the final vote took place on January 16, Senator John Sharp Williams delivered, in flagrant violation of Senate rules, as personal and vituperative an attack on Dad as was ever delivered in the history of the Senate. Williams repeatedly called Dad disloyal and a liar. The vote was fifty to twenty-one to dismiss the disloyalty charges. Dad wrote to me: "It took all the guts I had to sit still throughout Williams' drunken attack."

In the pages that follow, Phil describes his military service during World War I. But even before America formally entered the war, he sought some means of making a positive contribution. The following letter was marked "strictly personal":

Maple Bluff Farm,
Madison, Wisconsin,
January 19, 1917

Daddy dear:—

I am going to try and write this letter to you just as I would say it to you. And all I ask is that you read it *through* without becoming prejudiced at my first statement. Further I ask that you try and put yourself in my place and see it from my point of view. Now I'll begin.

I want very much—more than I have wanted to do anything in a long, long time—to go to France and join the American Ambulance Corps there.

I am not asking your consent or approbation without knowing full well that you will object, largely I think, because of fear that something will happen to me there—that I would probably get killed or wounded, or something like that. These are the facts: There have been some four hundred and twenty-five odd American College men over there doing what they can to alleviate what suffering they can, and there have been just TWO killed and four wounded. . . .

I want to do it because of my inner feeling towards the war: I really do not believe in war, but if I were going down the street and came across two fellows who had been fighting and they were both badly knocked up, I would be a good deal of a chum if I didn't do all I could to help them out, no matter what they had been fighting about—and so it is with this war. This work would not prolong the war a half hour—but it does give a lot of poor devils a lot of comfort and help. . . .

Now Dad, I really feel that I know what my weaknesses are as well if not better than anyone else, at least some of them. This kind of thing is what I need (from a purely selfish point of view), it would make a man out of me. In a great many ways, I am weak and childish, I need something to bracen me up—to make me stronger morally and physically—something that will give me assurance in myself physically—assurance that I have the real stuff in me. This will do it as nothing else will. I say this to you—as I have never said it to anyone else—I feel that in some ways I am not a real "guy" when it comes to meeting real problems— But I am just as confident that going through a thing of this kind will develope that in me—that I have the will power and the courage to make my self do what a man should. . . .

Dad, if I am ever to amount to what I aspire to—if I am going to be able to live the life that I have hopes of living, I have got to have something I haven't got now—you can give it to me—by letting me go?

All I ask is that you will look at it with the future in view, and I'll be always the same,

Phil

The letter was not mailed. Later, Phil added the notation, "Changed mind to other view."

Like most young men, I had given lots of thought to what I should do personally about the war. I would be twenty-one on May 8, 1918. Should I enlist or wait for the draft? I never seriously considered anything but enlisting. The question was which service I would choose. In the spring I learned from a brother Beta, John Richards, the head football coach at Wisconsin, that there would be a Reserve Officers Training Corps camp at Fort Sheridan, Illinois, the coming June. John was a lifelong Progressive and a close personal friend. I never knew whether he agreed or disagreed with Dad's stand on the war, but I knew he would give me good advice. I did not know anything about soldiering, but John took me to the commandant, and he arranged for me to go to Fort Sheridan. The camp was for only one month, and at its close one could enlist or not, as one chose.

Those who went to this camp were excused from final examinations. I was glad of this because it had been difficult to concentrate on academic work. I had, in fact, flunked two courses simply by neglecting to study. So early in June, Joe Farrington and I took the train for Chicago and nearby Fort Sheridan. On the first day, when we lined up for assignment to squads according to height, Joe shrunk a bit and I talled a bit, and we got into the same squad. I certainly was a candidate for the awkward squad. On the second or third day I was called on to give the commands in close order drill. I promptly got the company completely fouled up, and it took one of the officers to untangle it.

That same day a call came for a typist. I had had a typewriter for years, and with the hunt-and-peck system I wrote everything with reasonable accuracy and at good speed. For the first few days I was company clerk, but when the company commander found that I could think as well as type, I suddenly found myself made first sergeant.

The company officers had been passed over for overseas duty and were disgruntled with their assignment to a training camp, so they had little enthusiasm for their jobs. During the second week a crisis arose: the camp commander arrived to inspect our company area. One of the second lieutenants was out with the company on a field exercise and the other officers were absent— as I remember it—at a ball game. Apparently I did the honors satisfactorily enough, for the next day the camp commander complimented our commanding officer on the condition of his area. From that day on I was "in solid," and aside from military training I was left to run the company.

Shortly before the camp closed, a notice came from camp headquarters to the effect that after a few days' leave the camp would continue for another nine or ten weeks and at its close those qualified would be commissioned as second lieutenants of infantry. I telephoned Dad, and he urged me to come to Washington. I went to see the family and to talk over my plans. There was never any question in my mind of my not staying in service. During the first days at Fort Sheridan I was interviewed, and asked what my father wanted me to do. I replied: "He wants me to do just what I feel is right."

When I arrived in Washington I visited Bob. For more than six months he had been bedridden, battling the infection. His legs would swell; when that subsided, it would be his chest and arms, then his face, then a repetition of the cycle. He was skin and bones, but he was still fighting, with Mother, and especially Dad, at his bedside night and day.

Dad said he could arrange for a Marine Corps physical examination for me through Secretary of the Navy Josephus Daniels, who had disapproved of the vicious attacks on Dad. So I went down to the marine base at Quantico, Virginia, for the physical. I passed the examination and was eligible for the corps. That night Dad and I discussed whether I should stay at Fort Sheridan or join the marines. Once we were in the war, Dad felt that it was altogether honorable for me to enlist. He emphasized that the choice of service was mine, but he favored the Marines because he feared that in the army I might get under the control of someone who, from hatred of him, might single me out for "special" treatment. He was confident that Daniels would see that I got, not any favors, but fair treatment in the Marine Corps. But I had been treated well at Fort Sheridan and decided to return there.

Before leaving for the train, I visited Bob. Both of us were too choked up to talk, so I left a note for him with Mary. I wrote: "I have just told you good-bye but could not express to you dear old pal what my old heart felt. I didn't want to try because it would have been a miserable failure. . . . You have faculties and a personality possessed by one in ten million. If you could only know the hold you have on people's thoughts and affections you would believe me when I say you have an untold future of service to the world of thought and and action. . . . Thine to the end of Time's Journey." Later Fola wrote me that Bob said again and again: "I love Phil so—no one knows what he means to me. All the quarrels we used to have have gone into love. He is such a wonderful boy. He has such a wonderful future before him."

Just before going to the train I talked with Dad about the war. Like millions of others, I had been impressed with President Wilson's Fourteen Points and expressed the hope that perhaps the world might get a just and lasting peace. But Dad had no illusions on the subject. He said the war had started over the commercial rivalry between Britain and Germany and that the Allied secret treaties, exposed by the revolution in Russia, made it clear that our Allies—especially France, Britain, and Italy— had no intention of following the Fourteen Points but intended to collect the spoils of victory and sow the seeds of another war.

So I went back to Fort Sheridan. Within a few days I received word that Bob had been taken to Hot Springs, Virginia, and in the succeeding weeks that he had turned the corner for the better. Early in September I learned that Dad, Mother, Mary, and Bob were going to California and would pass through Chicago en route. I got a leave and met their train at Lafayette, Indiana. Bob was still so thin that I carried him in my arms across the station. It was a brief visit but a happy one because, though it would take months for him to recover fully, Bob at last was on the road to good health.

In mid-September I received a commission as second lieutenant of infantry and was ordered to report to Norman, Oklahoma— the home of the University of Oklahoma. On arrival at the Student Army Training Corps headquarters I was assigned to the job of personnel adjutant. After the Armistice of November 11 I took a quickie course at Dallas, Texas, on discharge procedure. I learned enough so that when the order came directing the release of all military personnel, everyone except the captain and myself was out of the army by the day before Christmas, 1918, and all records were boxed and shipped to Washington.

I had planned to go to Washington to be with Dad for Christmas, but he insisted that I should go to La Jolla, California, to be with Mother, Bob, Mary, and Aunt Jo Siebecker. With the war over, we had much to be thankful for. Dad summed it up in a letter to the family: "How favored we have been and are. We have lived with an awful fear in our hearts for our beloved boys so long that as we begin to come back toward normal life and conditions with both of them still with us and the balance of the flock well—that I want to pray or cry or sing my thankfulness for all our blessings.

"And then my heart goes out to the millions who sit in their broken, desolated homes suffering the unspeakable horrors which this wicked, brutal war has brought upon them. Peace can bring them nothing until they find the peace that passeth all understanding."

Mother, Bob, Mary, and Aunt Jo were living in a small cottage on the beach at La Jolla. The warm, balmy weather, the peaceful Pacific, and the awful load that was lifting from our lives gave us an inner peace at Christmas that seemed almost unbelievable. Until those burdens began to leave us I don't think any of us had realized how horrible those two years had been. There were deep scars within each of us that we would carry as long as we lived. But the ceaseless strain and daily apprehension were gone.

6

THE OLD MAN

". . . MY GOD,
WHAT GUTS HE'S GOT!"

It was wonderful to be with the family, but I stayed only a few days. I was eager to get back to the university and to finish my senior year. I returned to Madison in time for the second semester and roomed again at the Beta house with Joe Farrington.

During this last semester Joe and I both fell in love. Joe's girl, a fellow journalism student, was very good-looking. He was head over heels in love with her and married her a year after he graduated. He and I were to remain friends until his death—a friendship without discord or discontent for forty years.

The girl who attracted me was Betty Head. We had known each other from childhood. Her father was a Madison physician, and her mother a woman of strong character, intelligence, and charm. Betty was extremely good-looking, and intelligent. She sparkled with vitality, and she attracted me like a powerful magnet. On a warm spring night we agreed to become engaged. I went back to the Beta house walking on air and intoxicated with love. Betty had a job in New York for the next year. I had decided to go to Washington to take my first year of law at the George Washington University Law School.

The decision to study law was greatly influenced by my mother. She had studied law at Wisconsin as a bride and was the first woman graduated from the Wisconsin Law School. Her main point was valid for anyone who is undecided about a career: She said that the study of law is invaluable even if one never practices it. It is not the learning of rules of law that is so important as learning to think—especially in legal terms. The cornerstone of that thinking is that in issues between people, or peoples, there are at least two sides, so do not take sides until you understand and weigh the problem as a whole.

From the day in September, 1919, when I entered George Washington until I received my LLB from Wisconsin in 1922 I was fascinated with the law. The law is often described as a jealous mistress. During my law school years I gave her no reason for complaint. I devoured the law books and digested from the leading cases the rules or principles of law that they set forth. Before the end of each semester I drafted an outline for every course and knew one or more cases illustrating each point. And with important questions I could quote from memory a paragraph or so from leading cases. While in law school, I took time to listen to the arguments in some of the important cases before the Supreme Court of the United States. Justice Brandeis often alerted me to some case of special interest before the court.

From September, 1919, to June, 1920, I ran the family checkbook. From the time I was a youngster we went through periods of family financial feast or famine. The magazine's deficits were especially high at times, and it would show up in the family car's standing in the garage for want of a spare tire—or in Dad's wondering if the help might be pilfering a bit from the larder. I felt the painful frustration of stretching Dad's salary further than it would go—the task of so much "on account" on this bill and so much on that one. This experience, on top of all that had gone before, gave me a horror of debt that stayed with me.

Dad and Mother wanted all of us home for Christmas, 1919. Mary was studying at an art school in New York. She, Fola, and her husband, Mid, came down from New York, as did Betty Head and Mike Colean. Joe and Betty Farrington and Ralph Sucher were in Washington, too. So on the night after Christmas we rolled up the rugs and had a gay, wonderful party. This was the first chance the family had really had to know Betty, and they took her into their hearts at once. But on the morning after our party the first "rift within the lute" appeared between Betty and me. I was born with great reservoirs of energy, which I expended lavishly; but this energy had to be restored with sleep, and Mother had always encouraged my long naps and late sleeping (when possible) in the morning. So, on that morning after our party, I slept and slept while Bob chafed with impatience at my woeful lack of gallantry. Finally he routed me out of bed with angry comments. Betty was returning to New York that afternoon, and I rode on the train with her as far as Baltimore in an endeavor to make my peace.

This episode was a warning to her that perhaps I would not "break into double harness" very easily; and her reaction to it warned me that marriage was a double harness affair which, to be lasting, had to be based on attractions, interests, and values beyond the physical. Our relationship was not improved by one of her brothers-in-law, who was a "LaFollette hater" of the first degree. That summer we became, by mutual agreement, unengaged. Shortly thereafter she married, happily, a distinguished doctor. She was a wonderful person whom I shall always happily remember. I think we were both right in recognizing that we did not share enough of the same values in living—what one wants to give to and take out of a marriage for the long pull.

During the same Christmas vacation, Professor Max Otto of the Department of Philosophy at Wisconsin came to our house on Sixteenth Street for a brief visit. I had taken (as Isen did later) Max's course Man and Nature. Few students who came under his teaching were left unchanged. He taught no absolutes other than integrity. He was the flint to the tinder of our minds. He brought light to the dark, thoughtless corridors of our brains. He could unfold the mysteries of life in a tree, a plant, or in the face of a great soul deftly sketched on a blackboard. Loving, loved, shy, and tender, he had in his small body a heart of oak that never faltered under fire.

This great teacher wrote his impressions at the time of his visit with us:

"I have long had a kind of apologetic admiration for his [Dad's] fighting qualities and great admiration for his mind. Like many other people, I was repelled by what I regarded as a ruthless streak in him. I had heard him mercilessly brand men in public life, some of whom I admired. . . . I did not relish the thought of sitting next to 'Fighting Bob.'

"Then he came in.

"We shook hands and he looked at me with friendly, affectionate eyes, not at all the platform eyes with which I was familiar. All stiffness vanished. He won me over immediately. If 'immediately' is not quite the correct word, that is because his first gaze was searching, disconcerting.

"At any rate, my impulse after breakfast was to run upstairs and write a card to everybody I knew, and another one to the world at large, saying to them all: 'I have met Senator LaFollette and I am his without reservation!' It was almost as if I had returned to my boyhood and had met my first hero."

Of our family he wrote:

"All who live here are individual persons; the father, the mother, the children. There is spontaneous, obvious appreciation of the Senator as a great man, but they all speak up, they disagree, they give advice. They seem to be doing the job as a group. Even the maid is a person."

Our first political test in Wisconsin since the end of World War I would come in the election of delegates to the 1920 Republican National Convention. Dad was not feeling well; his gallbladder seemed to be kicking up again. So he and Bob went to the Mayo Clinic late in January, 1920, stopping off in Madison for conferences with our leaders. The Mayos advised Dad that his gallbladder should come out, but because of the prevalence of influenza they felt that the operation should be delayed.

Dad and Bob returned to Madison to help our leaders put our candidates for delegates to the Republican convention on the ballot. Dad was called back to Washington for the votes on reservations to, and the final vote on ratification of, the Treaty of Versailles. The treaty failed to receive the required two-thirds majority because twenty-three Democrats joined twelve Republicans, including Dad, in voting No (the Democrats, of course, because of President Wilson's opposition to the reservations).

Dad and Bob got back to Wisconsin less than two weeks before the April primary. Consequently we would not have time for any real campaigning, and our forces concentrated largely on getting out our vote. In view of all that had happened in the previous three years, the results were a tremendous comfort, as we elected almost all our convention delegates.

After this victory came the question of agreeing on a slate of Progressive candidates for nomination in the Republican primary in September. Because of the excellent showing he had made in the 1918 special election, James Thompson was the Progressive choice to oppose Senator Irvine Lenroot. Three men were eager to be our candidate for governor. They were John J. Blaine, state attorney general; Edward Dithmar, the lieutenant governor; and Joseph D. Beck. All three had been lifelong Progressives and had stood fast during the bitter attacks on us during the war. It was obvious that if we had two—let alone three—Progressive candidates running against a sole Conservative, we would be licked.

Dad met with these three eager candidates and with other leaders from all over the state, trying to get them to agree on one candidate. He was overdue at the Mayo Clinic for the operation; yet he did not want to leave with the question up in the air. Day after day he went to his law office on West Main Street —six rooms on the second floor over a grocery store. There he sat and talked hour after hour for days—then into weeks—while he tried to get these three men to agree on which one would be our candidate. He expressed no preference among them. At long last Beck withdrew. That left Blaine and Dithmar. Both were Dad's personal friends. Both were ambitious. Neither was a big man, though Blaine was far abler and more intelligent and better equipped for the governorship.

I often wished that those who saw Dad as a boss or dictator could have sat through these seemingly never-ending conferences aimed at getting two ambitious men to agree to act in the common cause—even if only to decide by drawing cuts. They were adamant. Finally they both promised to hold the situation "as is" while my father went to the Mayo Clinic.

He went to Rochester. His gallbladder was removed. And Ed Dithmar announced his candidacy for the Republican nomination for governor almost before Dad was out from under the anesthetic. In response, Dad endorsed Blaine.

The prolonged delay in the weeks before he went to Rochester, with the day-by-day comments in the press on his efforts to bring unity to our ranks, made it clear to our leaders throughout the state that "Bob" was not dictating but pleading—delaying until our supporters could themselves see what was going on, until they grew exasperated at the failure of these men to agree on a common course—until Dad's followers had themselves grown impatient with him for *not* interfering.

This is an important lesson for political leaders: Often it is not enough to make the correct decision. You must wait until the passing of time itself makes clear that your decision is inevitable. Words—explanations—are hard to see. Events—disclosed slowly enough for all to see—are often more eloquent than words of justification.

Another factor in the 1920 picture was the increasing recognition by friend and foe alike that Bob LaFollette was a great human character and political leader who was leaving an imprint on the life of his generation. He was still hated by some, but the virulent tide was ebbing.

Warren Harding and Calvin Coolidge were nominated at the Republican convention in Chicago. Progressives disappointed at that outcome turned their attention to two other political groups. The Committee of Forty-Eight, mostly comprising Progressives who had supported Theodore Roosevelt in his third-party campaign in 1912, opened a convention in Chicago on July 10. The Labor party—a "left" to "close to Communist" group—called a convention for the next day.

Neither group had an effective national organization, but the men at the core of the Labor party were skilled in Marxian tactics. Committees from the two conventions tried to agree on a platform that would satisfy Dad and secure him as a third-party candidate. I do not dwell on the details because their efforts failed. The only importance of the incident was to make clear that Dad and his type of American progressivism understood the

Communist tactic of "boring from within" and would have no part then or later with "united fronts." So, with that short delay, we all went back to our real job of the 1920 campaign in Wisconsin.

The 1920 campaign was, of course, not the first one for Bob or me. We had followed with intense interest—conscious of intimate family involvement—each campaign from 1904 on. And in 1916, Bob and I drove our Model T Ford for Dad all over Wisconsin. But in 1920 I began to really get my feet wet.

At Rome (not Italy but a village in Jefferson County), I made my first political speech. In the years that were to follow I would make thousands—and I mean *thousands*—more. Even now, I can see that enormous audience at Rome; there must have been all of fifty people. The seats were planks supported by empty beer kegs. The hall was lighted by two or three kerosene lanterns hanging from rafters. Though I was not even the main speaker, I had made the plunge. I found I could swim.

Of course, I was going to law school. But I began a pattern I was to follow for the next twenty years: Work during the day seven days a week, then at night—two or three times a week— a round trip drive of eighty or a hundred miles and a speech.

Blaine, with Dad's endorsement, won the gubernatorial nomination but by only a plurality. In politics, unless the head of the ticket wins by a substantial margin, the rest of the ticket—the other state officers and members of the Legislature that support him—only squeak by, or fail, depending on their individual strength. It takes a landslide to pull the whole crew to victory, and we failed to achieve that goal in 1920. We were unable to prevent the renomination of Senator Lenroot. Nevertheless, Blaine had won the gubernatorial nomination, and that was really something in that still overheated war atmosphere, and especially considering the usual tightness of our meager financial resources and the ever present hostility of the press. In November, Blaine and Lenroot both won in the Republican sweep that carried Warren Harding into the White House.

In February, 1922, I graduated from law school and was admitted to the bar. I hung out my shingle at my father's law office in the Bank of Wisconsin building on the Capitol Square in Madison. My father never practiced law after he was elected governor in 1900. He felt that it was a conflict of interest for a public officer of high rank to handle legal matters for private individuals or corporations. However, he maintained an office for use on his visits to Wisconsin. His partnership with Alfred T. Rogers was purely nominal. And so was mine.

During the war there had been a moratorium on political meetings. It was too dangerous to hold them. People were too frightened to come out. And in 1920 my father was recuperating from his gallbladder operation. So in March, 1921, when he came back to Madison from Washington, he had not made an important appearance in Madison for four years. Friends arranged for him to speak in the Assembly chamber. Before he appeared, he conferred with his trusted friends, who were old hands at politics. They loved the "Old Man." They desperately wanted him to be vindicated in the next senatorial election. They cautioned him. "Don't talk about the war." They unanimously urged, "The war hysteria is receding. Don't stir it up. Talk about domestic issues. Spread balm on the scars. Let your old friends who deserted us in the war days come back to our camp. This is no time for a fight. Just take it easy, Bob." They *all* advised this. The Old Man listened. He was a great talker, but he was also a great listener. He made no comment, no commitment. He just listened.

The day came. The Assembly chamber in the Capitol was packed to the roof. Dad began his speech with the formal graciousness typical more of his generation than of ours. It was not artificial or stilted. It followed a measured tempo and rhythm permissible before the day of television and radio.

On first sight people were often surprised at my father's size. Though he was always thought of as being tall, he was only five feet six inches, and weighed around 170 pounds. Especially in photographs his pompadour hair, square jaw, high forehead, and stocky frame gave an impression of power and height. It was the figure of an indomitable fighter with high intellect and depth of emotions—all controlled by an iron will.

My father was a man of deep affections. No man who does not feel and express warm affection for others ever stirs reciprocity of devotion in others. He loved people. They knew he did and loved him in return. He was hated by some. And in particular cases, that, too, he returned with compound interest. It was this intrepid fighter—with such warmth in his heart—who stood before that audience in the Assembly chamber in the Capitol. He was back home after the war. He expressed his thanks to his friends and to his neighbors—friend and foe—for cordially welcoming him back to the place where he had been born and had made his home for a lifetime.

Then he changed. The muscles of his jaw tightened. His blue eyes shot fire. He raised his right arm, fingers together, hand upright and waving aloft like a banner. The words came out like salvos from a sixteen-inch battery:

"I am going to be a candidate for reelection to the United States Senate. I do not want the vote of a single citizen under any misapprehension of where I stand: I WOULD NOT CHANGE MY RECORD ON THE WAR FOR THAT OF ANY MAN, LIVING OR DEAD."

A few moments of deathly silence followed as the audience began to grasp what he was saying and what it meant. There he stood—sixty-five years old. After four years of as wicked a beating as ever came to a man in public life in American history: Defiant! No quarter asked or given! The fight was on!

Pandemonium broke loose. He got the greatest ovation of his life. A member of the state senate who had fought Bob La-Follette for nearly forty years—and would still fight him—sat in his seat, tears running down his cheeks as he shook his head, repeating to himself: "I hate the son of a bitch; but, my God, what guts he's got!"

Thus began the campaign of 1922. There was nothing like it in Wisconsin history. It was a triumphant march up and down and across the state. No halls were large enough to hold the crowds. It was grueling work for a man of his age, after all the pounding he had taken—and given—through the years. But it was balm to his soul.

Five years had passed since he had taken his stand against our entry into World War I. He had known what lay ahead. He had known what nations did to leaders who stood out against war. One of my treasures is Trevelyan's *Life of John Bright*, so carefully marked by Dad at poignant paragraphs setting forth Bright's experiences in his opposition to the Crimean War: One such passage reads: "To attack the justice and wisdom of a popular war while it is still in progress requires more courage than any other act in a political society that has outgrown the assassin's dagger and the executioner's block. And it requires not only most courage but most power and skill. To perform it well is not only the rarest but one of the most valuable of public services, because to arraign an unjust and unwise war is the only way to prevent another."

There had been no histrionics when Dad said to his intimates back in 1917: "You may live to see the day when people understand the awful mistake we are about to make. I never will." But he did.

In the 1922 campaign I was on my own for the first time. A friend loaned me an old Lewis car for the campaign. It was a big, seven-passenger touring car. The wheels were nearly as big as I was. Changing a tire was quite a job. And every time the wheels turned, the car seemed to swallow a gallon of gas. I was alone. It was hard work physically—five speeches a day, covering the west side of the state. This was the less populous area of Wisconsin, and I figured the campaign managers felt that I could do less harm there. In any event, there was such intense interest in the campaign that even a young fellow, with my name, could draw crowds—nothing like my father's, of course, but good-sized audiences of hundreds in the daytime and a thousand or more at night at the county seat. It was strenuous. It was exhilarating. It was fun. I was hitting my stride. By September, 1922, I had made more than two hundred speeches. I was not bad by then. At twenty-five I had become a seasoned campaigner.

The primary election fell on September 5. We had a set routine in the LaFollette family for election days. In the morning we all went together to vote. That was accomplished with the usual news photographers taking their shots. Then we returned to Maple Bluff Farm. Then came long hours of waiting while hundreds of thousands of men and women from the farms, villages, and cities trooped to the polls.

If you have an intimate stake in a hard-fought election, the only suspense like it is the long wait for a jury's verdict. Indeed, it *is* the verdict of a jury, the verdict of thousands of people instead of the vote of twelve. The minutes seem to stretch into hours, and the hours into days. You pick up a book. You read the newspapers for the third time. You put them down. You go for a short walk. You come back and sit down. You wait—and wait. There seems to be a pervasive stillness. You think you can hear those paper ballots dropping into those boxes in three thousand precincts across the state.

Every election night the family gathered around the dining room table to tabulate the results as they came in over the telephone. Open before us was the *Wisconsin Blue Book*—published biennially by the state and containing the results, precinct by precinct, of every election district in the state in the most recent primary and general elections.

As I listened, many years later, to the Presidential election returns over television—with all the charts and the grunting and wheezing of complicated computers—I could not help thinking: None of those machines can yet equal the accuracy of a smart politician with a pencil and paper—one who knows his precincts. If you know a precinct, you know far more than its geographical location. You know the people in it—whether they are farmers, workers, business, or professional people. You know whether they are predominately Yankee, Irish, German, or Scandinavian—Catholic, Jewish, or Protestant. And you have before you in the *Blue Book* exactly how they voted in the previous election.

Armed with this experience and with the record, you will catch a trend almost at once from the first precincts to report in. And after you have a comparatively few scattered returns from the state—they must be scattered so that you have a sampling that will not reflect a purely local political current—you will know whether it is a landslide or a photo finish.

So we waited around the dining room table—the family and a few very close friends. In this business, experience has taught you not to plan a party, just have those who are your most intimate friends. If the results are bad, you will find it more agreeable to be alone. If you win, then the rush to congratulate the victor will come with astonishing speed.

The phone rang. The first precinct was in. It was the village of Butternut. The vote: LaFollette, 111; William Ganfield, president of Carroll College, 6. The phone rang faster and faster, reporting such fantastic results as: LaFollette, 184; Ganfield, 3. LaFollette, 141; Ganfield, 1. LaFollette, 401; Ganfield, 12.

No one had doubted that Dad would win, and by a large enough margin to carry in the rest of the ticket as well. But nothing like this had happened in Wisconsin's history. It was the greatest, most overwhelming victory since Wisconsin was admitted to the Union. He carried seventy of the state's seventy-one counties, including areas that had always voted for his opponents. He and Mother—and the rest of us—who had gone through such dark, bitter years, could hardly believe it. It was far more than a political victory. It was an astonishing tribute to a man's character. Doubtful friends—and theretofore implacable enemies—all had come to a well-nigh unanimous verdict that, differ how they might on this or that issue, Bob LaFollette was a great man and a great leader.

Alf Rogers, with his accustomed practical foresight, said: "Let's chew this down to the rind. Enjoy it to the last shred. In this old world you get so damned many kicks in the pants, or elsewhere in your anatomy, you had better really chew on this one."

The overwhelming victory in the primary meant that the November election was a foregone conclusion. It had reverberations in Minnesota and North Dakota. What looked like a one-sided scrap was on in Minnesota. It looked hopeless. The Farmer-Labor party had picked a small-town dentist, Henrik Shipstead, to run against Frank B. Kellogg, a Republican, for the United States Senate. (The Democrats were not a serious factor in the election.)

Dad had a very special interest in that fight in Minnesota: Frank Kellogg had presented to the Senate the resolution to expel my father on the grounds of disloyalty—in plain words, as a traitor. It would be payment on a long overdue account with Frank

Kellogg if by some chance he could be given even a close race. And if, by some remote chance, he could be beaten, that would make Dad's cup really overflow.

Dad decided to go to both North Dakota and Minnesota. He spent two days supporting Lynn J. Frazier, the Republican nominee in North Dakota, and then went to Minnesota to endorse Shipstead. I was to meet him for the Minnesota trip. The first meeting was scheduled for Mankato.

With the announcement that Bob LaFollette was coming into Minnesota, the press, divers and sundry patriotic organizations, and public officials let out a roar of angry protests. Overnight the senatorial race became front-page news. People in Minnesota who had never heard of Henrik Shipstead were now reading about him every day—not favorably, of course. His name was inevitably carried along with every attack on Dad. At once Bob LaFollette was "running" for the Senate in Minnesota under the name of Shipstead.

This was going to be fun, but we did not know it when we arrived in Mankato. It was dark. The air was raw as the train pulled into the station. The weak light bulbs made the station platform look unfriendly. It was. There was no one—not a soul —to meet us. This did not look like a good beginning. We thought that perhaps we should have stayed home.

As we walked over to a taxicab, a down-at-the-heel figure slunk out of the shadows. At last a greeter! He was that, but he was not at his best. He had fortified his weakened courage with several drinks, and he left us on the platform. We took the taxi to the rather moth-eaten hotel. The clerk at the desk informed us that feeling against Dad was running high and that we could expect trouble that night. We had some sandwiches and coffee sent up. We ate. Neither of us had much to say. Dad was obviously worried and troubled. What troubled him was me. Should he go over to the hall and start the meeting himself? Or should he send a twenty-five-year-old alone to face what might be a mob?

When we got to that hall we were met by a delegation from Minneapolis and Saint Paul headed by Floyd Olson. Floyd was the real stem-winder of the Farmer-Labor party of Minnesota.

He was a husky, tough, Norwegian-descended lawyer who later became governor of his state and a national figure. All in all, he was a great guy. No local personage would introduce us, so Floyd did the honors.

The hall was packed to the rafters, and I started in like a rocket. I gave them the same kind of speech I had been making in Wisconsin all summer. It wasn't bad. It took that audience by storm, especially when I picked out a couple of prosperous, pompous-looking fellows sitting in mid-center and gave them both barrels. It happened that they were superpatriots who had led nasty attacks on helpless people whose only sin was their German name. The pent-up fury—built up in those five years of abuse by political bullies—exploded. A tongue-tied stutterer could have succeeded with that audience, and I was not that. My speech was built around the theme that Dad and the five others who had voted against America's entry into the World War had done so from the conviction that our vital interests as a nation were not at stake, that our entry would inevitably involve us in the economic and territorial ambitions of our Allies, and that the six senators had been hounded from one end of the country to the other as traitors for saying what later events proved to be true.

In his own speech, Dad did a magnificent job. Then we went back to our dingy hotel. Before we got into bed, Dad walked over to me. He took my cheeks in his hands. Tears streamed down his face. He said: "You are *my* boy."

The sensational success of the Mankato meeting caused the powers-that-be in Minnesota to see red and their anger made them more than usually stupid. They tried to stop Dad from speaking in Minneapolis and Saint Paul. A big meeting had been planned for the hall at the fairgrounds, but the Old Guard Republicans controlled the state government and the state board that controlled that hall, meeting in emergency session, prohibited its use for the LaFollette meeting. Arrangements were then made for meetings at the Saint Paul municipal auditorium and the Minneapolis armory.

More headlines! More excitement! The whole state was aroused almost overnight. The white hot intensity in Minnesota was as great as in Wisconsin. And Kellogg was going to speak the same night in the same town.

Senator Kellogg was a thin, white-haired, rather cadaverous-looking individual. He had grown rich as the lawyer for the big financial interests in the state, including one of the biggest corporations in the world—United States Steel. He had a stoop that gave the impression—only the impression—of a small hump on his back.

That night the Saint Paul auditorium was packed with ten thousand people. The police estimated that more than twenty-five thousand were in the streets outside, and no one could estimate how many more went home, unable to get nearer than a block from the hall. We were pleased to hear, as we struggled through the crowds, that Kellogg hardly had a corporal's guard to hear him.

If anything could heal the Old Man's wounds, the primary victory in Wisconsin and then this outpouring of men and women in Minnesota would do it. You could smell victory in the air. We were going to win in November, not only in Wisconsin but in Minnesota as well. Every man and woman in that packed auditorium knew and felt the drama. Here was Bob LaFollette in the same hall where, five years before, he had been misquoted as saying that we had "no grievances" against Germany. And his opponent was the selfsame man who had relentlessly spearheaded the campaign to crush—to blacken—to smear his name forever: to make the name LaFollette a synonym for Benedict Arnold.

As I looked at Dad through the tears I could not keep back, the years of age faded. He was young again. He was more than my father; he was my triumphant leader. He had prepared an address on domestic issues—principally the tariff—in which he read the roll call in the Senate showing Kellogg's votes. His only reference to the war and the 1917 Saint Paul speech was: "All that I said at that time has been demonstrated to be true. Not one word . . . will I ever need to retract or to modify in the slightest degree."

His speech was one of his best, but everyone felt an electric tension as they waited for him to go after Kellogg. The audience hungered for some way to release their pent-up emotions—some way to show their feeling for Dad and to vent their resentment against Kellogg. As Dad approached his conclusion, you could feel it coming. And it came:

"God Almighty, through nature, writes men's characters on their faces and in their forms. Your senator had bowed obsequiously to wealth and to corporations' orders and to his masters until God Almighty has given him a hump on his back—crouching, cringing, unAmerican, unmanly."

Back at our room in the hotel we had a drink. Dad was tired, relaxed, relieved. He said, with a mischievous grin: "Your mother will give me hell for saying that about Kellogg." She did—but with the restraint of an understanding partner in his life. She knew it was not unprovoked.

We went back to Madison. The November elections brought triumphs in Wisconsin, Minnesota, and North Dakota. Frazier and Shipstead won, and our victory in Wisconsin was the greatest in the history of the state.

7

ISEN

"I'D SURELY LIKE TO VAMP HIM. . . ."

While Phil was attending Wisconsin Law School, Isabel Bacon of Salt Lake City was enrolled as an undergraduate at Wisconsin. She was the oldest of the five daughters of George M. Bacon, a civil engineer. On November 15, 1920, she wrote to her family:

Had a marvellous Walrus meeting last night. I sat by Phil La. Follette, and well—! he is about as fas-kinating as you could wish for. He's quite a flirt and was darling to me. He has absolute poise and charm! It's perfectly killing how all the girls just play up to and act for him. Of course his life in Washington has added a romantic flavor I suppose, but it surely is attractive. You should see him talk to older people. I'd surely like to vamp him, but don't know how. Too much competition anyway.—We talked on Russia and had a great time.

Casual meetings at the Walrus Club, a campus discussion group, took a serious turn, as Isen describes in her memoirs, written many years later:

I met Phil during my senior year. I had heard that his father was a United States senator, distinguished but very controversial; some spoke of him with the gleam of fanatic devotion in their eye. Campus gossip had it that Phil was engaged to "a girl back east" and when he began "rushing"

me I did not take it seriously, feeling that he was exciting
company and that doubtless he knew what he was doing.

When on a spring night Phil stopped his little car on Park
Street near the lake, and said he wanted to talk to me, I
settled back resignedly. I seemed to be fated for many confidences of unrequited love. I sighed to myself, "Well, here
it comes."

To my utter astonishment, with that admixture of Gallic
fire and Scotch caution that I was to know so well, Phil
wanted to know if and when in that far-distant future he
could earn a living, would I be interested in considering
the matter of marrying him? I seemed to have indicated
that I might.

Looking back, I should have had some inkling of Phil's
trend when he took me walking in the cemetery, showed
me his grandfather LaFollette's grave where the then
Senator LaFollette had personally transferred his father's
bones from the little country cemetery where they had
originally rested. I was deeply impressed when Phil told me
that what first attracted him to me was my attitude toward
life—that it was an adventure to take hold of with both
hands—and that he would like to "play it that way" with
me. We were very serious.

What my poor mother and father could not understand,
with all their perspicacity, was that we were living in the
twenties, with "freedom" in the atmosphere, and psycho-
analysis on our lips. Instead of announcing our engagement,
borrowing money for a diamond (Mother remarked, "You
will never get one"—she was right), and setting a date some
two years hence when Phil would be "established," we
continued to talk in terms of "if" and "when." We spent
hours on the moors and beaches of Nantucket, at the historic shrines of Washington dear to Phil's heart, and on the
shores of Wisconsin's Lake Mendota, discoursing on how
to retain the greatest amount of freedom with the fewest
strings attached.

*On May 31, 1921, after Phil and Isen had become engaged,
Isen's father wrote to her:*

Word from Mother has just come of the understanding
between you and Phil. My first feeling is one of unmixed

pleasure at your prospects of happiness; my second, that of gratification that you are still justifying what we have tried to do for you the last twenty years.

As to the future, the older I grow the more thankful I am that it is in the hands of something higher than the sum of mere human effort. All that is asked of us is that we do *our* share and play the game according to our lights. That you have done this and will so continue has been demonstrated to my entire satisfaction. My hunch is that this applies to Phil. So I wish you God-speed in the conviction that however you work out your future it will not be by fudging and cutting corners.

I am proud of you, and that because you have made very much of a woman of yourself. As such you have earned my trust in addition to the love you should always have. Parents are too prone to think they can always lead their children by the hand, but a time comes when that is a harm rather than a help. They *should* have taught their children to walk upright and alone and then they can sit on the side-lines and cheer!

Isen and I planned to be married when I was earning enough money to support us. I was deeply in love with her but was cautiously hesitant about fixing a definite date. Isen gave up her job in Bayonne, New Jersey, and stopped off in Madison in September, 1922, to spend a few days. She found she could get a job on *LaFollette's Magazine* in the spring of 1923, so we decided to be married on April 14, 1923.

As that fateful date approached, I grew more and more apprehensive. I wanted to get married. I loved her and no other. But I wondered what marriage would do to my "freedom." How she ever stuck out those months I will never know. But she did.

Then a week before our wedding date, the barn at Maple Bluff Farm burned to the ground. Unconsciously, I suppose, my fading bachelorhood grasped at that fire as the possible out. I phoned Isen at Salt Lake City. Her family did not get long distance phone calls as frequently as we did. She expected it to mean a major catastrophe. Our conversation went something like this:

PHIL: "Isen, the barn burned down last night!"

ISEN: (silence) "What did you say?"

PHIL: "The barn burned last night."

ISEN: "Oh, you said 'The barn burned.'—So what?"

PHIL: (rather weakly) "Well, maybe we should postpone getting married?"

ISEN: "But what has the burned barn to do with our getting married? We weren't planning on living in the *barn*, were we?"

PHIL: "Oh, no, but—I thought I ought to tell you."

ISEN: "Well, I am sorry about the barn. But are we still to meet in Chicago on the fourteenth?"

PHIL: (very meekly now) "Why, of course. See you in Chicago on the fourteenth."

So I met her in Chicago on the morning of April 14. Before she left Utah, her father had told her, "If Phil isn't there to meet you, go to a movie and come home."

We were married by Dr. Eustace Haydon of the University of Chicago Divinity School, in his apartment. We left Chicago that afternoon for Madison and began our life together at Maple Bluff Farm.

From the beginning, Isen and I had a financial understanding: she was to have a check for family finances on the first of the month. It was to be my job to see that that check came on time and also my prime responsibility to say how much that check was to be. It was her prime responsibility to spend within that amount. We were free, of course, to look over each other's shoulder and comment—discreetly, to be sure—and occasionally make a suggestion or two. For us, at least, our system worked. Isen is thoroughly economical. But she always spent, and spends, any money that reached her hands—no thrift but no waste. Not once during our marriage has there been any thought that we ought to own this or that "to keep up with the Joneses." In our entire married life she has never had a full set of dinner dishes. Yet we have always lived in comfort amid the warm glow that the inherent artist with the skills of hand and brain can create in a modest home.

In those days, though there was Prohibition, Wisconsin never believed in it. Those of German, Polish, or Italian descent looked on wine and beer as part of their daily food. Hard liquor? Quite another matter. Those of Yankee or Scandinavian descent were often ardent supporters of Prohibition. They voted dry but drank wet. And for them it was usually hard liquor.

Our friends, in the early days of our marriage, were mostly our age. They loved good food, good drink, and spirited talk. Nobody was bored. Nobody got drunk. We had robust, healthy, exciting fun, and returned Monday morning eager to get at our jobs. Then, as for decades afterwards, our friends were graduate students, members of the university faculty, journalists, foreign students, Americans and foreigners interested in American politics, and close friends and associates in law and Wisconsin politics.

We have always made lasting friendships wherever we have touched down—for short or long periods—in Madison, Chicago, Washington, New York; in Britain, France, Belgium, Germany, Italy, Austria, and Scandinavia; and in restaurants, on trains, planes, or ships. Our life has been difficult, often exhausting, but never by any count dull.

From the time of our marriage, politics was central to Isen's and my life. Ripon, Wisconsin, was the birthplace of the Republican party. The main political battles in the state, from the Civil War until 1934, were fought within the Republican party—with Progressives in one camp and the Conservatives in the other. Occasionally a Democrat would be elected governor (1890 and 1932), or senator, but this was the exception. The Conservatives had the money, federal patronage—except under President Wilson, when it went to "deserving" Wisconsin Democrats, largely Conservatives—and the almost unanimous support of the state's daily press and of the Chicago, Saint Paul, and Minneapolis press as well. Beginning in the early 1920's, I learned how our more skillful candidates overcame these handicaps. Some were fair to excellent speakers. Others were masters of direct, person-to-person politics.

Merlin Hull, later a congressman, was an example of the person-to-person politician. Hull ran a newspaper in the small city of Black River Falls. He was intelligent, honest, and courageous, but he lacked dynamic appeal. However, he carefully tended his political fences and rendered outstanding service to the voters in his district. In the rear seat of his auto he carried a large index file. When he approached any city, village, or hamlet, he would stop his car at the edge of the business district and refresh his memory from this file on contacts he had had with people living there. He then went from door to door. As you went with him, you found there was scarcely a place where he had not had some personal relations with those with whom he shook hands. It might have been some problem for a war veteran, congratulations on a marriage or a birth in the family, some achievement of an honor student in high school, graduation from the university, or just some seeds sent from the Department of Agriculture. There was almost always some personal note to be struck, and he was warm and gracious as he struck it. Anyone running against Merlin was running against the personal friend of many individual voters in his district.

When the Progressive legislators held their caucus before the Legislature met in 1923, it seemed natural to me to accept the invitation to attend—with Dad's approval, of course. Most Progressive Legislators did not look on Bob or me as "outsiders"; on the contrary, they recognized us as leaders who, they knew, always consulted our father on any important suggestions or move we made. Bob, who was then twenty-seven, had been elected chairman of the Republican State Central Committee. With three years' experience as Dad's secretary, he was already demonstrating what, before long, would be recognized as mastery of legislative procedure and the tactful maneuver that "got things done."

Early in the 1923 Legislature it became clear that Governor Blaine was going to play a different political game than Bob or I had theretofore known in Wisconsin. Blaine had been a moderately successful country lawyer. He had served in the state Senate and as attorney general. After his election as governor in 1920 and again in 1922, he saw only two possibilities for his future— being reelected as governor in 1924 and then to the United States Senate; or returning to his country law practice in Boscobel (population, 1920: 1,648).

Personally Blaine was abstemious in his habits, but he knew that Wisconsin did not approve of the Eighteenth Amendment or the Volstead Act. Because his opponent in 1926 would be Irvine Lenroot—a dry—he, Blaine, would therefore become known as a wet.

It was Dad's policy to avoid what he considered extraneous issues and center his fire on the great economic, political, and social problems of his time. We avoided religious and racial appeals by having a "balanced" ticket, *i.e.*, candidates of German and Norwegian extraction, as well as of both the Catholic and Protestant faiths, were always on the state ticket. Those of Polish and Italian origin were always represented on the legislative slate from Milwaukee, Racine, and Kenosha. We ignored the Prohibition issue. Dad voted for the submission of the Eighteenth Amendment on the theory that the several states were entitled to vote on it—as a sort of referendum—and he voted against the Volstead Act. Again, his justification was that he did not want vital issues of peace or war and progress in the social, economic, and political fields beclouded by Prohibition. Most of our leaders agreed until Blaine became governor.

People of Scandinavian, and especially Norwegian, descent were the backbone of the Progressive Movement in Wisconsin, and when Blaine brought the issue of Prohibition to the front, it divided our forces. In the 1923 and 1925 sessions of the Legislature, Blaine established himself as an out-and-out wet. I did what I could at our Progressive caucuses, and Bob made a special trip from Washington to attend one of them in an effort to get our forces to present a united front, especially on tax legislation. But it was a difficult task against a governor who wanted to "save" issues for a future campaign of his own. However, Bob again displayed his enormous gifts in handling difficult legislative conflicts, and by a large majority we put through the Assembly a satisfactory tax bill. This experience gave me some basic schooling on how to get on with the Legislature and how later to deal with two that were hostile to me in my own administrations.

In the 1923 Legislature, State Senator Henry A. Huber introduced a resolution directing the superintendent of public property to remove from the State Historical Society and destroy by burning the university petition that had charged Dad with disloyalty.

As soon as I heard of this resolution, I knew that Dad would never approve of it. He always wanted the record kept straight. I sent him a draft of a letter to Henry Huber and he sent it back signed—though I wish he had improved its wording. It read:

Dear Henry:

I deeply appreciate the spirit which prompted you to introduce this resolution and the desire on your part to rectify in so far as possible what has seemed to you to be an unfair and libelous attack upon me.

The signing and promulgation of that resolution by members of the faculty of the University of which I am an alumnus was a source of deep regret and disappointment. Many of them had been life-long friends and associates. Before the experience of the war, I would not have believed that they could bring themselves to impugn my loyalty and devotion to the best interests of this country. However, the support and steadfastness of you and many others gave me great compensation which was a source of strength to me in doing my duty to my state and my country as it was given me to see it.

Time is the great sifter and winnower of truth. The formal destruction of that document cannot change the fact of its existence. I stated many times from the public platform in Wisconsin during the recent campaigns that I would not change my record on the war with any man in the United States Senate. History alone can judge impartially. So far as I am personally concerned, I am well content that this document shall remain as physical evidence of the hysteria attendant upon the war.

It seems to me that our energies should be devoted toward bringing our institutions back to the principles upon which they were founded, and which are the true source of our greatness.

This applies with special significance to the University, and we can perform no greater service toward all our institutions than to see to it that the great University of Wisconsin ever continues that winnowing and sifting by which alone the truth can be found. . . .

Of this letter the New York *Times* said editorially: "On that platform the Senator deserves the support of all his fellow-alumni, and of everybody else, no matter what may be thought of his war record."

8

LaFOLLETTE
FOR
PRESIDENT

"I WANT TO DIE, AS I HAVE
LIVED, WITH MY BOOTS ON. . . ."

Throughout 1923, Dad; Bob Jr.; Mary's husband, Ralph Sucher; myself, and our close political friends had our eyes on the 1924 Presidential campaign. One of Dad's doctors had told him that if he took care of himself and lived more quietly, he would live for a number of years; but that if he continued at his accustomed pace he would die within two years. This was disturbing news for all of us, because Dad was considering running for President in 1924. A definite decision was delayed until later in the year.

Meanwhile, I undertook some campaigning in Minnesota. Senator Knute Nelson, an Old Guard Republican from Minnesota, had died in April, 1923. The Republican candidate for the Senate at the July special election was J. A. O. Preus, governor of the state. The Farmer-Labor candidate was Magnus Johnson, who had lost to Preus in the 1922 election. Senator Henrik Shipstead and other political friends urged Dad to come to Minnesota, but his physicians dissuaded him. However, he got out a strong statement for Johnson which was widely circulated.

Magnus Johnson was a dirt farmer who spoke with a marked Swedish accent—which did not hurt him in Minnesota—and who based his campaign on support of "Bob LaFollette," and what he stood for. Preus supported "regular" Republicanism. This special election attracted national attention as a trial contest between President Harding and my father.

Senators Burton K. Wheeler of Montana and Lynn Frazier of North Dakota came to Minnesota to help Johnson, and Wisconsin contributed Lieutenant Governor George Comings and five of our Progressive congressmen. I spent four days in the state, and the LaFollette name attracted fine crowds. The Saint Paul *Pioneer Press*, the Old Guard Republican paper, said on its front page; "The star attraction to which the audience responded with the most spirited demonstration [was] Phil LaFollette, son of 'Senator Bob.'" As in 1922, so in this special election, Dad became the issue. Johnson was elected by 95,000 votes. This election, with our other victories in 1922, gave Dad and his Progressive associates in the United States Senate the balance of power in that body.

We had a wonderful family Christmas in 1923. By then, Dad, Bob, Ralph, and other close advisers were talking over the approaching Presidential campaign in earnest. It was agreed that if Dad were to be a candidate, it would not be on a "third party" ticket but as an independent. An independent candidacy might have more appeal to Progressive Republicans and Democrats than a third party.

An important reason for choosing an independent candidacy was that we felt that we could avoid "boring from within" by the Communists and fellow travelers. In 1920, Dad had refused to accept the Presidential nomination of the Labor party mostly because of this infiltration. And in 1924 he wrote a letter to Herman Ekern, attorney general of Wisconsin, in which he repeated his strong opposition to communism and its methods of infiltration, and warned Progressives to stay clear of that group. Any new political movement has to turn away persons who may be well meaning but who can be very troublesome.

You may well ask why Dad decided to undertake the 1924 campaign. He faced heavy odds: he was sixty-nine years old; his health was not good; outside of Wisconsin, and to a lesser degree in Minnesota, he had no political organization; and adequate financing was not available. None of us for a moment thought we had any chance to win. But we hoped that we might get enough votes to deprive any candidate of a majority in the Electoral College and thus throw the election into the House of Representatives, where Progressives might hold the balance of power. At the very least, we might get a large enough popular vote to lay the foundation for what most of us wanted above all —a new political alignment in America that would unite the Progressive forces.

When Isen and I returned to Wisconsin after the holidays, we set up a committee to promote sentiment for Dad for President. The temporary or starting committee was composed of W. T. Rawleigh of Illinois, chairman: Dante Pierce of Iowa; John F. Sinclair of Minnesota; and Harry Sauthoff of Wisconsin, secretary.

W. T. Rawleigh was born in southern Wisconsin and began his business career with a borrowed horse and buggy, selling medicines for "man and beast" from farm to farm. He built this "farmers' drugstore" into a multimillion-dollar-a-year business, and he was a lifelong supporter and friend of Dad's. He was by far the largest contributor to the 1924 campaign, but even his great generosity was small compared with the large sums available to both the Republicans and the Democrats. However, it was Rawleigh's donation that gave the LaFollette committee its modest start.

From New Year's day to election day in November, the 1924 Presidential campaign absorbed all the interest and energy of the LaFollette family. Early in January we opened a "LaFollette for President" headquarters in the old Auditorium Hotel on Michigan Avenue in Chicago. I can still see those rooms, with the moth-eaten, bedraggled, overstuffed furniture. We had one typewriter, some stationery and stamps—and Harry Sauthoff. Harry was a heavyset, slow-moving, deliberately spoken, fast-thinking Madison lawyer who from boyhood had been a devoted and fearless Progressive. He later served four terms in the United States House of Representatives.

I trust that no reader believes in a "spontaneous" demand for someone to become a candidate for office. If there is such a thing, I have never seen it. It is considered good political manners to arrange matters so that the candidate seems to be drafted or at least comes forward in response to a wide demand to achieve this impression. The LaFollette for President committee sought to secure as many signatures as possible to the petitions asking Dad to become a candidate.

In addition to the job of circulating the petitions, I visited the midwestern and northwestern states to organize a state committee in each. It was our clear-cut policy that these state committees should remain aloof from all contests for federal or state offices and concentrate solely on the independent candidacies for President and Vice-President.

As I covered the Midwest and West I found a ground swell of sentiment—and among many, a deep devotion—for Dad. Though our lack of organization, and money, was appalling, somehow the enthusiasm we found kept us going just as if we had a chance to win.

Early in March, Bob called to say that Dad had pneumonia, and I left for Washington at once. I found Mother and Bob concerned by Dad's illness and disturbed even more about his Presidential campaign. At the first opportunity alone with me, Dad assured me he would be well in a week and had no thought of not going on with our plans, but he was needlessly concerned that Mother and Bob might make some statement taking him out of the race.

He said: "I know perfectly well what Doctor Kellogg told me last summer—all about my having to slow down—that if I kept up the same pace I'd be dead in a couple of years.

"Well, Phil, I have had a wonderful life. I'd like to live it all over again. But I don't want to—I just can't—live rolled up in a cotton blanket in a damned wheelchair. I want to die, as I have lived, with my boots on. . . . We are going right ahead with our plans, with a full head of steam in the boiler."

And we did.

I am sure that Dad knew deep down that Mother and Bob would not take any action against what they knew Dad really wanted to do. They regretted his decision, but they both understood the hard-learned but basic lesson of satisfactory human relations—that no one can change the essential fabric of another person's character—that much of the unhappy friction between humans, especially between man and wife, arises from attempts to do so.

Because of our plans for an independent candidacy, Dad decided not to enter his name on the Republican Presidential preference ballot in the April primary in Wisconsin. We did, however, have a Progressive slate of delegates to the Republican convention. On April 1, we elected twenty-eight of the twenty-nine delegates. Dad received more Presidential preference votes, all write-ins, than did President Coolidge, whose name was on the ballot. Although he had formally withdrawn his name from the Presidential primary ballots in Michigan and North Dakota, there were enough write-ins in North Dakota to instruct nearly half of its Republican delegates for Dad.

At the Republican convention, our Wisconsin delegation submitted a minority report on the platform, as had been done at each convention since 1908. Coolidge, President a year since Harding's death, was nominated. Charles Dawes was named his running mate.

The Democrats, balloting 103 times for President in New York's Madison Square Garden, chose John W. Davis, a New York City lawyer, and Charles Bryan of Nebraska as their candidates.

On the Fourth of July, the Conference for Progressive Political Action (CPPA) met at Cleveland, with William H. Johnston, president of the International Association of Machinists, as chairman. The CPPA comprised representatives of organized labor, of which the railroad brotherhoods were the backbone, and included representatives of agriculture, the Socialist party, and a fine roster of distinguished names including the poet Edwin Markham, Andrew Furuseth, Congressman Fiorello LaGuardia, Senators Henrik Shipstead and Lynn Frazier, and others.

On the previous day the LaFollette for President committee

presented to Dad petitions bearing 250,000 signatures, and the chairman of the CPPA wired that organization's request that he become a candidate.

There were some one thousand delegates and another nine thousand persons in the auditorium. The New York *Evening Post* reported: "There is little organization and no machine, but there is a sort of self-imposed discipline." The New York *Times* reported that "a more complete cross section of American life was never assembled in one hall." In the late afternoon of the first day, Bob read Dad's statement addressed to both the La-Follette committee and the convention, announcing his candidacy. He made clear that his was not a third party candidacy, and why:

"I stand for an honest realignment in American politics, confident that the people in November will take such action as will insure the creation of a new party in which all Progressives may unite. I would not, however, accept a nomination or an election to the Presidency if doing so meant, for Progressive Senators and Representatives and Progressive State Governments, the defeat which would inevitably result from the placing of complete third party tickets in the field at the present time."

This was Bob's first public appearance, and he did a magnificent job in presenting his father's announcement. The convention unanimously endorsed Dad and instructed its national committee to cooperate with the LaFollette for President committee in naming a candidate for Vice-President. The national committee was authorized to call a national convention to form a third party, in the event that the November returns were sufficiently encouraging.

Burton K. Wheeler became Dad's running mate. Born and raised in Massachusetts, Wheeler went west as a young man and settled in Montana. Throughout his public career as a state legislator, United States district attorney, and in the United States Senate, he demonstrated intelligence, conviction, and indomitable courage. He had faced the power of the mighty Anaconda Copper Company and beaten it. He had courageously opposed our entry into World War I and had been elected as a Progressive Democrat to the Senate in 1922. Dad had secured his appointment to the Senate committee investigating the Department of Justice, where he took the lead in exposing the scandalous administration of Attorney General Harry Daugherty.

We had our candidates for President and Vice-President. We faced the task—a gigantic one—of getting their names on the ballots in forty-eight states. No federal law provides any legal machinery for national political parties or independent candidacies. Political parties are controlled by state laws. About the hardest laws to change are those governing elections. State legislators think that the existing machinery that chose themselves must be the best ever, and vigorously oppose change, particularly any change that opens the ballot to additional parties or individuals.

So, with Congressman John M. Nelson of Wisconsin in our Chicago headquarters; Gilbert E. Roe, dad's beloved friend, in New York for the eastern division; and Rudolph Spreckels in San Francisco, we went to work to get on every ballot. We succeeded, but it was a tough assignment. In California, for example, the state supreme court, by a four-to-three decision, turned down petitions signed by some fifty thousand voters to put LaFollette-Wheeler electors on one ballot. The only way that their names could and did appear on the ballot in California was under the Socialist label.

Now for the campaign itself. I think I can give you a hint of the problems one faces in organizing such a campaign by quoting from letters that I wrote Isen.

REDFIELD, S.D. JULY 26, 1924

It has been literally impossible to get a moment to write you even a line. . . . Got to bed about 12:00. Was up at 7:30 and started to confer. . . . The difficulty here was the Farmer-Labor Party . . . had put five Presidential Electors on their party ticket. . . . Richards' [president, State Federation of Labor] group had put five electors also in the Independent column, which left us with a divided electors column. . . . I began by calling the whole bunch together and giving them a general talk on the reasons for an Independent candidacy. . . . I then started in talking to the several groups separately. I finished with the groups at Huron at 6:00 P.M. and left for Mitchell. . . . Arrived there about

9:00 P.M. There I met another group of the F-L crowd—some 50 or so. I was with them until 12:45 this morning. I returned to Huron and got to bed at 4:30. Up this morning at 7:30 for further conferences. . . . I finally got all groups to agree. . . . I leave by auto for Aberdeen and go from there to Butte. . . .

SEATTLE. AUGUST FIRST, 1924

This trip would be a wonderful one to take if one weren't being pushed for time—as well as a lot of contending factors each pushing and pulling in its particular direction. It all takes enormous patience and quite a lot of decent firmness and *judgment*. As to the latter, only subsequent results can tell.

SUNDAY A.M. AUGUST THIRD, 1924

I arrived in Seattle late Thursday night. Began Friday morning to see people. Kept it up without interruption, except for a night's sleep, until last night at 8:15, when I left for here. . . .

Yesterday was a hard one—conferences from 9:00 until 4:00, without a stop, with the leaders. The difficulty here was the same as elsewhere—too much local politics. . . . Believe me, Old Dear, this sort of work is harder than campaigning. The campaigning entails meeting people. But this sort of thing brings in *all* the elements of human nature that want something from you specifically—and to refuse and yet not antagonize takes lots of time and patience. All patience is, as I see it, listening to the other fellow—without irritation—until he agrees with you.

THURSDAY, AUG. 7, 1924

I arrived in Denver yesterday afternoon. . . . The various leaders began coming in about 7:00 o'clock. . . . I finished seeing the last person at 2:45. Went to bed and up at 8:00 and saw more people until the train left at 11:30. I am bound for Lincoln, Nebraska, where I arrive at 12:50 tonight, then to Kansas City tomorrow and to St. Louis tomorrow night. . . . Hope I have a solution here in Colorado as elsewhere. Got an agreement as to the policy but question of manager open. . . .

Dad opened his speaking campaign on September 18 in Madison Square Garden before one of the largest crowds that ever attended a political meeting in the Garden. Burt Wheeler, too, was soon on a nationwide tour that would take him to twenty cities in fourteen states. A unique feature of our campaign was that at Dad's and Burt's speeches about half of the hall was reserved, and these seats were sold. In addition, a collection was taken up at all meetings. Thousands of people buying tickets to a political meeting struck a new note in American politics.

Both Dad and, I think, Burt Wheeler had private railroad cars for their tours. Both were paid for largely by the ticket sales and collections. Aside from Dad's, Mother's, and Burt Wheeler's, my name was as good as we had for drawing audiences. So I was out speaking on my own through September and the first week in October. Here again, quotations from speeches, newspapers, and letters to Isen will give you a glimpse of the excitement of the campaign:

KALAMAZOO, MICH., SEPT. 24, 1924

Got to Benton Harbor last night. . . . Well, the hotel was of Civil War vintage. I got a room with a bath—no toilet. "The other room with bath and toilet" was taken. . . . But I did have a fine meeting in the Opera House—which must seat about 1,000 —and people stood packed to the doors for two hours while I harangued the multitude. In addition, at my suggestion they put a few baskets at the door as the crowd left, and they collected $95.00 for their campaign fund.

I speak at Paw Paw tonight—about 18 miles from here—and here tomorrow (Thursday) night—Muskegon and Grand Rapids Friday, and Toledo Saturday night.

TOLEDO, OHIO, SEPT. 27, 1924

Left Muskegon last night—arrived Detroit at 6:00 this morning and caught a train over here which got me in at 9:30. Have been out meeting people and got back in time for an hour's nap. . . . Had an audience last night of about 1,000 or more.

The only snag I have run into thus far is a row at Youngstown, Ohio because the Speakers Bureau asked them to make it an indoor meeting. They seem to have taken it somewhat in the nature of an insult to ask for a hall—and especially for an "upstart" like yours truly. . . . But that's all in a lifetime. To Cleveland tomorrow—Dayton Monday—and then back thru Indiana to Chicago the end of the coming week. I have four or five days to myself beginning next Sunday P.M., which is going to be spent

home . . . to have some peace and quiet and *your* company
again. . . .

Bob talked over the phone today and indicated I might possibly be called to go with Dad when and if he starts out.

Louis Seltzer of the Cleveland *Press* wrote of the Cleveland
meeting:

Young LaFollette is of his father's short stature. Like his father,
he is handsome in a strong, vigorous way. He has his father's
great shock of hair—although his father wears his pompadour
style; Philip parts his.

Slender, nattily dressed in soft blue, soft-collared shirt, blue
striped coat and vest with gray trousers, LaFollette looked much
like any well-dressed young man in Cleveland—until he began
to talk. His father is rated one of the best orators in the country.
Philip got his share of his father's ability as a talker.

My speech in Dayton included the following:

We represent the same principles as did Thomas Jefferson . . .
and Abraham Lincoln. . . . The two big parties of today have
lost sight of their original ideals—the very ideals which we seek
to revive. . . .

The fundamental issue of this campaign is: Shall the government of the United States be a government of, by, and for the
people or a government in the interests of the pampered favorites
of Wall Street?

Again, a letter to Isen:

TERRE HAUTE, INDIANA, OCT. 1, 1924

Arrived here yesterday morning from Dayton at 4 A.M. Went
back to bed and slept until 10:00 when I was called for, and all
started for another town for an afternoon meeting. Had good
meetings both yesterday afternoon and last night. I leave in a
short while for Princeton for a meeting late this afternoon and
at Evansville tonight—then Murphysboro, Illinois tomorrow—
Hammond, Ind. Friday—Belvidere, Ill. Sat.—and Chicago Sunday
and then, pray God, *home.* . . . I am getting rather anxious for

Sunday to come to end this trip. It will be mighty nice to be home, Woman.

> Your friend, with respect,
> "Putz"

But I did not get home. The latter part of that week, Bob called and asked me to meet Dad at Rochester, New York, on Monday, October 6. I was to take up my role as a "curtain raiser" to lessen the strain on Dad.

I wrote Isen:

> SCRANTON, PA., OCT. 7TH, 1924
>
> I met the car yesterday morning. Dad and Bob, Bas Manly, Fred Howe, a publicity man, and three or four stenographers, etc. make up this car. There is one ahead for the newspaper men. We have been very comfortable thus far. We had a splendid meeting last night . . . the largest ever held in Rochester. Extremely enthusiastic. Dad stood it splendidly.
>
> We go from here to Newark tomorrow—then to Detroit, then Cincinnati, and then Chicago.

After the Rochester meeting Bob telegraphed Mother: "Biggest meeting ever held here. 4800 jammed the hall and filled the aisles. 3000 outside. . . ."

The same enthusiastic, packed halls, with an overflow crowd outside, met us in Scranton, Newark, Detroit, and Chicago. The Detroit *News* reported that the meeting there "was one of the most enthusiastic political meetings in the history of Detroit." The story went on: "It was estimated nearly 7,500 heard the address at Arens Gardens, most of whom paid $1 for the opportunity. . . . In addition, a tin-plate collection is understood to have produced about $1,000."

After Dad's meeting in Chicago, Frank Kent of the Baltimore *Sun* reported that "no such electric meeting as he [LaFollette] held here last night would be possible for either of the two other candidates. Beyond compare, this flaming old man and his two attractive sons present the one dramatic, colorful spectacle of the campaign, and the fight they make surpasses in ardor anything of which the others are capable."

The Chicago League of Women Voters asked the Republicans, Democrats, and Progressives to send a representative to speak for twenty minutes. The Chicago *Herald Examiner* reported, on October 12, 1924:

Young LaFollette was received with much interest and little enthusiasm. He looked like a college boy all set to explain the Einstein Theory.

After he had spoken but five words, however, the situation was decidedly different; and when his allotted time for speaking was up, the women refused to allow him to leave the platform.

But I got safely away.

At the close of the first week of campaigning, John W. Owens wrote in the Baltimore *Sun:*

The effect of last week's appearance after appearance before great cheering crowds, far from wearing down the vitality of a man nearing 70 years has been tonic to him. . . . The tour, taking it all and all, is a marvelous performance. . . . What has there been in politics in years that is comparable?

These great meetings gave our supporters tremendous encouragement. But they likewise roused the enemy—especially the Republican. The checkbooks came out, and the heat was turned on labor and farmers. By the last week in October one could feel the vast, spreading tentacles of organized economic power beginning its squeeze to drive people—especially labor— by fear into voting for Coolidge. Dad had received copies of orders to railroad foremen from superintendents urging the formation of Coolidge or Davis clubs, stating that the names of the officers of such clubs should be reported back to the boss.

Before election day, economic pressure (slips in pay envelopes warning: "Don't come to work after election day if Coolidge is not elected." Word passed over the banks' counters to farmers, small businessmen, to all and sundry: "Bad times ahead unless Coolidge is elected.") was doing its work. It was effective. We had vast reservoirs of enthusiasm. But we had no effective political organization except in Wisconsin.

Organization in war and politics spells victory or defeat. If, when the final rush of the enemy hits you, you are organized and disciplined, you can withstand that assault and launch the winning counterattack. Without it your forces disintegrate. We had no organization—just millions of individuals fighting, singly and in small groups.

The *reported* campaign expenditures were: Republican, $4,-360,000; Democratic, $820,000; and Progressive, $222,000. Remarkably, only two persons contributed as much as five thousand dollars to Dad's campaign, and about one third of the total came from ticket sales and collections.

When Dad, Bob, and I arrived in Chicago, we drove through the Loop, the downtown business section. People lined the streets. They looked, some smiled—but there were too many who stood silent. There was fear in the air.

We went on for another three weeks with enthusiastic, overflow meetings in seventeen cities. The campaign for us closed on Friday, October 31, in the Cleveland Auditorium before twenty thousand people, who, according to the Cleveland *Plain Dealer*, were "swept away in a frenzy almost religious."

We left our private car at Chicago and returned to Madison. After a warm reception at the station, Dad spoke briefly to his friends and neighbors from the Capitol steps. On Tuesday, November 4, Dad, Bob, Isen, and I voted—Mother was in Washington to be with Mary for the arrival of her first baby. For the first and last time in forty years we did not listen to the election returns at Maple Bluff Farm. At Governor Blaine's insistence, we went to his office in the Capitol to get the returns via radio. It was a gloomy occasion. We had no thought of winning, but we had expected to carry several states at least. LaFollette and Wheeler carried only one—Wisconsin—and ran second in California, Idaho, Iowa, Minnesota, Montana, Nevada, North Dakota, Oregon, South Dakota, Washington, and Wyoming. Our ticket had received the largest popular vote ever given independent candidates. One out of every six persons voted for LaFollette and Wheeler.

As we drove back to the farm that night, both Bob and I spoke out in wrath at "labor's betrayal" of our cause, but Dad brought both of us sharply to task and let us have it.

He said: "You have never known real poverty. Oh, we have had hard times but never the haunting fear of losing your job, of losing those paychecks that are all that stand between starvation for those workers and their families. Don't blame the folks. They just got scared."

Bob and I went to bed that night tired—and still bitter. The next morning when I awoke it was another day. In the excitement, stress, and strain of Dad's campaign, I had almost forgotten that I had just been elected district attorney of Dane County— the job Dad had won in 1880, forty-four years before.

Dad's campaign was a baptism for thousands of Americans. Ten years later, in the days of Franklin Roosevelt's New Deal, the activists who flocked to Washington had one sure and certain password among themselves to prove they were not "Johnny-come latelies"; they had fought for "Old Bob" in '24, and they had Gutzon Borglum's bronze medallion of LaFollette and Wheeler to prove it.

9

DISTRICT ATTORNEY

SHALL THE CAPITAL . . . SHELTER A NEST OF MURDERERS?

Early in 1924 I thought I had a good chance to be nominated and elected district attorney of Dane County. Even though I had spent so much time on the national campaign, I won by a good majority. Once elected, I faced a real challenge—to break up organized murder in a section of Madison.

Immigrants of Italian birth had settled in an area roughly six blocks square, known as Greenbush and commonly called the Bush. It was within six blocks of both the Capitol and the university campus. With the coming of Prohibition, the market for homemade wine soon gave rise to stills and a booming bootleg liquor trade in the Bush. The profits attracted gangsters from Rockford and Chicago and in the early twenties, rivalry in this business led to sawed-off shotgun murders, none of which was prosecuted.

Because of the unsatisfactory record of the district attorney's office in the preceding years, the county board had cut the salary to eighteen hundred dollars a year. I had by this time been prac-

ticing law for two years and had made a good start. To take on
the district attorney's job at that salary did not look inviting. I
called on state Supreme Court Justice Burr W. Jones to discuss
the problem with him. I remember listening to this tall, erect,
keen-minded master of the law speaking from the vantage point
of fifty years at the bar:

"Two years as district attorney—especially with the great
challenge which confronts that position at this particular time—
will teach you more: more law, more of the rules of evidence
and trial procedure, and above all, more about people, all kinds
of people—than you would get in years of private practice. All
this experience will become a part of you and thus acquired, it
will never leave you to the day you die. But take it for only the
one term of two years. Do not yield to any pressure for more.
You will have all it can teach you in two years."

I was extremely fortunate in having Glenn Roberts, an able,
loyal, and courageous friend and later my law partner, as my
assistant district attorney.

Dad and Bob stayed on at the farm after the November election. In the evenings Dad, Isen, and I would sit in front of the
wood fire, and Dad would reminisce about his days as district
attorney. I soaked up all he had to tell me. What he impressed
on me most deeply was that an alert DA should get to the scene
of an important crime faster, if possible, than immediately. Thus
you see the evidence, collect facts, interview witnesses while the
scene is still fresh. Seeing and hearing it yourself, it registers in
your memory and enables you to paint it vividly to the court
and jury. It does not blur nor strain through the brain of someone else.

Before I took office I made an agreement with the sheriff and
the chief of police that both Glenn and I were to be notified of
any major crime. Most particularly, anything that looked like
murder must be reported to us instantly, wherever we might be.
Both the sheriff and the chief agreed to this with enthusiasm.
They rightly sensed that exciting times lay ahead.

At noon on Monday, January 5, 1925, Glenn and I took our
oaths. Two mornings later I got my first call—a shooting in a
rooming house on University Avenue. I got there fast. In the

parlor of this residence for French students, a young, good-looking man lay on the floor. He had shot and wounded a young girl. Then he had shot himself fatally. The girl was not seriously hurt. The suicide had denied me a trial, but I should have been patient: there were others to come.

The problem in the Bush was simple: A shooting would occur in broad daylight. Though people would see it, eyewitnesses could never be found. The threat of a sawed-off shotgun in the murderer's hands was much closer to them and more to be feared than subpoenas, district attorneys, and criminal courts. What could be done? Instinctively I looked for an expert. My father's former law partner and intimate friend Gilbert Roe had moved to New York City to practice law about the time Dad was first elected governor. I turned to him, and he conferred with New York City Police Commissioner Richard Enright, who told Gilbert: "That kid has guts if he is really going after such a gang. Believe me, I know. You tell him for me that he needs protection and he needs it all the time." As a result of this visit there arrived in Madison a New York City police officer who was a specialist in offenses occurring among those of Italian descent living in that city. This man was a strapping, dark-complexioned six-footer in his early thirties.

So far as I ever learned, there was no leak about his coming. No one in Madison except Glenn Roberts knew anything about him. I felt sure that now we had the answer. It surely would not take this able New York, Italian-speaking police officer long to solve our problems. Within a week, I had two interviews with him—the first when he arrived, and the second when he left for New York. During that period he had—so he said—roamed through the Bush. I believe he did. He walked into my office, explained frankly that the situation in the Bush was "too hot," asked for his pay and expenses, and told me he was returning to New York. He got his money and left. I have never heard of him since. He came. He saw. He flunked—cold feet.

So Glenn and I were back where we started. As I learned later, one seldom finds the answer to problems in the head of some fellow a long way from home. Usually you have to find the answers right at home and among people you already know.

Our first move was to have the Bush patrolled around the clock by police walking in pairs. It is harder to kill two armed men than one. If you try for two, one is likely to live to tell the tale, or shoot to kill.

Alcohol was the prime factor in crime in the Bush. We decided that if we could not get witnesses to murder, we could get witnesses to bootlegging—possession or sale of liquor. To hazard a guess, I would say that perhaps 25 per cent of the American public supported the "noble experiment" of legislating human habits and morals. The other three-fourths were equally violent in their opposition—hatred if you like—to this attempt to interfere with what they considered their private lives. As I've pointed out, Wisconsin largely opposed Prohibition. So how were we to get juries of twelve members to convict by unanimous vote enough people in the Bush to clean out crime in the area?

We did it by telling the people of Dane County exactly what we were going to do. The issue was not "wet" or "dry." The issue was, Shall the capital city—the seat of the University of Wisconsin—shelter a nest of murderers? Will you forget your feelings about Prohibition while your district attorney uses the laws on the statute books to blot out this gang of organized criminals? The men and women of Dane County backed us to the hilt. The folks will, with rare exceptions, do this if you make the issue clear and simple—and get it to them.

Glenn, Bill McCormick, then lieutenant of detectives, a selected few from the Madison police force, and I laid our plans. We proceeded as if we were in a military campaign. Success or failure would depend on split-second timing—and complete surprise—as overwhelming numbers hit the enemy in his vital spot.

First we hired our witnesses-to-be. Most of them were bums. They could buy liquor from vendors in the Bush without arousing suspicion. However, we took meticulous care to provide irrefutable corroboration. Each witness was accompanied to his destination by one or two reputable citizens. He was then given an empty bottle, carefully identified by his respectable companions. They watched him enter the door of the bootlegger. His going and coming were accurately timed. He returned to his companions and delivered the bottle and its contents to them, and immediately it was on its way to the laboratory and then to a vault. We set out to forge chains of evidence for the courtroom —clean, clear, unbroken, irrefutable legal evidence.

The Bush lay quiet. The patrolling, paired policemen aroused apprehension at first. As days passed with no interference with the making and selling of liquor, bootlegging came out of hiding and went its merry way as our witnesses made their repeated purchases. The vaulted evidence grew day by day. The pungent smell of alcohol permeated the room that held the vault.

We kept our fingers crossed against ruinous exposure. Strangely, we were to find later that one of the judges of the court that would take the arraignments of our prospective defendants was up to his ears in shady financial dealings with bootleggers appearing before him. But he did not betray us. Perhaps he knew that if he did and was caught, he would go straight to prison. He took bootlegger money as "loans," but he did not deliver the goods, and we dealt with him later.

Late on a foggy Saturday afternoon in February we made our move. Every available police officer except one, and every deputy sheriff in the county was assembled at the police station. They were divided into squads. Each squad leader was armed with both an arrest warrant and a search warrant. Each squad hit its target at the prearranged time. Each returned with its prisoner and the fresh evidence.

All the cells in the central station and the county jail were packed that night and all day Sunday. No judges were available for writs of habeas corpus. So win, lose, or draw, the defendants had thirty-six hours of jailing for a taste. The event really startled people. Nothing quite like that had ever happened in Dane County.

Monday morning the defendants—joined by wives and children—packed the courtroom and overflowed into the halls. Nearly all the defendants pleaded guilty. The judge who took their pleas and gave the sentences was August Hoppmann. He was of German extraction and did not view violation of the state Prohibition act as serious. Though he was an essentially honest and conscientious judge, he made no pretense that he was learned in the law. He was a good judge, but the light sentences he gave that morning infuriated me. I urged that he give stiffer fines accompanied by jail terms for the more flagrant violations.

When he was finished, I voiced my boiling indignation. I was clearly out of bounds. The DA's job is to prosecute, not to sentence. In retrospect, Judge Hoppmann's fines proved adequate, and our continued vigilance really put a crimp in the bootlegging in the Bush.

Meanwhile, the paired patrolmen kept their round-the-clock vigils in the Bush. We kept the pressure on bootlegging sufficiently tight to make the business unprofitable. As 1925 ended, we thought we had won our fight, and perhaps we relaxed a bit. A cold night in January would wake us up. Until then the victims of the sawed-off shotguns had been Italians. On that night in January, a bootlegger killed a policeman in the Bush.

Rudolph Jessner ran a small restaurant. He did some bootlegging also, though we never caught him at it. We never looked on him as a major factor in our problem. Two police officers— Palmer Thompson and Earl Hessling—had been keeping an eye on Jessner, and this interfered with his business. It irritated him. He decided to shoot.

The Ku Klux Klan had revived in the twenties, especially in the Midwest and South. For a time the Klan ran Indiana. Even a man of the character of Hugo Black joined because, in many places, the Klan was on a par with the Elks or Eagles. In any event, the Klan had supporters in Madison, and there were a few on the police force.

Jessner, who was a Jew, was convinced that Thompson and Hessling were Klansmen. Hessling later testified that he *had* joined the Klan. I never had the slightest doubt that they were first-class policemen, and their interest in Jessner was solely centered on his liquor business. But Jessner was obsessed with hatred for policemen in general, and for Thompson and Hessling in particular. He had saved heaps of newspaper clippings referring to the Madison police.

Palmer Thompson was shot in cold blood, but convicting his murderer would not be easy. Jessner retained a competent Madison lawyer, but a new figure appeared almost at once—William

Rubin, a Milwaukee lawyer. Shrewd, keen, organ-voiced, he had defended (according to him) fifty-eight homicide cases when he turned up as the chief defense counsel for Rudy Jessner. He had political ambitions as well. He saw the Jessner case—with a LaFollette prosecuting—as his meat. He was not going to defend Jessner; he was going to flay the police department alive. He was, in effect, going to indict and convict the Ku Klux Klan, the district attorney, and Palmer Thompson and Earl Hessling.

In Wisconsin, any jury of twelve will have, on an average, four Catholics. In criminal cases it takes only one holdout to block a conviction, and any Catholic might justifiably feel sympathy for one who claimed he had been persecuted by the Klan. Bill Rubin was certain he could get at least a hung jury for Jessner.

Rubin threw the book at us. He pleaded not guilty by reason of insanity. Glenn Roberts and I did not underestimate our opponent or the appeal that his defense might have. We wisely knew we needed help, and for my first and only time as DA, I asked the court for special counsel.

Harold Wilkie, who had taught Evidence in the Wisconsin Law School, was appointed. He was a lawyer's lawyer, an indefatigable worker with complete power of concentration. His job was to riddle the insanity defense. He did. Glenn was to handle the defense witnesses—except Jessner, who was mine. I had the affirmative case as well. From start to finish every step was thought through.

We took a room at the Loraine Hotel. There, free from interruption, we—Glenn and I—worked for four weeks preparing our case. Before I go into a bit of detail, I must tell you about two features of Wisconsin criminal law. Wisconsin provides for a grand jury, though it is rarely used. Instead, we have the "John Doe" procedure. It is simple, inexpensive, and provides greater freedom than a grand jury. In addition, it is the most effective weapon ever devised for a district attorney. So far as I know, in all Wisconsin's legal history it never has been abused. There is a safeguard, of course; were it abused, any court of record could issue a writ of prohibition and stop it instantly.

Under this procedure, the DA swears out a complaint before

a judge. He charges that John Doe (that ubiquitous character so familiar to law students) on such-and-such a date committed a specified crime at such-and-such a place. This starts the legal machinery. It is in law a real case. Then the DA starts issuing subpoenas. Witnesses appear before the judge in chambers. The proceedings are secret, as with a grand jury. Thus no one is exposed to needless publicity. The DA can fish for evidence with complete freedom. This procedure enables him to have the sworn testimony of all the known witnesses for both the defense and the prosecution. He is prepared to impeach at the trial any witness who changes his testimony on any material point.

Under the law, the district attorney is duty bound to present all material evidence in any criminal case. More, it is his duty to protect the innocent as well as to prosecute the wrongdoer.

The John Doe procedure was so accepted in Wisconsin that it was never mentioned in our state Supreme Court reports until the Jessner case.

The second feature is this: Long ago Wisconsin adopted the procedure for the court, in cases of insanity pleas in criminal cases, to appoint its own psychiatrists. The defense can employ its own if it wishes to do so. If it does, the money is usually wasted. Where the court appoints the experts it works like Gresham's Law about money—only in reverse. Gresham said that cheap money drives dear money out of the market. Court-appointed experts drive private psychiatrists out of court. Faced with the choice of believing the court-appointed psychiatrist or one hired by a defendant, the jury properly believes the witness who has no private motive.

Glenn Roberts combed the Bush with subpoenas for possible witnesses. He did it so thoroughly that each witness actually called by the defense (except an expert) had been thoroughly examined under oath in the John Doe proceedings. The pretrial testimony ran to some thirty thousand words.

The legal maxim about cross-examination is, Never ask a witness on cross-examination a question unless you know what his answer *must be* or you *don't care how* he answers it. Jessner was smart, and a smart witness is a dangerous witness to cross-examine. (Jessner, I should add, was not insane—not even under the terms of modern psychiatry.) Within the confines of his limited world—that small, six-block area of the Bush—he was an expert. He would most certainly see the questions coming a mile away.

I wrote out longhand every question that I proposed to ask him. There were a lot. Read in order, they pinned him—pinned him so tight he could not move. These were typed. Then I tore each question into a separate slip of paper. One question, one slip. Then the slips were shuffled all out of order. In this disorder they were retyped. That was Mr. Jessner's cross-examination. He never got a glimmer as to where these questions took him. They took him—with the masterly aid of Harold Wilkie and Glenn Roberts—straight to a life sentence for first-degree murder.

Wisconsin does not have the death penalty. My Uncle Robert Siebecker once told me he could never have sat on the bench if Wisconsin had had the death penalty. It degrades anyone who has anything to do with imposing it. But more important, it hinders justice.

When I was DA I talked with an old-time jailbird who spoke more wisdom than many a Ph.D. He said:

"All us guys are gamblers. It is built in. There is no deterrent to crimes of hot blood. When your blood boils you don't think. You just feel. A gallows, a gas chamber, or an electric chair can't get in a head that boils with blood.

"Now, with every crime that takes thinking, we are gamblers. We calculate the risks. It is not the severity of the sentence that stops us. What stops us dead in our tracks is the certainty and speed of a conviction.

"That's why this damn state of Wisconsin is so disliked by we guys. Why in hell I ever stopped off here, I'm damned if I know."

Well, there it is. Wisconsin is comparatively free of crime because its legal machinery moves fast and with good aim. *State v. Jessner* was one of the longest murder trials in our history. Yet Rudy Jessner was in state prison—properly, thoroughly tried and convicted—within three months of the murder. Speed—proper speed—is certainly a key to preventing crime.

The figure who dominated the Bush was a man named Tony

Musso. He did not live in Madison but in Rockford, Illinois. He had connections in Chicago with Al Capone, but he kept out of sight in Madison. Then one day shortly after the Jessner case I had a call at the office by one of Musso's friends. He said Tony would like to see me on a business matter, and I answered that I would let him know.

I talked the matter over with Glenn and also with Frank Gilbert. The latter had been attorney general of Wisconsin and was one of the ablest trial lawyers in the state. I wanted his advice on seeing Musso and on having any conversation with him taken down in shorthand by an official court reporter. He urged me to do exactly that, and I arranged to have Musso come to my office at an appointed hour.

I had a microphone installed in one office and a court reporter at the receiver in an adjoining office. Musso, a big man, swarthy and muscular, and well-dressed, came into the office; we shook hands, and he sat down across from me at the desk. The conversation went something like this:

"I want to do some business with you that will be worth your while. I have some places in the Bush. I'll tell you where they are. I am not asking you to stop your raids down there. In fact, keep them up. All you got to do is tip me off before the raids. For that I'll guarantee you thirty thousand dollars a year—maybe more."

To that I replied, "Musso, you have just committed the crime of attempted bribery, which is a state prison offense."

At that point Musso grabbed his hat and rushed out of the office and beat it for the state line.

The next day an Italian whom I had come to know fairly well came to the office with his attractive daughter. With the news of Musso's departure, fear had lifted from the Bush, and this father was ready to, and did, sign a complaint charging Musso with statutory rape. Warrants now were issued against Musso on the charges of attempted bribery and statutory rape. We did not try to extradite; we knew he would not return to Wisconsin.

Further evidence of confidence in law enforcement among the Italian-Americans in the Bush came shortly after the Musso affair. Two Italians came to the office to complain about the then judge of Superior Court whose shady dealings I have already mentioned in passing. To both Glenn's and my astonishment we were told that they held promissory notes of the judge for money they had loaned him. We gravely doubted their stories, but when Glenn and I confronted the judge he admitted it—and added that there were other similar notes. This was not bribery because the records did not indicate that the judge had "delivered" anything to these creditors of his. It was, however, highly unethical for an officer of the law to accept favors from people he knew were boot-leggers. The only remedy was disbarment proceedings, which we instigated and which resulted in the judge's departure from the legal profession and from the bench.

As my term neared its end, Glenn Roberts, quite naturally, wanted to be the district attorney in his own right. He became a candidate in 1926 and was elected without opposition, and I returned to civil practice after benefiting from the DA experience.

10

TRANSITION

HIS NAME WAS
ROBERT M. LaFOLLETTE, JR. . . .

Isen and her sister Dorothy planned to sail for Europe in June, 1925. She and her sisters had inherited equal shares in a small trust fund from their Grandfather Bacon. Isen was packed to leave, when the phone rang. It was Bob calling from Washington. He told us to come at once; Dad was seriously ill.

A cold he had caught at election time in 1924 had hung on. He and Mother had gone to Florida to bake out the cold and rest his tired system. They came back to Washington from Florida feeling better. But Dad's cold came and went and came again. Now he was seventy—on June 14—and he had pneumonia again.

When Isen and I got to Washington, Dad was perfectly conscious. But he was so tired. He died early in the afternoon of the eighteenth. As his life ebbed away I saw him as two individuals— as my father but, perhaps more, as my chief. He knew he was at the end. He died as he said he would: when his ship went down, the flag still flew, and there was no fear. His old heart just did not have another beat left.

At urging from my family, Isen and her sister went on with their trip to Europe. We went back to bury Dad and to face the political consequences of his death.

Five years earlier, at the time his father was suffering from gallbladder trouble, Phil wrote a note to himself that reads in part:

Whenever death strikes our family it is going to be bitterly sad. We have all lived so close together—so much a part of each other, that the passing of one of us will be like the going out of a part of ourselves. I feel I must do my suffering, outward or confessed suffering before the rest do. Fola, Mary & Bob, or Dad will be hit hard—but Mother and I will have to let it go deep and let it lie there—I know I must help them—not myself. Sometime long after perhaps I may let myself loose—but not when the blow comes. I don't have any overestimate of my comforting qualities—but what they may be, I must use. We all must live, & live for the future as well as the present and past. Whatever Gods there may be, whatever strength I may have . . . I call up to help me to help them. Dad, Mother, Bob, Fola, Mary—what a group they are.

After his father's funeral, Phil wrote to Isen, in Europe:

MADISON, WISCONSIN, JUNE 26, 1925

Beloved Girl,

The days have slipped past and I have not written. Even now it is hard to write—not that I haven't things I'd like to say, and things I'd like to pass on to you that are in my mind. Somehow I am still in the air, and it is awfully hard to come down to the realities of things.

We left Washington a week ago today at 3:00 P.M., and came straight through on special trains arriving in Madison last Saturday at 1:30 P.M. All along the way there were silent signs, people standing in doorways—gathered at little stations, that were heart touching. At Madison a large crowd was gathered—most of them silent and tear-eyed. Mother, Fola, Mid, Ralph, Gilbert and Bas Manley went directly to the farm, Bob and I took Dad to the Capitol, where we left him in the Governor's reception room. The Legislature had designated four members, who staid with him night and day until the funeral on Monday. Sunday morning at 11 people were let in, Dad having been moved into the Rotunda of the Capitol; it was a hot day, but they filed past, in two columns until 7:30 that night. Somewhere between 40 and 50,000—and so few, if any, were curiosity seekers. Monday at 1, the funeral. First a Hymn by a chorus of 50 voices,

Nearer My God to Thee; then Dr. Haydon read some of those passages he likes; then "Abide with Me," and then Dr. Haydon spoke. His talk was eloquent—the eloquence of simplicity. I am sure it was the finest thing he had ever done. Then it all ended with the chorus and the thousands in the Capitol singing America. Then thru a lane of silent people all the way to the cemetery, and there more thousands of people, and a few words by Haydon, and it was done. It was as simple a funeral as ever was, the only thing different were the thousands of people. . . .

I miss you my dear girl, but I am peaceful and content in knowing you will get all there is to be got out of this journey. I am with you in heart and spirit. . . .

I am yours, dear, ever,
Phil

The Constitution requires that a United States senator be at least thirty years old. I was two years too young (assuming— and it takes a lot of it—that I might have other qualifications). Henry Clay had been elected when not quite thirty. A few months might be ignored in pioneer America, but you could not ignore two years.

After Dad's funeral, the politicians began to cluster in groups. Who would succeed him? Smooth—too smooth—politicians of all shades of allegiance had a unanimous choice—my mother, Belle Case LaFollette. Select her, all said, to serve Dad's unexpired term of three years. Fitting recognition for a woman of rare ability and special qualifications. All politicians—but all— in Wisconsin were for her. With Belle Case LaFollette elected for that short term, the field would be wide open for one and all in 1928. Also, thousands of women—not only in Wisconsin but all over the country—wanted this honor for her and for their sex.

If those eager and, in this instance, foolish politicians had stopped to think, they would remember that my father termed her, with sound reason, his "wisest and best counsellor." Mother issued a public statement expressing her appreciation to all who had so urgently asked her to be a candidate, and took herself out of consideration.

Governor John Blaine had the authority to call a special election. Blaine himself considered running, but he had geared his well-planned steps to run against Irvine Lenroot in 1926 for a full term of six years. When Blaine decided not to run, the way was opened for Bob. He was thirty years old. He had had almost the identical upbringing as I, but he had three other facets that would soon prove him an outstanding member of the Senate:

First, for the past six years he had been his father's secretary, with the privilege of the Senate floor. In that period he had absorbed to a remarkable degree all the intricacies of parliamentary procedure. He was a thorough master of the workings of the Senate.

Secondly, he had an extraordinary gift for working with other people. This was to glow when the "other people" were his Senate colleagues. Bob was firm and had deep convictions, but he could state his side of a disagreement without offending the other side. And he could work marvels in finding common ground among men of diverse views.

Finally, he had a first-class mind which, put to work on a given subject, could master it.

Bob's university studies had been interrupted by two sieges of streptococcus infection. They had sapped his physical reserves, which would tell on him later. In temperament and outlook he had much of his mother. He loved fun. He had wit and charm. The long, dreary, painful months of his illnesses had shown his patience and demonstrated his character. Far, far deeper down within him there brooded a dark melancholy that seldom came to the surface, and none but his most intimate friends knew it existed.

Experience teaches that human beings are intricate, complicated. There are few out-and-out blacks and whites in the endless variations in emotions and thought processes within us. So with Bob. To most he seemed a natural, skilled, accomplished public official. He was. Yet, were it not for circumstances over which he had little control, he—like his mother—would never have chosen public life. Under different stars he would have attained a top position in science—most probably medicine, in which, though a layman, he acquired extraordinary knowledge.

He was thirty. His name was Robert M. LaFollette, Jr. He became the Progressive candidate for the nomination on the Republican ticket for the United States Senate in the special primary and election called by Governor Blaine in the summer of 1925. Bob opened his campaign at Stoughton, a small city near Madison. Until then he had made only one real public appearance, at the Cleveland convention in June, 1924, where he read his father's announcement of his Presidential candidacy. He had done this extremely well. His Stoughton speech before a warm, friendly audience was a bit rough, and afterwards, Alf Rogers and others had plenty of suggestions on how to make it better. Don't misunderstand me, Bob's speech was not a flop—far from it. Compared with most speeches, it was good. But according to LaFollette family standards, it left much to be desired.

Within a matter of days, at four speeches a day, Bob hit his stride. Thereafter, in the Senate or on any other platform, he was an eloquent and forceful speaker who marshaled his facts into a disciplined army, marching to his skilled commands.

The total vote in the primary and final special election was not large. It seldom is in special elections. But Bob won by handsome margins. He was a United States senator at thirty, and would hold that office for twenty-one years.

Isen came home from Europe in September. She and her sister had had a wonderful trip. She had special news for me: I was advised we ought to start a family. This we proceeded to do, and in 1926, after the usual excitement and what seemed like interminable waiting, Isen produced a nine-pound, ten-ounce boy. Mother was in Madison and spent the long day with me at the hospital. When she went to see Isen the following day she was amazed to hear Isen refer to "the next time." Mother commented on the effect of modern anesthetics—that her children were born at home (in the bed I still sleep in) and that her deliveries were long and hard, so when her babies arrived she was thankful and content without thought of the future.

When Isen asked her what we should name the baby, Mother replied, "Whatever you and Phil want, but it would be fine if you named him after Daddy." A few hours later my brother ar-

rived at the hospital, and Isen asked his advice on a name for the
baby. Bob replied, "Whatever you and Phil want, but it would
be nice to name him after Daddy." Isen inquired, "But what if
you have a boy of your own?" Bob laughed—he was still "playing
the field" and answered, "Better not count on that!" So Isen
designed a card announcing the arrival of "Robert Marion La-
Follette, Tertius."

In the spring of 1926, I was invited to lecture in criminal law
at the university law school on a part-time basis. I accepted and
began in September with two classes each week for the school
year.

The University of Wisconsin Law School—when I was a
student and later a lecturer there—combined the two principal
methods of teaching—the so-called Socratic and the layer-down-
of-the-law. The emphasis was on the former, though it was
good to have some of the latter.

Since the nineties, under the leadership of the Harvard Law
School, the case method has overwhelmingly predominated. In
the case system the student learns the law from specific, actual
lawsuits rather than from textbooks that set forth legal principles
and rules.

In my father's and mother's time, law was taught by more or
less eminent local lawyers "laying down the law" in lectures.
They knew and told you the leading case at each point. Minority
opinions—even opposing decisions—while cited perhaps, were
not usually emphasized.

Stare decisis—the point has been decided—must have given
to most students the idea that the law was a stable, established
structure. In other words, students must have had the impression
that somewhere in a far-off, mysterious realm open only to the
high priest of the law there was a vast, definite, fixed law. This
the judges found and delivered, like mined ore, in massive decisions.

The genius of the English common law is the opposite. From
its inception it has grown, often slowly, at times perhaps too
slowly, but it has grown; and it grows today like the living beings it governs and who "find it"—not in some mysterious place,

but out of the specific, often comparatively minute, problems of human lives.

At Wisconsin Law School we had an outstanding example of the "layer-down-of-the-law" in Professor Howard L. Smith. We read cases, of course, but there was never any doubt in his mind or speech about which of any conflicting decisions was right. None of this gray area business for him. It was definitely black or white, and no nonsense about it.

The Socratic teaching, of course, seeks to compel the student's mind to find the better, not necessarily the best, answers in the shaded areas of conflicting, honest differences of opinion. Eugene A. Gilmore, later president of the State University of Iowa and vice-governor of the Philippine Islands, taught constitutional law. He was an ideal Socratic teacher. In constitutional law I was greatly bothered by a glaring inconsistency in the interpretation of the Thirteenth and Fourteenth amendments by the United States Supreme Court. The first prohibits slavery and involuntary servitude. The second prohibits any state from depriving any person of due process of law. Both were adopted over the issue of Negro slavery, both at nearly the same time.

The Supreme Court construed the Thirteenth Amendment narrowly. It was intended to apply to Negro slavery, and it did not permit a seaman, no matter what the provocation, to jump his ship. If he did before his contract expired, even in a safe port, he could be sent to jail. Quite the opposite position was taken by the court on the Fourteenth Amendment. A broad view was taken wherein its due process clause was applied to corporations and not just to persons, as it actually says.

Why? I chased Professor Gilmore politely but relentlessly through his constitutional law course, in and out of class, for an answer. It took months. Finally he said, "In most governments there is some special, mysterious, awesome, respected spot, almost like the high altar of a cathedral, where sit the protectors of Private Property. In Britain it *was* the House of Lords. With us it *is* [1922] the Supreme Court of the United States."

To most, teaching gives joy. You feel the minds of those you teach grow and flower, and you have the sense of deep satisfaction akin to the act of creation itself. No, not exactly, for you are not creating. It is there. You help it become free, alive.

I was approached by the heads of both Wisconsin and Chicago universities about the law deanships, and I was sorely tempted to accept. As I look back, I know how my mother craved that I would surrender to the temptation to make teaching my life's work. But the pull of action and the tempting hazards of life outside the cloister were too deep, too strong, and I declined.

In 1927, I got my first real experience as a professional lecturer. In January of that year I signed a contract with the Redpath Lyceum Bureau to deliver thirty-one lectures beginning the middle of July and continuing through August. At that time Redpath operated the Redpath Chautauqua, mainly in Indiana, Michigan, and Illinois. The Chautauqua took its name from the New York lake of that name. In the nineties and until the 1930's it was a distinctive feature of small town life in America. For six days or one week—usually in July and August—there would come to the county seat or some other center, a big tent with platform and folding chairs for an audience of 1,500 to 2,000. There were morning, afternoon, and evening performances. Domestic science, sewing, singing, music, travelogues, art—all these brought entertainment, education, and some culture to these towns and their environs. There was always a lecturer on the program.

Six weeks on one of those circuits would prove whether you were a professional or not. Never was a tougher audience assembled. Everybody bought tickets for all performances. Some liked this, some that. Their particular interests induced them to buy their tickets, and unless he was a prominent national figure, few really wanted to hear the lecturer. The whole family would attend and sit there staring, generally with arms folded, cold as icebergs, shouting in stony silence, "Entertain us if you can!" And, mind you, the local potentate had taken you aside and whispered emphatically in your ear: "No politics here! Nothing controversial!"

Lecturing tests a speaker's character. There is a strong temptation to deal in pious platitudes—to entertain and avoid anything controversial. If one can avoid that error, and if he makes the grade, lecturing can be of enormous help for a person in public life, especially if he is without inherited wealth.

Toward the end of the lecture tour Mother urged me to take a trip to Europe, at her expense. From the time of Dad's death I had handled her legal and property affairs. We had sold off enough of Maple Bluff Farm to pay the mortgage and leave enough so that Mother, with her modest needs, felt a financial freedom she had so often been without.

I hesitated about going to Europe. I would be away from the office, and from Isen and the baby, for six weeks; but both Isen and Mother urged me to go. So with mixed emotions I left for New York after my last lecture. I visited Fola's husband, George Middleton, in New York and saw a new play of his that had just opened.

Among the mail awaiting me on the ship was a wonderful letter from Bob, which illustrates the deep and abiding bond between us:

August 22, 1927

Dear Phil:

I cannot tell you how happy I am that you are started on your first vacation in years. God knows you have earned it. You have been so generous with your time in every way, without thought of self, during the last few years that I feel even this fine trip is too short.

The thrill in store for you seeing Paris for the first time! To see it with Fola as your guide and companion is ideal. Don't fail to see the Cluny Museum. This is the history of France before your eyes, from Roman times on. . . . Be sure and see the old houses. I think they are on the left bank, which were there when the Three Musketeers were performing their wonderful feats.

You mean so much in my life, Phil, that I feel poverty-stricken when I attempt to express my affection. I must rely on your marvelous intuition and understanding. . . .

Fola and Mid had taken an apartment on the Left Bank in Paris, at No. 20 rue Jacob. Of my arrival in Paris I wrote Isen:

Saturday, Sept. 3, 1927

Yesterday afternoon I arrived at St. Lazare [Station] at 5:37. I had wired Fola of my train, but we missed each other at the station—so your good husband creaked his terrible French into action, got a taxi, and told the driver—very slowly: 'Vang—Ru—Ja—Kobe'—and he started on his way down the streets of Paris. The way from St. Lazare to Rue Jacob takes one across the Seine through the Tuilleries Gardens, past the Louvre—the Place de la Concorde—where one gets the sweep up and down the Champs Élysées. . . . When I got into that taxi and started out I got a thrill! which increased into a real crescendo as I saw the Place de la Concorde and the Arc de Triomphe.

I reached 20 Rue Jacob but the front looked like the shopping district, so I stopped the taxi and rang the concierge's bell. . . . I said "LaFollette" and . . . he immediately replied in the affirmative. So I climbed the 6 flights to the apartment and was admitted by the dear Old Marie. When Fola arrived I was already shaving and in quite a settled state. The apartment is a charming place—looking out over the roofs of Paris and down into an old garden, part of which was once Racine's. The house is some 300 years old, with quaint charm one would expect.

Fola and I spent the next day at Versailles, and that night Jo Davidson, the sculptor, came for dinner. He and I hit it off right from the start. He was short and stockily built, with a full beard, twinkling eyes, and a mischievous, sensual mouth. He and Fola were old friends. He and Lincoln Steffens had accompanied Dad and Mother to Russia in 1923, and while they were in Paris, Jo had made a bust of Dad. And he had been commissioned by Wisconsin to sculpture a statue of Dad for Statuary Hall in the United States Capitol in Washington.

After dinner, Jo suddenly jumped up and said, "Fola, this young feller ought not to be sitting around talking—in Paris! I'm going to show him the town." So Jo and I started out in his uniformed-chauffeur-driven Peugeot. We made the rounds of the night spots, and Jo, with his reputation as an artist and with his red ribbon of the *Légion d'Honneur* in his lapel, got the red carpet treatment. In several places the hostess would greet Jo with open arms and set us down with champagne as they reminisced about the days when Jo and she were young—and about this or that girl who was now the mistress of a member of the cabinet; then about another who had married a millionaire; and about others who had died in the gutter. We got back to Fola's at about dawn. It had been quite an experience for the "young feller" from Madison.

Under Fola's masterly guidance I saw everything choice to see in or around Paris—Versailles, Saint-Denis, Chantilly, Chartres, Cluny Museum, Saint-Eustache. Fola wrote Isen: "You will have a French husband at the end of twenty days. He is already fluent with the taxi drivers, and followed the French farce we saw last night as if Paris were his home."

Before I left Paris for Strasbourg, Munich, and Vienna, Fola and I went to Jo's studio for lunch with him and his wife and to see the still uncompleted statue of Dad. It impressed both Fola and me very favorably. The hands of the statue were not satisfactory, so Jo, noting that my hands were like Dad's, used mine for a sitting; and Jo remarked that "at least your hands, Phil, will be in Statuary Hall in the Capitol."

11

THE DEMANDS
OF POLITICS

...WITHOUT HOPE
OF PROFIT OR REWARD.

On my return to Madison I found Isen and our baby fine, and my office desk loaded with work. And, of course, I also found the ever present and always urgent demands of politics. Bob would be up for reelection in 1928 for the first full six-year term of his own. The first hurdle of 1928 would come at the spring primary, when delegates to the national conventions would be chosen.

We obtained the consent of Senator George W. Norris of Nebraska to enter his name in the Presidential preference primary. Norris won the endorsement by 163,000 to Herbert Hoover's 17,000 write-in votes, but because Hoover's name had not been on the ballot the result was inconclusive. Bob led all others in the election of delegates-at-large to the national convention. We won control of the delegation, but the results indicated that the September primary fight in the Republican party would be a tough one—at least over the governorship.

Because we had elected a majority of the national convention delegates, we could name the state's representatives on the various committees. Bob was chosen for the platform committee, and he would thus present the minority report to the convention and, via radio, to the nation.

Nineteen twenty-eight marked the first real impact on American politics of radio. It was, I recall, more startling than the subsequent introduction of television. At each Republican convention since 1908, Wisconsin Progressives had presented a minority report in the form of a substitute platform. At each of the five prior conventions, it was received with hoots and yells of derision. Now, twenty years later, Bob could point out the remarkable fact that almost all the planks presented by the Progressives since 1908 had been enacted into law.

Bob did a superb job in presenting the platform. Although most delegates did not agree with him, they and the audience were friendly to this serious young senator who proved that Progressive dissenters were not stubborn roadblockers but instead had a constructive program that, over the years, had won national support for most of its proposals. When Bob concluded, he was given a generous and rousing ovation. Overnight he was a national figure. And of vast importance politically, hundreds of thousands of people in Wisconsin had heard him by radio. Whether they agreed with him or not, citizens of Wisconsin were proud of their young senator. One correspondent wrote: "Hoover got the votes; LaFollette got the cheers." We knew that LaFollette would also get the votes in Wisconsin that year.

As I have said, the real contest in 1928 would be for the governorship. To understand the dilemma we faced in choosing our candidate for governor, we must consider first the gubernatorial election of 1926.

Dad had persuaded Herman Ekern to run for attorney general in 1922. That post has been a good launching pad for the governorship. Dad was looking ahead to 1926, when Governor Blaine would be our natural candidate to oppose Irvine Lenroot for the Senate. Objectively, Herman was an ideal candidate to succeed Blaine as governor. He had been an outstanding leader in the state legislature, and he had made a national reputation in the insurance field. He, more than anyone else, was the author of the federal War Risk Insurance Act, which has been such an inexpensive boon to the millions of Americans who have served their country in wartime.

Ekern had intelligence, integrity, courage, and vision; and he was prominent in the Norwegian Lutheran Church. He was a perfect candidate on paper. Unfortunately, he was a flop as a live candidate.

Herman had opened a law office in Chicago. He kept his home in Madison, but he traveled all around the country. He was the acknowledged legal light in the field of mutual insurance. Generous with his money, he himself lived modestly. During his travels he contracted the worst case of Pullmanitis ever known. He just could not stay out of a Pullman berth. During the period of twenty-five years that I would meet Herman on the street, in a conference, or in an office, I invariably asked him the same question:

"Herman, when are you leaving?"

"On the sleeper tonight. For [and here was the only variation] Minneapolis . . . Chicago . . . San Francisco . . . Washington . . . New York." The destination varied; the method of departure never varied.

Herman ably discharged his duties as attorney general, but his own political fences were sadly neglected. When he agreed to run for governor in 1926, no strong Conservative appeared against him. But a fellow Progressive—Fred Zimmerman—vastly inferior to Herman in essential qualities but a master as a political mixer and hand-shaker, entered the race. He was secretary of state, and the requirements of that office in Wisconsin are not high. In fact, its maximum needs are those of a competent office manager, but it carried with it an important political asset. Fred Zimmerman handled the issuance of the license plates for automobiles. His name—usually printed in black letters big enough to read across the room—went into the home of every automobile owner in the state. Every year that name was seen with greater frequency.

Fred Zimmerman would not have defeated Herman if the Conservative Republicans had not switched a substantial bloc of their votes to him. They preferred a backsliding Progressive if by switching they could defeat the "regular" progressive candidate.

By 1928, we had the two United States senators, Bob and Blaine (who had defeated Lenroot in 1926), but the governorship was in the woefully inadequate hands of Zimmerman. Our problem would not be Bob's reelection but the governorship. Should we support Herman Ekern again in 1928, or should we seek another candidate? Herman wanted to have another try at it. His great abilities, his character, and his record of unwavering loyalty to our cause gave him the inside track.

But an objective review of the 1926 campaign showed conclusively that Herman should have won. We had tried to get Herman to concentrate his energies on that campaign but had failed. Victories or defeats often have many explanations. But if you find an explanation that is within the control of a candidate himself, you do not need to look further. If the candidate fails to do his best, he must accept the blame if he is defeated. Bob agreed with me that if Herman would not devote himself exclusively to the 1928 campaign for a minimum of three months, we would not support him again.

The Conservative Republican candidate in 1928 was virtually certain to be Walter J. Kohler, a plumbing manufacturer. As a newcomer to politics, he had two advantages: he was a millionaire, and he also was known to many thousands of Wisconsin voters who saw his name not once a year like Fred Zimmerman's but several times every day, when they used a Kohler toilet.

What were we Progressives to do? Our conference was to meet in Milwaukee. A day or two before we were to meet I got Herman over to our home. We talked, it seemed, for hours. I pleaded with him to promise that he would spend June, July, and August campaigning. He would not budge. I am convinced his years of ceaseless travel had become a form of sickness. (He often said, "I sleep so well in a Pullman berth.")

Bob and I had had many talks with other leaders in the state. All those who understood the problem agreed that it would be better to get licked with a candidate for governor who attended to business rather than go through another campaign with Herman in a sleeping car.

Finally, exhausted, I told Herman that Bob and I would support Joseph Beck for governor. Joe Beck came off the farm, but it never left him. He had graduated from the university, had been in state service, and had a fine record. Now he was serving his fourth term in Congress, representing a largely rural district in western Wisconsin. Joe was overweight. He always carried a handy tool—a combination nail file, scissors, and ear cleaner. He was devoted to chewing tobacco—and was very accurate in its outward propulsion. A friend who had a peek at his trunk in his hotel room claimed he saw its entire contents—two shirts, two suits of underwear (long, winter), some handkerchiefs, four pairs of socks, and the rest, packed in neat rows, fine-cut chewing tobacco.

If Joe had been a university professor, for which he was fully qualified, he would have been readily accepted by more "sophisticated" persons. But he carried the farm with him all his life—everywhere. So he seemed to many a bit rough at the edges. He had an excellent mind. He had courage, integrity, complete devotion to his cause, and he was a hard worker. He wanted very much to be governor of Wisconsin, and Bob and the rest of us knew that Joe would put his heart and soul into the campaign.

Our conference in Milwaukee was well attended. As usual, it was made up largely of dedicated men and women. It was a volunteer force, and all came at their own expense. Only a few had ever held, or even expected to hold, any kind of a salaried job in politics. These people knew Herman Ekern and valued him highly. None of us could explain in public why we preferred Beck to him.

By a close vote, our conference endorsed Joe Beck. Herman, with great grace, gave warm support to the decision. Later, in 1938, on the death of the incumbent when I was governor, I appointed Herman lieutenant governor. He liked the well-earned recognition which did not seriously interfere with his law practice—his travels and the Pullmans.

The 1928 campaign developed as we expected. Walter Kohler led the Conservatives. Joe Beck was our candidate. Fred Zimmerman, the governor, was also on the primary ballot and would divide our vote as he had in 1926. Bob was opposed by George Mead, a paper manufacturer and banker. The results for governor were Kohler 224,000, Beck 203,000, and Zimmerman 83,000. Bob won by a two-to-one margin.

Zimmerman's vote and the Kohler campaign funds gave the nomination to Kohler. The Kohler family and the Conservative Republican organization spent money lavishly, openly, and on a scale never before seen in Wisconsin. It was a clear and flagrant violation of the Wisconsin Corrupt Practices Act, which would present a challenge to Progressive leadership in 1929.

Bob had clear sailing in the general election in 1928, polling 85 per cent of the vote. His smashing victory in the primary had made it clear that he would have no trouble in November. Indeed, the Democratic nominee withdrew, and Bob's only opponent was a Conservative Republican running as an independent.

Bob did not support Hoover, the Republican presidential candidate. He devoted his efforts to campaigning in other states for Burton Wheeler, Henrik Shipstead, and Lynn Frazier—and at the Mayo Clinic trying to clear up recurring attacks of various *streptococcus* infections. Blaine enthusiastically supported Governor Al Smith, the Democratic nominee for President. I lent a hand with a few speeches, for I had long admired Smith's record as governor and the progressive principles that he held. Hoover carried Wisconsin over Smith by 94,000 votes, and Bob, in winning his race, ran 91,000 votes better than Hoover.

Progressives faced a real dilemma in January, 1929. We had talked—no, more, shouted in words of wrath—about the wickedness of the lavish, corrupt use of money in politics. Now it had happened in the Kohler campaign. It smelled so badly you could not ignore it. Were we going to put up or shut up? Were we going to do something about it or admit that our righteous anger was fake?

The Wisconsin Corrupt Practices Act has sharp teeth. Any citizen who can present to a Court of Record a prima facie case that the law has been violated can start judicial machinery moving that can declare an election void for abuse and oust the guilty official from office. Yet we faced one of those facts of political life every politician must know: Any man in public life who resorts to law to right a political or personal affront invites almost certain trouble for himself, because people in this country expect political leaders to be able to take it, and with a smile. It is not "playing the game" to resort to the courts, but the Kohler campaign had been so blatant in ignoring the law that we had to do something about it.

In July we filed the complaint, sworn to by myself, William T. Evjue of the *Capital Times*, and others. It was entitled *State ex rel. LaFollette* v. *Kohler*. Harold Wilkie accepted appointment as special counsel by the attorney general at twenty-five dollars a day, the rate fixed by law. As was to be expected, top lawyers represented Governor Kohler. Before this lawsuit, Harold's professional reputation was very high, but he was almost unknown outside a limited circle. This case enabled him to demonstrate, in the glare of publicity, what a master craftsman he was—especially in his cross-examination of the governor, which was devastating to Kohler.

During the initial maneuvering, the Wisconsin Supreme Court held that the Corrupt Practices Act was constitutional. The case was then tried in Governor Kohler's home county, with a judge from Milwaukee. This judge did everything in his power to shelter the defendant, but this helped us, the plaintiffs, because the prejudice was so obvious that it removed all element of "persecution." This politically untutored judge helped us by overhelping the defendant. The case went to the Wisconsin Supreme Court again, but before a final decision could be reached the case became moot because of the expiration of Governor Kohler's term.

That lawsuit is memorable. It gave Harold Wilkie the opportunity to demonstrate his great gifts publicly. It showed that Progressives were not political cowards. And it proved what had been obvious, that Governor Kohler had spent too much money. Far worse, the defendant's two lawyers let him so testify that he was made to appear either quite foolish or careless with the truth.

People who do not know Wisconsin have never understood the hostility of the press and the bitterness of people of wealth toward Progressives and progressivism. Throughout my father's life no more than two daily newspapers supported him at any given time. My father could carry his story to the public only by campaigning in person in every village, hamlet, and crossroad or through the LaFollette weekly. He established the standard of a long campaign—eight or ten weeks, with four or five speeches during the day and a fifth or sixth one at night at, perhaps, the county seat.

Strangers to Wisconsin and, indeed, some who are not strangers, find it difficult to understand how Progressives during these years could run a successful campaign covering a state of 55,000 square miles and a population of more than three million people, for between $25,000 and $30,000, and that sum would include the campaign of five state officers and a United States senator.

A campaign at that cost was possible for these reasons: One headquarters at Madison would run the campaign for everything outside Milwaukee County; at the second headquarters in Milwaukee County, most expenses would be raised locally. The state campaign manager would be paid perhaps fifty or seventy-five dollars a week. Aside from him and perhaps five or six stenographers, all the help were unpaid volunteers, and there was no such thing as a paid speaker. Rent was kept at a minimum by holding the day meetings out of doors in good weather or in a country schoolhouse or village hall. The night meetings would be in the courthouse or the auditorium of a school building, where the charge was nominal. In some large cities the local committee engaged a hall and paid for it out of their local contributions. Then, the Railroad Brotherhoods were a tower of strength. They would send into Wisconsin—as they did in other states—a special edition of their militant weekly newspaper, *Labor,* which would reach every rural mailbox holder and which volunteers would distribute house to house in the cities.

Through the years there have been repeated references to the LaFollette Machine. Let me tell you exactly of what it consisted. In the inner circle of Wisconsin Progressives we had "a little black book." This book was indexed by counties and then sub-indexed by townships, villages, and cities. It contained the names of four thousand men and women who were farmers, workers, small businessmen, professional people, teachers, and, here and there, a manufacturer or a big businessman whose enlightenment led him against his immediate and shortsighted self-interest. This volunteer political army, formed under the leadership of my father, was the backbone of the Progressive Movement in Wisconsin.

If one were to translate into dollars the value of the services of our volunteers, the Progressive campaigns undoubtedly would have cost far more than the $25,000 I have mentioned. But the Corrupt Practices Act in Wisconsin, and everywhere else, is framed on the theory—and, I think, a fundamentally correct one—that there is a vast difference between an individual who is contributing large sums of money to influence an election, on the one hand, and an individual giving of his time, effort, and thought in support of a candidate or candidates in whom he believes, on the other hand. The corrupt use of money has, all through history, been an ever constant menace to the life of democracy itself. The greatest defenders and supporters of democracy are those who give of their time freely, without hope of profit or reward. They do it to support principles, policies, and candidates in which and in whom they believe.

Isen and I had found a comfortable but modest home on the west side of Madison. We continued to live on the west side because of Isen's belief—which I share—that we should live where our children could walk to school. This, uniquely in Madison on the west side, was possible from kindergarten through grade school, high school, and the university.

On December 13, 1928, Judith Bacon LaFollette had arrived. When she and her mother came home from the hospital it really seemed as if we had a family.

During this period, a new and fascinating client, the architect Frank Lloyd Wright, appeared in our office. I had read in the newspapers that he had been arrested and jailed under the Mann Act and released on bail. His wife had refused him a divorce without assurances of alimony for her lifetime. The mortgage on his home-studio, Taliesin, near Spring Green, Wisconsin, had been foreclosed, as had the chattel mortgage on its furnishings, including his valuable collection of Japanese paintings. He was in real trouble and wanted our firm to help get his affairs untangled. Because, as a child, I had attended the Hillside Home School conducted by his two maiden aunts, I had a personal interest in helping him to get his affairs in order.

Wright's loyal supporters recognized his genius, and some were ready to help financially providing that he put himself and his affairs in the hands of a responsible lawyer. They had agreed that I would be satisfactory.

Every time Frank came to the office his procedure was the same: he either talked walking around the room, or he talked sitting on my desk. He was indifferent about any papers on the desk and about where his cigarette ashes might fall. But he sparkled with wit and humor, and like so many geniuses, he had a firm opinion about any subject that came up for discussion. Some people thought him conceited and vain. I do not agree. Conceit and vanity are obnoxious if there is no solid foundation for supreme self-confidence. Those rare people who have the spark of creative genius usually have in them something of the actor. Frank was a great actor, and his play was Frank Lloyd Wright.

He had humor but not the gift to see one's self in perspective. Only once did I hear him tell a story on himself. That was about the visit of a great opera singer—I think it was Mary Garden—to Taliesin. As I remember Frank's version, the story went something like this:

"Mary Garden asked me to give her my views on modern architecture. So I gave her my best. She sat there looking at me, her eyes sparkling with what I thought was rapt and fascinated attention. I talked on and on for nearly an hour. I stopped, and she apparently thought I had finished. She looked at me with her winning smile, and said: 'I have always wanted to ask an expert like you a question. May I?' I assured her she could, and waited for some gem. This is what I got: 'How do they get those wonderful little ships in a glass bottle?' "

To return to Frank's affairs: We retained another firm to negotiate with Mrs. Miriam Noel Wright for the divorce. We organized a corporation to manage his affairs. Frank was to work for the corporation, which would pay him a salary and handle all his financial affairs. Frank's friends put money into the corporation to pay for Mrs. Wright's alimony: the divorce was obtained; and Taliesin and its furnishings and Japanese paintings were restored to Frank and the new Mrs. Wright.

Once freed from his harassments, Frank went back to his work with the energy and fire of a young man. But it was obvious that he disliked having his finances controlled by someone other than himself. It was only a question of time until he would assert his independence. Late one afternoon I saw a brand new Cord car coming up the street. At the wheel was Frank, proud as a potentate, as his expensive car proceeded west toward Taliesin. Up to this time we had not been paid a cent for our services, and I knew that our professional relations were over.

Just as Alf Rogers and I were preparing to withdraw from the corporation, Miriam Noel Wright died. Under the terms of the trust, the funds reverted to the corporation. We then garnisheed (attached) the fund for payment for our services. Frank did not like that at all, and our paths did not cross again for many years. Then one day I encountered him on the train for Chicago. His face brightened, and we shook hands. He said something like this: "Phil, you know I was all wrong about you and Rogers. Can't we just forget about the whole thing?" So our friendship was back on an even keel and remained so until he died.

12

CANDIDATE
FOR
GOVERNOR

... A NATURAL EVOLUTION
OF PUBLIC SENTIMENT ...

In March, 1929, when Jo Davidson's statue of Dad arrived in Washington and was placed in Statuary Hall in the Capitol, I was designated to express the LaFollette family's appreciation.

Before a large and distinguished audience the statue was unveiled by Mary's son, Robert Sucher, and by Marion Wheeler, daughter of Senator Burton K. Wheeler. In every mind in that audience dwelt the astonishing fact that, only eleven years before, the Senate of the United States had before it petitions to expel Robert LaFollette from that body on the ground of disloyalty because he opposed our entry into World War I.

Though I had made many speeches during the previous ten years, this was my first at a formal and, for all Dad's friends and supporters, a most important occasion, so I read from a manuscript:

He first took me through this Hall. He knew that critics found fault with some of these statues as works of art, but it was not in that spirit he viewed them. His background and his intimate knowledge of American history made him venerate not the statues but the lives they commemorated. . . .

Trevelyan says: "The character of a public man can best be judged when he is opposed to some violent and almost universal passion of his fellow-countrymen. Then will be seen the stuff of which he is made." All of us recur to the period of the War, not alone because of the change in public sentiment toward that undertaking, but because the intensity of feeling and passion of that period were a supreme test of the inherent character and qualities that directed the course of my father's public career. . . .

He had no narrow sense that he represented any single state, or that his duty was confined alone to the people of Wisconsin. . . . [But] he would want us to remember that whatever service he was able to render his country was made possible by the unmatched loyalty and affection, existing without interruption for a quarter of a century he was in the Senate, between the people of Wisconsin and himself. In the most trying hours of his public career he was sustained by their confidence and, above all, by their understanding. Enemies swarmed upon him, leaders betrayed him, friends forsook him, but in some mysterious way the silent masses reached out through it all and spoke to him. He was born among them, fought their battles with them, and went to his grave, after the holocaust of bitterness and animosity of war, sweet and untouched by hate, because of his love of them and their love of him. In an age of doubt and disillusionment, of betrayal of faith, this mutual trust and understanding made even stronger his profound confidence in the masses of the people and their ability to work out their own destiny.

With Bob's sweeping victory in 1928 and the defeat of our candidate for governor, speculation began in the fall of that year and continued increasingly through 1929 as to "What is Phil going to do in 1930?" And the interest and speculation were not limited to Wisconsin. The October 2, 1928, issue of *Time* magazine carried a story on the LaFollette brothers, with my photograph on the cover. And the May, 1929, *World's Work*, a monthly magazine that dealt with contemporary issues, carried an article by Henry Pringle. I quote from it because it gives an interesting analysis of Bob and me:

Philip LaFollette . . . is an essential part of the story of Robert. Out of Madison the consensus of opinion is that "Phil is more like the Old Man; Bob is like his mother". . . .

Bob . . . is logical, calm, and judicial. Phil, whether in conversation across a luncheon table or on the platform, is likely to depart into the cold and luminous realm of idealism. . . . He thunders denunciations where Bob points a cool, accusing finger. . . .

Bob and Phil differ in these primary characteristics. Their secondary traits, it is obvious, are those of each other. . . . The differences are just pronounced enough so that they complement each other perfectly.

In the hands of these two brothers rests, to no small degree, the future of the Progressive movement. They are visionary, but they know the machinery of practical politics as do few men in this country.

Naturally, I gave no hint of my own thoughts on the campaign of 1930. I say "naturally" because I had not made up my mind, and I knew that the inevitable charge of "too much LaFollette" could best be answered if, when I became a candidate, it was clear that no other leading Progressive wanted to run and that Governor Kohler would be difficult to beat.

So, during 1929 I "sawed wood." I kept up my practice, did my usual professional lecturing, taught two hours a week at the law school, and filled speaking dates in Wisconsin. The speeches, of course, were nominally nonpolitical, but Dad had drilled into me the effectiveness of speeches made outside formal campaigning.

When in 1929 President Glenn Frank of the University of Wisconsin urged me to accept the deanship of the law school, I wrote the family:

There is a side of me that this appeals to very strongly, especially as I contemplate the likelihood of disappointments and defeat in the world outside. When one puts his effort and personality into the academic field, he works in a smaller field—he can see and sense the results of his effort more easily and more immediately. . . . If he reaches out beyond the academic world in his work and thinking, he may have quite as important results. If one considers and assesses the relative value of men like Karl Marx, William James, Kant, Voltaire, etc., with Jefferson, Lincoln, Bright, Dad, etc., one's first reaction is that perhaps the former have a more profound and lasting influence. Perhaps, if one goes deeper, however, he sees that this is due to two things. First: The fact that the academic group does not deal primarily in the world of reality enables them to avoid the necessity of compromise—and thus to appear as individuals who laid down profound and inflexible plans—and second: The academic influence is the direct influence of one leader upon other leaders, and the other leaders preserve the ideal of their teacher as an ideal untarnished by practice. From this, if it be correct, it follows that the greatest job of all is the leadership which preserves itself in the conflict of the open field unprotected by the softer influence of the University World.

If the choice could be made, I should like to spend some years in this atmosphere of reflection. I would welcome an opportunity to write, think, and act, so that when and if the time came for me to return in some way to public affairs I could come with better preparation. But that choice is not possible . . . because my accepting this position now would leave our forces with a sense of being left somewhat without leadership—and while I seriously doubt whether I have the qualities which they hope I have, they nevertheless *think* they are here. And if those inherent qualities are not in me now, that kind of quality will not be developed by a period of incubation in a university. . . .

I don't need to add that I have concluded not to take it, and that I am ready to take what may come in the world of politics.

I think it correct to say that at the time I wrote the family about the offer of the deanship I had not definitely decided to run for governor in 1930. What I had decided was that I would wait for the opportunity to get into public affairs. As for 1930, the final decision was a year away, and many things can happen in a year.

Then, something of political significance did happen. The late twenties was the period of skyrocketing stock markets and booming prosperity. In tune with this atmosphere, the largest bank in Wisconsin, the First Wisconsin National Bank, organized a holding company to take over the choicest banks in the state. I spoke out against this move of the "chain system" into banking. For years Progressives had opposed the concentration of vast economic and financial power in a few hands. This issue of chain banking reached into every city and county in the state. The small businessman in Wisconsin had seen the "corner grocer" go out of business under the fierce competition of the food chains, and the chains were moving into merchandising of clothing, shoes, and other commodities.

My attack on chain banking got a good press throughout the state. Invitations to speak poured in from Rotary, Kiwanis, and Lions clubs, Chambers of Commerce, and similar business groups. The speech was a good one, and it went over with every audience.

The chain banking issue gave me the opportunity to talk to thousands of men, most of whom had never voted for a Progressive or listened open-mindedly to a Progressive candidate for high office. These meetings continued through the winter and into the spring. Isen and the children had gone to Biloxi, Mississippi. Though this was not an ideal situation, we felt that it was a necessary safeguard because the children had been exposed to tuberculosis, which had stricken Isen's sister Lois. On the credit side, their absence left me free to put in a hard, double-time schedule—practicing law, lecturing, speaking two or three times a week, and meeting and conferring with Progressive leaders in Wisconsin.

Alf Rogers, my law partner, dreaded seeing me get into active politics so soon. He hoped I would wait until I had built up some financial competence, but he was shrewd enough about politics to say: "With Bob in the Senate, you may never have another chance. It happens that right now no other Progressive leader wants to run—hardly anyone thinks Kohler can be beat—so the way is open for you as it may never be again."

During the winter and spring of 1930 scarcely a week passed that I did not stop for a visit with State Supreme Court Justice

Charles Crownhart. He had been a lifelong Progressive, had managed Dad's campaigns for reelection in 1910 and 1916, and was a master strategist in politics. He was a mild-mannered man with innate wisdom, who smoked his pipe with a slight drivel and looked out the window through steel-rimmed glasses as he pondered his advice to me. He had strongly advised against my accepting the deanship, feeling that I was "made for politics." Still, during the early weeks of 1930 my mind was not made up. I wrote Isen on January 8:

"Nothing is settled. We are really just marking time and letting the situation develop as political currents [show] a natural trend. There may be a change in the situation—but at present it continues as it has been for the past six months: a general feeling among our people that I should be a candidate. If I become a candidate, it will be a natural evolution of public sentiment among our people. I see no reason for altering my present attitude, which is simply awaiting events—with my mind open—and without commitments either way. If you get any reactions, let me have them."

George Middleton had gone to Hollywood under a profitable contract, and Fola, on her way to join him, arranged to stop over in Milwaukee to meet me and to hear one of my speeches on the chain bank issue. She wrote Mother on March 29:

"I heard him give a fine speech. He has gained tremendously in ease and control since I heard him speak extemporaneously in New Jersey with Daddy. The quality of poise and emotional modeling of his material which he had in his speech at the unveiling of the statue is now a part of his extemporaneous speaking. There is great power and intensity but [it] is directed. . . . This makes the whole more telling and gives a greater sense of power. . . ."

We had decided not to hold a statewide Progressive conference. Instead, we held conferences by state senatorial districts. As these were held, I was endorsed as the Progressive candidate against Governor Kohler.

I cannot say now when I actually decided to run. I just grew into it. As the months passed, it became clear that the Progressives had no other candidate. Though I was by no means the unani-

mous choice of the Progressive leaders, the controlling factor
was that the great majority of politicians as well as newspaper-
men did not think Kohler could be defeated. If the Progressives
were to have a serious contender, it had to be me. Charlie Crownhart always said a trend set in early in an election year, and
what a candidate had to do was get on the right side of that
trend, nurse it, and not make too many mistakes. He was sure
by January that the trend had set in for me. Alf Rogers saw it,
too—though with reluctance.

In April, I had a matter before a federal commission in Washington and arranged to meet Bob at Atlantic City. Mother
came, too, and this gave us a quiet weekend to talk over the
situation in Wisconsin. It was now certain in all our minds that
I should be a candidate in the September primary. But naturally
it was sound politics not to announce the decision until the time
for filing nomination papers.

April 14 was our seventh wedding anniversary. I wrote Isen
from Atlantic City:

We both appreciate fully how completely out of our own
control are all the external things and events of life: health,
illness, sorrow, death, so-called success and so-called failure—
but with the passing of years I think each of us has got a sense
of the unlimited possibilities of one's inner self. It is like a vast,
unexplored Empire—of which one can be master and of which
no outsider or alien foe can either know or upon which he can
set foot. . . . While we may be separated, while life may cut
us short or otherwise act upon us, we have established, I believe,
a subtle union of our inner lives—and the real beauty of it, if
only we can always remember it, is that it has been and it can
never be taken from us as long as the sweet recollections of it
stay with us.

May and June were busy months, indeed. Volunteer Progressives were circulating nomination papers throughout the state,

and the speed with which they came back indicated real enthusiasm. Petitions are a good way for the candidate to get his name known and create interest for many signers: they have a proprietary feeling for *their* candidate.

Next, we had to prepare the announcement of my candidacy, draft a platform, and organize the reference material to take with me on the campaign. I started with the formal announcement. I sent the first draft to Mother and Bob. After one reading, Mother was on the telephone. She and Bob did not like it at all, and she said she was sending out Mary's husband, Ralph Sucher, to lend a hand. But before she finished, she wanted to talk with Isen. Isen had written for *LaFollette's Magazine*, later known as *The Progressive*, and Mother had been impressed with her writing, so she wanted to know what Isen thought of the draft. Isen replied that she did not know anything about politics. Mother said to her, "You are an intelligent woman. If what Phil writes doesn't appeal to you, rest assured it will not appeal to others." Since then Isen has been my best critic.

Ralph, Isen, and I went to work on the dining room table at Maple Bluff Farm. The meat was already in the draft, but Ralph was of great help in smoothing and polishing the rough edges. When finished, the statement read, in part:

The fortune of birth does not justly entitle any candidate to the support of a single voter. It does impose upon me a special obligation to uphold the noblest traditions of a great public office and to render to all the people of Wisconsin the best that is in me in faithful service to the State. . . .

Under the present administration the State government is a virtual partner of powerful and selfish interests. If I am nominated and elected Governor, that partnership will be dissolved.

Wisconsin's heritage was not won without sacrifice. Thousands of men and women fought from the beginning to build the Progressive Movement in this state. . . . Against tremendous odds, they won the greatest victory for representative government in half a century.

It is an inspiration and a grave responsibility to fight in such a cause and for such a tradition. I am deeply conscious of both

Above, left: Belle Case LaFollette, about 1905 (*State Historical Society of Wisconsin*)

Above, right: Robert M. LaFollette, Sr., about 1906 (*State Historical Society of Wisconsin*)

Opposite: Phil LaFollette, about 1907 (*State .Historical Society of Wisconsin*)

Left: Belle Case LaFollette with Bob, Jr. (standing), and Phil, about 1905 (*State Historical Society of Wisconsin*)

Below: Phil and his younger sister, Mary, with their Shetland ponies at Maple Bluff Farm, about 1910 (*State Historical Society of Wisconsin*)

Top: The former executive residence, Phil's home for eleven years during his father's terms as governor and during his own.

Bottom: Maple Bluff Farm, the family homestead, purchased by Robert LaFollette, Sr., in 1905 (*Donald Young*)

Top: Election night, 1924: Robert LaFollette, Sr., an independent candidate for President of the United States, listens to the returns over the radio. With him, left to right, are Mrs. Phil LaFollette; Mrs. John Blaine; Phil; Governor Blaine of Wisconsin; and Bob, Jr. (*State Historical Society of Wisconsin*)

Bottom: Wisconsin's foremost family, in the early 1930's: seated on the steps of Maple Bluff Farm (left to right) are U.S. Senator Robert LaFollette, Jr.; his wife, Rachel; George Middleton, the playwright and husband of Fola; Mrs. Robert Siebecker, sister of Bob, Sr.; Fola LaFollette; Mary Sucher; Governor Phil LaFollette; and Ralph Sucher. Seated on the grass are Robert LaFollette III, Phil and Isen's son; Robert Sucher; Mrs. Phil LaFollette; and Judy LaFollette, Phil and Isen's daughter. (*State Historical Society of Wisconsin*)

Above: Phil LaFollette and his father during latter's presidential campaign in 1924 (*St. Louis Post-Dispatch*)

Opposite: Phil LaFollette, age 33, campaigns for governor of Wisconsin in 1930 (*State Historical Society of Wisconsin*)

Opposite: The LaFollette brothers at the zenith of their careers. After winning election as governor and senator, respectively, as third-party candidates in 1934, Phil (left) and Bob call on President Roosevelt at the White House. (*Brown Brothers*)

Below: Antagonists ignore each other: Glenn Frank (left) and Phil LaFollette attend the latter's inauguration as governor in 1937. Three days later Phil won his fight to oust Frank as President of the University of Wisconsin. (*UPI*)

Phil LaFollette and his wife, Isen, with the controversial symbol of the National Progressives of America. Phil's attempt to launch a new national political movement failed after the Republicans and Democrats combined to defeat him for reelection as governor in 1938. (*The Capital Times*)

Colonel Phil LaFollette and his son, Private Bob LaFollette III, visit each other briefly in Manila in June 1945, during World War II. Although the LaFollette family opposed the United States' entry into both world wars, Phil volunteered to serve in both wars and felt strongly that his son should have the experience of serving in the latter. (*State Historical Society of Wisconsin*)

With great-grandfather in Statuary Hall: Oliver Zabriskie, son of George and Sherry LaFollette Zabriskie and grandson of Phil and Isen, sits at the feet of Jo Davidson's sculpture of Robert LaFollette, Sr. The statue is in the United States Capitol in Washington, D.C. (*Sherry LaFollette Zabriskie*)

as I call upon the men and women of Wisconsin for their counsel and support.

A few weeks before I announced, a young man named Ed Littel called at the farm. He was an accomplished secretary and a good driver and volunteered his services. Mother gave me five hundred dollars with which I bought a new Ford four-door sedan. I had enough money in the bank to carry our living expenses and pay my traveling expenses. By September 12 there had been contributed to my campaign a total of $3,205. This was not all that would be spent on my behalf, but it gives an idea of our meager financial resources.

As the campaign was starting Mother wrote me:

You were surely right in thinking your announcement should convey the impression of reserve and steadiness. And I think that is the spirit to preserve above all else throughout your campaign. You know Daddy grew calm and self-controlled in proportion to the strain and excitement he had to meet, and I know you also have that power. . . .

I am convinced that you will gain strength in the long run if you plan your campaign so that it doesn't look like you are making a "whirlwind" tour of the state. . . . Conduct your campaign so as to leave on all your audiences the impression of poise and repose that is inherent in your nature.

We always looked on a political platform as a contract between an elected official and the people he represented. Before each campaign in which he was directly involved, Dad drew up and issued his personal platform, which, if we won, became the official platform of the Progressive Republicans. So did Bob and I. After each election from 1922 to 1928 I made a careful list of pledges and then the specific pieces of legislation that were introduced in the Legislature to fulfill them.

Before starting my 1930 campaign I sent the draft of the platform to Washington for Mother, Bob, and Ralph to work on. I had discussed the platform with Progressive members of the Legislature and, as usual, with Progressive leaders and also, as usual, with our friends on the university faculty on items where they were specialists. I was now ready to begin the speaking tour of Wisconsin. We had three headline speakers—Bob, Senator Blaine, and myself—and as the campaign developed we had a fourth—Isen.

A sound political campaign must be planned with the same meticulous care for tactics and strategy as a military campaign. If one draws a line from Green Bay to LaCrosse, the bulk of Wisconsin's population lives south of it. We made up our speaking schedules so that we covered the northern and western parts of the state in the beginning of the campaign and concentrated on the central, eastern, and southern counties in the latter weeks. Bob and Blaine made a foray into northern and western cities in the last week to hold up enthusiasm there, but we all worked hard the last ten days in Kenosha, Racine, and, above all, Milwaukee.

On Tuesday morning, July 15, I opened the campaign at Sauk City, northwest of Madison. Ed Littel was the driver, and two reporters came with us. I was a bit nervous for that first speech delivered to four hundred persons. By that evening I had hit my stride. In the next sixty days I would cover all but one county and deliver 261 speeches. At the end of that campaign my right hand had swollen to nearly half again its normal size from vigorous handshaking. To this day it is larger than my left, and I have to unbutton the right cuff of a shirt to get it on.

Long before I announced my candidacy, I was convinced I could win the primary over Kohler, but even I was astounded at the crowds that turned out for the meetings. The daily schedule usually called for two speeches in the morning, two in the afternoon, a conference with Progressive county and precinct leaders around seven, and the night meeting at eight. The day meetings were either in the township hall—free—or outdoors, except in the larger cities. The night meetings were outdoors in the park—free—or on the courthouse lawn—free. At the day meetings the crowds ran from 150 to 300, and at night from 2,000 to 5,000.

Loudspeakers were not common—and they cost money. So far as I now remember, I did not use one throughout the campaign. But both Bob and I had good carrying voices—and Isen had received training in the use of her voice. In this, as in later campaigns, Bob and I worked as a team, backtracking each other's itinerary, except for the last week, which was always devoted to the industrial centers.

Governor Kohler did not begin his campaign until August 11. By that time I had covered half Wisconsin's counties and had delivered 118 speeches. Throughout the campaign I never mentioned Kohler by name. I never lost my temper, but in the closing weeks Kohler lost his: he referred to me as an "upstart"—"a whippersnapper."

The last big meeting of the primary campaign was in Milwaukee. The auditorium there seats six thousand. Word came to us at dinner that the hall was packed and that thousands were outside. That settled it. We were going to win. It was only a question of what the majority would be. A correspondent for the *Wisconsin News* wrote that the crowd was "reminiscent of the overflow audiences that greeted the late 'Fighting Bob' LaFollette, the candidate's father, when he was at the height of his power in Wisconsin."

Following family custom, we closed the campaign in Madison at the university gymnasium. On Monday night the old gym was packed. Professor John R. Commons presided. Everyone knew that the voters had made up their minds and that we were going to win the next day.

On primary day, Mother wrote me from Washington:

Since the Milwaukee meeting, Mary and I have risked our reputation as prophets—at least I have—by predicting you were going to be the next Governor of Wisconsin. . . .

From this distance it looks as though the campaign had been the kind that satisfies our ideals of what a campaign should be. . . . After the count is made today, we will know where we are at and how much work there is ahead.

If you are elected, your personal responsibility will be very great. I know your endowment and how you have been seasoned, but I dread the long fight you will need to make before you get results. I am working on that period of Daddy's biography. What a struggle! You stand on his shoulders, but the task looks almost as tremendous as it did then. My constant thought is how he would glory in the way you and Bob are carrying on his work, each in your own way.

That evening Bob, Isen, Alf Rogers, Glenn and Melva Roberts, and other close friends gathered at Maple Bluff Farm. Bob and I, as usual, were armed with the *Wisconsin Blue Book,* and with tablets to take down the results. The first scattered returns, from rural townships and villages, looked like a landslide. But we could not be positive until we heard from Milwaukee. By nine thirty it was clear that we had won. The final primary vote was LaFollette 395,551, Kohler 267,687. The total Democratic primary vote in the entire state was only 17,004.

It gave Bob, Isen, and me deep pleasure to talk on the telephone with Mother, Mary, and Ralph. Then came the expected avalanche of congratulatory messages by telephone, telegraph, and letter. But any elation I might have felt was well tempered by what I knew was ahead.

A day or two after the primary, Bob and his secretary, Rachel Young, were married. Bob, Rachel, Isen, and I went to northern Wisconsin for a week, before beginning the campaign for the general election in November.

The stock market had crashed a year before my nomination. For months, in every waking hour, my mind had wrestled with one deep, haunting thought: What was the cause—what was the answer to the problem of hunger, want, suffering, for millions of human beings amid enormous plenty? Why, with unsalable farm surpluses, were people hungry? Why, with stupendous undone work, were people workless? Why?

13

THE
GOVERNORSHIP

...WE HAD TO
BE PREPARED TO ACT.

The 1930's were a revolution. They were not a "dip in the business cycle"—not a "recession" or a "depression." They ended
one epoch and began another. One important change that the
thirties effected was a reversal in the major function of the executive and legislative branches. For more than a century, the national Congress had largely taken a positive role, the Executive
largely a negative one, except in war and, of course, foreign
policy. The laws came from Congress; the veto, if any, from
the Executive. But the thirties would see profound changes as
many families that had regarded themselves as self-sufficient
found themselves dependent for survival on others. Political
institutions, both state and national, would need to change.

Under Wisconsin law, each political party holds a convention
in the Capitol to adopt its official platform. The nominees for
the five state offices and for the Legislature, plus the members
of the state Senate not up for reelection, are the delegates to
these conventions. We had no difficulty, therefore, adopting as
the Republican platform the one that I had issued in July.

Immediately after the convention, I started a campaign tour of the state. Although our victory in the primary made it certain we would win in November, this was an auspicious time to reach people's minds. As Mother put it in a letter to me: "When it is a foregone conclusion you are to be elected, the people are in a receptive mood—more open-minded. They are eager to meet you personally, and all except the rankest opponents will listen with less prejudice to your program." So I campaigned until November. I defeated my Democratic opponent, Charles Hammersley, 393,000 to 170,000.

After the election, I needed a rest, and I spent two weeks with Fola and George Middleton in California. Fola had a horse, and I rode, ate, and slept twelve to fourteen hours a day. I returned to Madison completely refreshed and rested.

The Depression was deepening. Bankruptcies and mortgage foreclosures were increasing rapidly. As the relief rolls rose, the public treasuries in industrial cities and counties were being drained, and their borrowing authority approached their limits. The state of Wisconsin was prohibited from borrowing the sum required to meet the crisis.

Under President Hoover, the federal government stubbornly refused all aid except to certain corporations through the Reconstruction Finance Corporation. "Prosperity is just around the corner," we were told, and state and local governments and private charity were obliged to carry this heavy burden of relief. But somehow, we had to be prepared to act. And our allotted time in which to act would be precariously short.

The governor's term in Wisconsin is two years—too short a time. Take from that short tenure the inevitable, time-consuming duties that go with the job—official functions; greeting flocks of visiting youngsters; interviews with the press, old friends, important leaders; inescapable hours to read, digest, and act on official documents; laws to be signed or vetoed. Finally, chop off six months from the rapidly diminishing margin of time; because only 1½ years later you face another two months of campaigning. Then, if you lose that primary campaign, you are a political eunuch for the remaining four months in office.

Thus, a Wisconsin governor can bank absolutely on only

eighteen months as an effective leader. And the composition of the Legislature for the 1931 session looked dark. We had firm control of the Assembly; but the Senate, with its four-year term, was controlled by Democrats and Conservative Republicans.

Under the Executive Budget Act passed in Governor Kohler's administration, hearings on the budget are held by the governor-elect before he takes office. In addition, we adopted another innovation before my inauguration: almost all important proposed legislation which, if adopted, would fulfill our platform pledges was drafted before the Legislature convened. An important feature of the "Wisconsin Idea" as it came to be called, was the Legislative Reference Library begun under the creative mind of Charles McCarthy, a brilliant political scientist at the university. It was ably and with equal brilliance carried on into my day by Edwin Witte, later chairman of the university's Department of Economics. This library, the first in the United States, made available to legislators reference materials to answer their questions and skilled drafters to transform their proposals into carefully written bills. I doubt if any governor had used the library to the extent that I did.

John Donaghey, chief engineer of the Wisconsin Highway Commission, came to me in November, 1930, with a plan to accelerate the state's program for eliminating railroad grade crossings, by constructing "overheads" above the crossings on important highways and railroads.

Shortly before Christmas, though I was not yet in office, I invited the presidents of the seven railroads operating in Wisconsin to come to Madison for a conference and to dinner at Maple Bluff Farm. All accepted. John Donaghey proposed to telescope a three-year program to change these crossings into a matter of months, which, it was estimated, would provide employment during that period to approximately ten thousand workers. The railroads would meet about one fourth of the cost. The state's share would be financed by a two-cent increase in the

gasoline tax. His proposed bill provided that after the state's
share of building the overheads had been fulfilled, the two-cent
tax increase would be returned to cities, villages, townships, and
counties, to be used exclusively for property tax reductions.

The dinner meeting was a success. Each railroad president
said that he would call a meeting of his directors and would
highly recommend approval. Word came back promptly that
the boards of directors of all the railroads had approved the plan
to eliminate the grade crossings designated in our program. The
grade-crossing bill would be the first major bill to be enacted
by the 1931 Legislature.

The dinner was a pleasant affair for everyone except Isen.
While we were enjoying her cooking, she had stood on a chair
upstairs to replace a light bulb, had lost her balance, and had
fallen and broken a rib. Good soldier that she has always been
she did not want to interrupt this important meeting, so she
would let no one tell me about it until our guests had departed.

The first tasks of a chief executive in America are his inaugural
address and his first message to the Legislature or Congress. On
both that inaugural address and first message (as well as later
speeches) I had help from two intimate friends and scholars
from the university, Max Otto in the Philosophy Department
and John Gaus, a political scientist, as well as from Isen and
others.

The inauguration was on January 4, 1931, at noon in the
rotunda of the Capitol. About 10:30 A.M. I went to my law office
to wait for the appropriate time to leave for the Capitol. Only
Alf Rogers, our old family friend, was with me. We sat together
looking out the window toward the Capitol. There had been a
heavy snowfall, and we could see the thousands of people
trudging through it as they entered the building. We left the
office about eleven fifteen, as it is only about a five-minute walk,
went up the "back stairs" to the executive office on the second
floor, and entered the almost empty offices. We looked around
for Governor Kohler because, by tradition, the outgoing chief

executive escorts his successor to the ceremonies. We found Kohler in the anteroom talking with his lawyer. I walked up to the Governor and introduced myself. This was the first time I had met him. He shook hands with me, but there was no smile on his face: he was coldly formal. So Alf and I withdrew abit and visited privately, as did Governor Kohler and his lawyer.

About eleven forty the procession began to form in the large reception room in the executive office. Bob, Rachel, and Senator Blaine had come from Washington for the occasion. When the procession had formed, we were notified, and we moved into the reception room. All the state officers were there as well as the chief justice of the state Supreme Court. My family was especially happy that Dr. Philip Fox, for whom I was named (and who was ninety years old), was present.

The procession moved into the rotunda, and we took seats on a platform constructed for the occasion. After the invocation, Governor Kohler escorted me to a place in front of Chief Justice Rosenberry and the microphones. After the oath was administered, I read a very short address. I said in part:

As a state and a nation we have astounded the world in production. Our energy and brains have shown the world how to produce the necessities and luxuries of life in sufficient quantities to satisfy the needs of all of our people; but in the midst of abundance of agricultural and industrial production we have want and suffering. Unless we can solve the problem of the distribution of this abundance—unless we can stop hunger and hardship in all of this plenty, we will be the actors in the greatest tragedy of history.

This problem can be solved if the same energy and intelligence that perfected our mechanism of production is mobilized for a cooperative and determined effort to meet the complex problem of distribution.

There has seldom been a time for greater intelligence, finer courage, and steadier hands.

After the inauguration we had lunch and then returned to the governor's reception room for a public reception. Bob, Rachel, and Senator Blaine were in the receiving line with me. For some time Isen did not appear. I sent word to her several times to hurry over from the Executive Residence. Finally she arrived and whispered, "I'll tell you later." We greeted the visitors as they came down the line for three hours, and then left for the residence. The snow was deep, and when the car came to the steep hill two blocks from our destination it got stuck and we all had to get out and wade knee-deep.

Isen told me why she was delayed. For years it had been the custom for the wife of the governor to invite the incoming hostess to visit the home and be initiated to its facilities. Not hearing from Mrs. Kohler, Isen went ahead and made her plans as best she could. Finally, just a week before inauguration, she received an invitation from Mrs. Kohler. Because Isen already had her plans made, she declined the invitation.

Isen had learned from good sources that the maid and cook employed by the state had been there for some twenty years and thought they owned the place. When Isen arrived at the Executive Residence on Inauguration Day, she rang the bell and waited. The maid finally opened the door and admitted her, her mother, Eleanor Weber (who for many years helped handle our household affairs), and our two children. The maid promptly announced that both she and the cook were leaving. Because we had scheduled an open house for that evening, this news gave Isen something of a jolt. Then it occurred to Isen that perhaps she was being tried out, that the help would like to be begged to stay and thereby gain the upper hand in their reputed way. So Isen came right back with: "Is that your firm decision?" When the maid said it was, Isen said: "In that case I want you to leave by four o'clock this afternoon." They did.

Isen had made a quick inspection and found disorder. Two of the seven bedrooms had no beds. The Kohlers had brought with them some furniture and pictures, which they naturally took back to their home, but there were no replacements, so the place looked something on the shabby side. Isen had ordered coffee and cookies for refreshments, and we had many friends who lent a hand. We had scarcely finished our dinner when the guests began to arrive. Everybody entered into the spirit of the occasion, and they all seemed to enjoy themselves. After another three hours of handshaking, the last guest had left, and we turned into bed exhausted but happy.

The next morning I went to the executive office for my first working day as governor. The functions, duties, and responsibilities of the governor of Wisconsin in 1931 were:

First: In association with the Legislature, the enactment, amending, or repealing of laws. I put this first because of the governor's platform pledges, 90 per cent depend on legislation to be fulfilled. As I noted in my first message, some chief executives felt inhibited from working closely with the Legislature because of the doctrine of separation of powers. I felt, and still feel, that when the Constitution gave the governor the duty to recommend and the power to veto, it became his duty to use every legitimate means he had to carry out his pledges to the voters.

Second: Chief executive officer of the state government, with the same day-to-day tasks that face the head of any large corporation.

Third: Leader of his political party in the state. Unless the governor is an effective leader, he and his associates and followers will not stay in power.

Fourth: Appointments to public offices. The most important of that time were to the Public Service Commission, Highway Commission, Conservation Commission, and Board of Control (penal and welfare institutions). The governor's patronage for political recognition was so slim that it was more than useless: it only made many disappointed friends disgruntled. Except for policy-making officers and a few other exceptions, all persons in state government were protected by civil service.

Fifth: State finances. In a state that is prohibited from borrowing, the governor is primarily responsible for seeing that there is cash on hand to meet the state's bills.

Sixth: Ceremonial and social activities. We cut the latter to a bare minimum and got out of as many of the former as one could with propriety.

Seventh: Receiving visitors, including journalists, commentators, students, delegations—small or large—desiring to press or oppose this or that, and state political leaders.

Eighth: Conferences with legislators on the progress of our program, and with leaders in agriculture, industry, banking, labor, education, etc.

Ninth: Consideration of applications for executive clemency. I discharged this important duty to the best of my ability. However, in my second term I created a three-member Board of Pardon Appeals, and I reviewed their findings. It worked well.

The Senate had thirty-three members elected for four-year terms. The Assembly had one hundred elected members with two-year terms. When the Legislature met in January, 1931, the Senate lineup showed that we were outnumbered slightly by the Conservative Republicans, though, on the vote for the president pro tem and for the committees of the Senate, we had the support of the Socialist and Democratic members. So we were able to organize the Senate, but our program would have rough sledding. Fortunately, we had a clear working control of the Assembly.

Thomas Jefferson, when elected President, abandoned the practice of Washington and Adams of appearing before Congress in person. Jefferson claimed it suggested too much a speech from the throne. Hence, the tradition grew for Chief Executives to send their messages to the legislative bodies to be read by the clerk. When father took office as governor in 1901, he addressed the Legislature in person rather than let his messages be "mumbled over by some clerk to a Senate or House busy talking amongst themselves."

On January 15, I also appeared before both houses of the Legislature in a joint session. Before a capacity audience I delivered my first message in person. I said, in part:

Thirty-seven years ago Professor Frederick Jackson Turner of the University of Wisconsin made a new interpretation to American History. He recorded the fact that both the character and the conduct of our democracy and of our institutions have been determined by the frontiers. He noted that the census of

1890 revealed the practical disappearance of the frontier. . . .

All this has a very direct and practical bearing upon the problems we are about to face in this legislative session. . . . In the days of our pioneer fathers, the free lands of the frontier gave this guarantee of freedom and opportunity. If the door of opportunity were closed to men in the East, it was open to them in the West. The frontier was thus a kind of social safety valve. . . .

The effort of this new political movement [the Progressive Movement] in Wisconsin was to find a new equivalent for the old opportunities offered by the frontier. As we look back upon this movement, we see it as an attempt to recreate the equality of opportunity that has been lost sight of in the society that was arising.

The premises on which, in the past, our program has been based are now fiercely assailed from two extremes. Often these extremes are identical despite their common antagonism. From one comes the assurance that the role of the individual is ended; that a bankrupt social system must inevitably pass into the receivership of a class dictatorship to be discharged in an unspecified Utopia. From the other extreme is an equally absolute assurance of the failure of democracy. The superior man, it is agreed, must be given absolute power; representative institutions are corrupt and time-wasting. There are some in our own country who find this superman in a section, narrowly defined, of the very rich. Let the Congress and the Legislatures adjourn, they argue, and this little group, which two years ago was assuring us of permanent prosperity, will solve our problems. . . .

Today the average citizen feels lost and friendless in a complicated world. New controlling forces have developed so rapidly that our institutions of government are often out of date and ineffective. In proposing that we call into our counsels the leaders, not only of the executive and legislative branches, but of our great basic interests and groups, we seek only to restore the neighborhood cooperation of the simpler days of the frontiers. . . . It is by no means clear that the American experiment of self-government will succeed. We must be prepared for genuine, profound readjustments, not merely of institutions but of mental habits, if it does.

During the budget hearings before I took office, I had seen the government of Wisconsin from a new angle. I had lived in a political atmosphere all my life and knew nearly all the heads of the various departments and agencies of state government by their first names. But as they appeared before me at the budget hearings, I realized that I was no longer an observer but a participant; that I not only could, but should, do something about the way they performed their functions. Ideas and plans have to be carried out by human beings, and the quality of these human beings will determine, in large measure, the character and quality of the results.

It has been my good luck to find and induce singularly able people to work with me.

Progressives had a comfortable majority in the lower house, but success in the Senate could be achieved only with the highest legislative leadership. The two Socialist senators from Milwaukee could be counted on to support our program. I decided to support one of them, Thomas M. Duncan, for chairman of the Joint Committee on Finance, which in effect would make him the administrative spokesman, or majority leader. I did this not because he was a Socialist but in spite of it. Tom Duncan was the son of well-to-do parents, a graduate of Yale, and a Phi Beta Kappa who had won his "Y" in track. He had tried banking but did not like it, and then became the secretary of Mayor Daniel Hoan of Milwaukee. Tom Duncan's agile brain had devised ways to free Milwaukee of its debt. At the age of thirty-seven he was the ablest parliamentarian and, by all odds, the greatest master of public finance that I had known.

We were also fortunate in having in the Senate Glenn Roberts, who had been my law partner and who was an intimate friend. His outstanding abilities made him a tower of strength in that body. These two were backed up by the experienced and loyal Herman Severson and Walter Hunt. The ability of these men enabled us to pass such of our program as was enacted in the 1931 Legislature.

In the Assembly we had three able men—Robert Nixon, floor leader; Myrwyn Rowlands; and Professor Harold Groves—aided by the experienced and benevolent Charlie Perry as Speaker.

I always worked closely with our Progressive legislators. It never made sense to me for a governor, after waging a hard campaign in which thousands of his supporters worked their heads off to get him elected, to sit back and wait for the Legislature to enact his pledges. On the contrary, as I have said, it was his job to do everything within his legitimate powers to get those pledges enacted into law. I did so—up to the hilt.

Before discussing the legislative sessions of 1931–32, I will go forward some seven months and set down a deep personal loss that came to us.

In mid-August of 1931 we received a shattering blow. One of Rachel's sisters called from Washington with word that Mother was in the hospital in serious condition, and that Bob and I should come at once. Bob caught the morning train. I was delayed by the rebandaging of an infected foot, but I caught up with Bob by taking a chartered light plane.

When we arrived in Washington on the eighteenth we learned that Mother had gone to a hospital solely for a medical checkup. During the examination, her intestines were punctured and peritonitis set in. There were no antibiotics in those days. When Bob and I reached her bedside, she was completely conscious, but within a few hours she slipped into a coma and was gone late that afternoon.

Her four children had lost their beloved mother, and Bob and I had also lost a great and wise counselor. As we began to arrange for Mother's funeral, my thoughts turned to my parents' religious beliefs. Mother's family were Unitarians—so far as they had any religious affiliations. Dad had been raised as a Hard-Shell Baptist, but the fire-and-brimstone preached by his stepfather had turned him away from formal attachment to any church. Dad liked to tell about an incident when he was in Congress in the eighties. He was visited by a group of ministers from his congressional district. It had happened that a few weeks before, he had attended the funeral of a fellow congressman at the Congregational Church in Washington. So, when one of the visitors popped the question, "What church do you attend, Congressman?" he replied, "Most frequently the Congregational here in Washington."

Mother and Dad had deep respect for the religious beliefs of others. All their children attended Sunday school, and our own three children did likewise. The particular Sunday school selected for our children was decided on our regard for the pastor, not on dogma. As a youngster in Washington, I attended for a time an Episcopal church and occasionally went to Catholic Mass with one of Dad's secretaries. Isen had been raised as an Episcopalian. We liked and respected the rector of Grace Episcopal Church in Madison, the Reverend H. H. Lumpkin. He had married Bob and Rachel, and we naturally asked him for the religious service for Mother.

In spite of the sorrowful memories of World War I, Mother never lost her devotion to the University of Wisconsin. Here came the first bloom of her intellectual awakening, and here she met and fell in love with Dad. Here she lived those years of adventure and happiness before the storms of politics began. We were pleased when it was suggested that services for her be held in the State Historical Society Library, where the services for President Van Hise and Dr. Stephen Babcock, the distinguished chemist, had also been held.

Our beloved friend, Professor Max Otto, delivered an appreciation of her life. It was a work of art, and like all real art, it was honest. It made no attempt to lift the mystery of life or death. Mother and Thomas Huxley would have approved it. Dr. Lumpkin read the graveside services.

Individuals, organizations, and the press all over the country paid Mother glowing tributes. An editor for the New York *Times* wrote:

Many women have figured in American politics. Some were the outstanding champions of woman suffrage. . . . A few have sought and gained public office. But Belle Case LaFollette . . . was perhaps the least known yet the most influential of all the American women who have had to do with public affairs in this country. . . . She had sound political sense, amazing tactical skill and a steady ideal of public service.

Some years after Belle Case LaFollette died, Mrs. Philip La-Follette recorded her recollections of her mother-in-law. The following paragraphs are drawn from Isen's memoirs.

From the time I first knew her Belle Case LaFollette was always very busy writing and speaking and otherwise occupied with such causes as woman's suffrage and peace. The whole atmosphere of the LaFollette home tingled with militant idealism. My relations with Mrs. LaFollette could have been difficult, as Phil adored his mother and thought that she could do no wrong. However, she was an ideal mother-in-law and never interfered with our affairs except to encourage us to enlarge upon our potentialities.

From what others have told me and from her early photographs, she was a beautiful young woman, with rosy cheeks and an infectious laugh. By the time I knew her, however, I thought of her as stoic and spartan, and sensed very early that, for all her devotion to her family and her circle of admirers, she was a lonely woman. When I mentioned this to an intimate friend of long standing in the LaFollette family, he thought for a few minutes, and then said in a puzzled tone of voice, "Why, of course she was. I wonder why it never occurred to me." By the time I knew the elder LaFollettes, neither one of them cared to go out socially although they dearly loved to have friends at their home. Although she loved gaiety, wit, and comedy, in which Bob, Sr., and Bob, Jr., were often sparkling, she was not amused by banter and "needling," which we used in my own family with vast pleasure.

His mother discouraged Phil's interest in politics and always insisted that she hoped for a writer's life for him —what she would have chosen for herself, Phil felt. By the time I knew her, her time was absorbed completely by her family and her work, and while I was beginning to understand the burdens of public life, I found myself wondering if there wasn't some way one could save time and energy for something beside work. Doubtless because of the onerous demands of public life which prevented her from following many of her natural interests, Mrs. LaFollette kept urging all of us to cultivate our talents and above all to get joy out of life.

I observed with deep interest the psychological change in Mrs. LaFollette that began at the time of her husband's death and that continued until her own death. The long years of fighting at her leader's side quite naturally caused her to transfer that allegiance to Bob, Jr., and to form a sort of partnership with him, because not only had Bob inherited his father's public office but he was then unmarried and still made his home with his mother.

On May 8, 1920, his twenty-third birthday, Phil had paid this tribute to his mother in a note to himself:

Today I pass again that shrine which marks in yearly intervals the way of my life. Four and twenty years ago I was conceived in my mother's womb, and after a period was wrenched forth from her warmth through her blood and pain, and as I was borned there passed into me part of her— To be true to that gift is the divine purpose of life.

14

THE GREAT
DEPRESSION

. . . THIS PARADOX OF
POVERTY-AMID-PLENTY. . . .

Before the Legislature adjourned at the end of June, 1931, it passed into law bills that substantially fulfilled our platform in a number of areas. It had taken steps to facilitate state entry into the power business; enacted an oleomargarine tax and other measures to protect the dairy industry from competition of butter substitutes; strengthened the powers of the Public Service Commission; exempted from taxation forty-two million dollars in personal property; enacted a statewide old-age pension system; placed farm cooperatives under a law that forbade misrepresentation of their status; adopted the most comprehensive and progressive labor code in the United States, firmly protecting the rights of workingmen in disputes with employers; revised and updated the Workmen's Compensation Law; provided for an executive council with ten members elected by the Legislature (five from each house) and ten appointed by the governor; imposed a tax on chain retail stores to balance the higher assessment on local stores; created interim committees to study and recommend legislation to deal with chain banking and the immediate and long-term problem of unemployment; and it provided additional funds for conservation—especially for fire protection in the forest preserves and to encourage forest cropping.

Still, when the Legislature adjourned, the Senate had not adopted a tax-raising method to meet the state budget or to aid communities with heavy burdens of unemployment relief.

As my next task, I began to prepare for the long and important special session that would come in November, 1931. The interim committees dealing with chain banking and unemployment were aided by the best expert and technical assistance we could find—such people as Professor John R. Commons; Arthur Altmeyer (later chairman of the federal Social Security Board); Paul and Elizabeth (Brandeis) Raushenbush; Professor Edwin Witte; Dean Lloyd Garrison of the Wisconsin Law School; my former law partners Glenn Roberts, Wade Boardman, Samuel Becker, and Frank Kuehl; and Tom Duncan (whom, on adjournment of the Legislature, I appointed executive secretary to the governor). I had two able private secretaries in Edward Littel and Jack Kyle. Many others helped the committees complete their work by early November.

After planning our legislative program for the special session my job was to prepare a message for the legislature analyzing the causes of, and offering a program to remedy, this paradox of poverty-amid-plenty, which was called the Great Depression.

Long before the election of 1930, and in the months after, I had talked with all the "experts" I could find about the causes and remedies of this evil. Now, in November, 1931, I came back to the advice of Melvin Traylor, that Conservative Republican banker: "Think this out for yourself. I probably will disagree with your conclusions—but you at least will have a fifty-fifty chance of being right."

So I went to Maple Bluff Farm to "bach it," as I had so often done before I was married, for complete seclusion, where I could think and write without interruptions of any kind. How many days I was at it I cannot remember. But I finished the message to the special session of the Legislature in ample time to have Isen, Tom Duncan, and other advisers shoot at it critically, and still had time to get advance copies to Bob and Ralph Sucher.

In his memoirs, Governor LaFollette does not deal at length with his message to the special session. Because of the importance of the message and of the political philosophy that underlay it, I have included some amplifying material by Mrs. LaFollette and by Walter Raushenbush. Excerpts from "Wisconsin Under Governor Philip LaFollette: A Study in Creative State Government," a senior honors thesis prepared under the supervision of the Department of Government, Harvard College, 1950, are quoted here with Professor Raushenbush's permission. His statements are enclosed in parentheses. The rest of what follows is taken from Mrs. LaFollette's memoirs:

Phil's interpretation of the governor's task was to aim at the welfare of all the elements of the constituency, of the worlds of industry and finance as well as agriculture and labor. He never deviated from this fundamental approach. Like so many things in life, however, it is all very well to approve a course but another to act on it.

His first term as governor came right after the 1929 financial crash and in the last two years of the Hoover administration, when the whole country was deeply depressed. In the LaFollette tradition, Phil went to work to get the best advice he could from people in all fields, regardless of political opinion. Then he stepped forward with a program. This was embodied in the special message to the Legislature. Of that message the eminent historian Charles Beard wrote at the time to a friend, "In all the history of American public documents there has not appeared a more important or more reasoned state paper."

In general, Phil suggested four courses "that we may pursue."

1. The direct control and ownership by the people through their municipal, state, and national governments of enough of those instruments of common necessity—the public utilities—to protect the public against extortionate charges, to ensure efficient service, and, to the extent of the ownership, thus to effect a better distribution of the earning power of those utilities.

2. The provision of machinery by the state that would enable business to govern itself. (He calls [an aspect of this matter] "collective individualism," and considers it a very

important part of what this country should be doing even today to meet its problems. The essence of the idea is that the people, through their government, agree on some policy it would be wise for private business or individuals to follow. Then instead of simply having government do it, or having the legislature pass a compulsive act, the people try to frame the policy so that business sees the advantages in following it, and also so that society gets the benefit of private initiative in the execution of the policy.)

3. The provision of machinery for undertaking and carrying on the profound research we need as a society; for the taking of economic and social counsel, and the definite attempt to plan continuously for the present and for the future of our communities. (Here again, collective individualism is a guide. The collective process of government can gather and publicize information by which individual farmers or businessmen can intelligently guide their activities. On a broader scale, government can lead attempts at planning for urban or regional development; within those plans, use can be made of the initiative of private parties that after all have the greatest interest in the plan's success. . . . This sort of planning is not the "planned economy" proper, yet it surely is conscious and effective community planning.)

4. The equalization of the burden of taxation. In Phil's words, "The intelligent and courageous use of the taxing power is the most effective thing that can be done immediately in the present emergency. . . . The use of the taxing powers . . . is an effective instrument with which to redistribute money to enable workers and farmers to trade with one another."

Phil centered his attention on the economic insecurity that resulted from the defective capitalist system, but his aim was to remedy those defects rather than to substitute any form of collectivism. His program was based on the conviction that the government, as our instrument of action, must act to protect the victims of this insecurity. While attacking the problem here in Wisconsin, he was at the same time communicating with other governors—Franklin D. Roosevelt of New York had ordered that Phil's state papers be sent to him at Albany as they came out—and with leaders

in business and finance. If the Hoover administration refused to act in the Depression crisis, Phil felt that the attempt should be made to get the ablest brains in the country
to work on the problems on a volunteer basis.

*An old family friend, Felix Frankfurter, wrote Phil on De-
cember 10, 1931:*

Your Message to the Special Session of your Legislature
is the most heartening state paper that has come out of the
Depression. It is easy enough to formulate against inade-
quacies and also easy to formulate general plans for the
reconstruction of society, but to a rare degree your Message combines forthright analysis of defects in the men and
measures of the past and condemnation of the evils they
have wrought with a matured plan for these specific reforms. . . . I have only one regret, that your pioneer Father
and your dear Mother are not here to glory in your leadership.

Phil resumes the narrative:

With the message delivered in November, 1931, we settled
down for a struggle with the Senate. As in the regular session,
we had no difficulties with the Assembly.

The two main issues at the special session were our relief program and the unemployment compensation plan. We also had
a constructive plan to curb chain banking, but because the state
Constitution requires a two-thirds vote in each house to enact
banking legislation, it was obvious the plan had no chance.

Wisconsin's unemployment compensation plan was based in
principle on our experience with the Workmen's Compensation
Act of 1911. That law had two objectives—to provide compensation to workers or their families following industrial accidents
and to give employers a financial incentive to reduce industrial
accidents. The latter objective was achieved by specifying that
each employer receive the benefits for a good safety record in
the form of a reduction in his individual insurance rates.

So our unemployment compensation plan of 1931–1932 provided that each employer had his own separate account. If he made a good record—if few of his employees were "laid off"— his contributions under the plan were reduced. And the employer who made a bad record had to pay for it. There was to be no common "barrel" in which the funds were poured and withdrawn regardless of the employer's individual record.

These two laws illustrate the basic difference in philosophy between New Dealers and Wisconsin Progressives. Both groups recognized that many economic and social problems had arisen out of the disappearance of the old frontier and the rise of industrialization that were beyond the power of individuals or even groups of individuals to remedy. Both felt that only government could deal with such problems. But our philosophy had an inseparable companion that we felt should, whenever possible, be tied to and made a part of each statute that prescribed governmental remedy: each statute or program should be so framed that it stimulated individual initiative by rewarding the individuals who did a good job and by penalizing those who did not.

I have always called this "harnessing the profit motive for desirable social and economic ends."

The Unemployment Reserves and Compensation Act was passed in the special session, and I had the privilege of signing this measure—the first of its kind in the United States—into law. Henry Huber, when a member of the Wisconsin state Senate, had introduced a similar proposal in 1921. He had been inspired to do so by Professor John R. Commons. Both Huber, then lieutenant governor, and Commons were present when I signed the bill in January, 1932. Also present were my close friends, Paul and Elizabeth (Brandeis) Raushenbush, who had taken up the cause. Paul became the first director of the Unemployment Compensation Division and remained such for more than thirty years. Both Paul and Elizabeth did wonderful work to perfect it, and Paul's record is another shining example of the best in public administration.

To the credit of Wisconsin's employers, they raised only one serious objection: that the Depression year of 1932 was not a propitious time to inaugurate unemployment compensation. Under the plan—as amended—no payments were made until 1936.

The Roosevelt administration accepted an unemployment compensation plan that gave each state the option of putting all contributions into one big pot, with no incentive for the individual employer to iron out the ups and downs of his hiring and firing. One of Wisconsin's large employer associations polled its members on whether they preferred that option, or the alternative choice, which resembled the Wisconsin law of 1932. I felt a deep satisfaction when I read sample replies. The employers of Wisconsin had taken a good look at both plans, and they wanted nothing to do with "one big pot." A vice-president of one of Wisconsin's largest industries told me: "Our Unemployment Compensation Law is the most constructive legislation affecting industry passed in America in fifty years. Until that law went into effect, we were firing at one door and hiring at another. That law made us do better housekeeping, and we are a better company for it."

It may be of interest to note that from 1936 to 1961, more than seventeen million weekly benefit checks, totaling more than $450 million, were paid under the Wisconsin unemployment compensation plan.

My message to the special session included a recommendation for an appropriation to provide work and an educational program for young single men. The work was to be done in northern Wisconsin as a conservation project. It did not pass the Senate, and many Conservatives in and out of the Legislature ridiculed the idea. President Roosevelt later told me that he got the idea for the Civilian Conservation Corps (CCC) from that message. When the CCC was put into effect by the federal government, many agreed that it was the most successful of all the administration's programs.

The real battle of the special session was on the question of how much money was to be appropriated for relief and how the money was to be raised. I recommended a total appropriation of seventeen million dollars. The program I recommended would not provide enough jobs for all the unemployed in Wisconsin: that was beyond a single state's resources. It was large enough, however, to make a real dent in the relief rolls and provide substantial aid to the overburdened real estate taxpayer.

I appealed by radio to the constituents of the Conservative senators to make their views known to their representatives. Finally, on January 5, 1932, I sent another message to the Legislature. It was tough because the facts were tough. I said:

I shall veto any bill which proposes to make the situation worse by loading the costs [of relief] upon those who have already been hit the hardest—the farmer, home owner, and small businessman.

If the Conservative majority in the Senate will agree that wealth must and shall contribute, then this legislature can complete its work and finally adjourn within 48 hours. Further delay will be but a continuation of the open and undercover defense of one form of wealth that has been on in this legislature for six weeks.

I was referring to the exemption of dividends from the state income tax. Hundreds of individuals derived their income almost exclusively from dividends. To take one example, the head of a paper company had a net cash income of about $290,000. His state income tax was $17.35.

Finally, a compromise measure was agreed to which removed the dividend exemption but appropriated only eight million dollars for relief. It passed both houses. I signed it, and the Legislature adjourned after ten weeks of hard fighting.

In reviewing the two sessions of the 1931–32 Legislature, what stands out is that Wisconsin Progressives understood that the Great Depression was not just another dip in the business cycle. It meant revolutionary changes in America and all over the world. We understood that our basic economic problem was not overproduction. Apparent "surpluses" existed not because we produced too much but because purchasing power had not kept pace with actual and potential production capacity. We realized that we should concentrate on finding ways to enable people to buy, and that the best—but not the sole—method of accomplishing this was the tax power.

This philosophy postulated that with the disappearance of the horizontal frontier, a perpendicular frontier could be opened only by governmental action. Although this doctrine still gives certain Conservatives hysterics, we should remember that the old horizontal frontier could never have been opened without the active leadership of government. Until the American Revolution, frontiers the world over were opened by government sponsored and protected colonies and settlements.

After the American Revolution, and as the years passed, all the land to the west belonged to the federal government. It did not have to sponsor colonies. It only had to plat the land into 160-acre homesteads and protect the settlers from the Indians, and the homesteaders could generally take care of themselves without governmental supervision. This absence of governmental supervision and controls stimulated American "rugged individualism" and self-reliance. In recent decades, broadly speaking, Republicans have cherished the qualities of individual initiative and responsibility, whereas Democrats have seen the need for collective action. In Wisconsin we tried to synthesize the two points of view.

To be more specific, if people are to have money to buy what we can produce, that money can get to them in three ways. It can be given to them, it can be loaned to them, or they can work for it. Although adequate money must reach the consumer to enable him to buy what we can produce, it is also true that how he gets it will affect his character and the future soundness of the American economy.

During the budget hearings in December, 1930, the financial needs for the state's penal and charitable institutions were presented by John J. Hannan, president of the Board of Control. Hannan had been my father's private secretary from 1903 to 1920. John was, in many ways, able and intelligent, but he had no training for or grasp of the problems of those public institutions. Like many administrators, he believed that the solution to complex problems was to be found in the use of more brick and mortar. As John presented the figures on the overcrowding in our penal institutions, I pressed him for new ideas: was there no

answer to the admitted fact of overcrowding besides more buildings and more walls? The expression on his face was one of hurt.
It seemed to say, Why, after all of my hard work, is this son of
my old chief attacking me?

Before I became governor, I had stopped at the Wisconsin
State Prison at Waupun. After transacting whatever business I
had there, I talked with the warden, Oscar Lee. He was not a
trained penologist, but he had a lot of common sense. I asked
him if he had any new ideas about dealing with the ever increasing overcrowding of the prison and the reformatory. He replied:

"You have to start out with this basic fact: About 85 per cent
of the prison population is a cross section of our people. They
are no better or worse than the run-of-the-mill of folks you see
everywhere. They got caught and were given sentences, largely
in accord with the particular judge's attitude toward the defendant or the particular offense of which he was found guilty.
Some way should be provided for them to work on prison farms
—or perhaps in reforestation. As for the remaining 15 per cent,
they never should be set loose—they will always be troublemakers."

I mentioned the reforestation idea to John Hannan at the hear-
ings. "But," he said, "they might escape!" I replied, "So what?
It is only a question of time when they will be released anyway.
Why not try this idea out?"

They did. In July, 1931, the Board of Control announced the
opening of the first reforestation camp on ten thousand acres
near Rhinelander. In 1964, Sanger B. Powers, director of the
Division of Corrections in Wisconsin, wrote to me, saying: "So
far as I can recall, we have had only two absconders from the
camps who became involved in serious offenses after running
away. This is quite remarkable when one remembers that several
thousand men have gone through the camps since their establishment."

Public utilities and public power had always been an important
item in Progressive platforms and policies in Wisconsin and in
the nation. One of our greatest Progressive leaders, Senator

George W. Norris of Nebraska, was the father of the Tennessee Valley Authority. We in Wisconsin have always favored public ownership of enough—not all—power utilities to provide a real yardstick of competition and to break the private monopoly control of this vital key to industrial and agricultural development.

One six-year term on the Railroad Commission, reorganized later in 1931 as the Public Service Commission, would become vacant in February, 1931. I secured a second vacancy by suggesting that a member of the commission with two more years to serve resign to accept a position on the legal staff. The latter was a workhorse and a Progressive, but I wanted two first-class members.

For the six-year term there was no question: It must go to Theodore Kronshage of Milwaukee, one of the state's outstanding lawyers. To fill the second vacancy on the commission, I decided to pick the most outstanding man I could find anywhere in the United States.

The great handicap was the salary of five thousand dollars a year. Donald R. Richberg and James M. Landis, both of whom would later render important service to the federal government, declined because of the meager compensation.

The third prospect was young (thirty-one), vigorous, highly gifted, skilled in the legal profession, and endowed with the sole foundation of greatness—*character*. His name: David Lilienthal. He was doing extremely well in his profession, earning more than twenty thousand dollars annually. He came to Madison from Chicago, and we had dinner at the Executive Residence. As we talked after dinner of the opportunities and the challenge of the job, his eyes sparkled and a warm smile lit up a face with character written all over it. He left about ten o'clock and said, "I'll see you here at breakfast if I may."

The next morning Dave came to the Executive Residence bright and early. After we ate, and over a second cup of coffee, he said:

"Phil, after I left you last night I walked the streets of Madison all night. I was intrigued with the challenge the job offered but was not certain what my wife's reaction might be to the salary. Finally I called her early this morning. Do you know what she said—I really had expected it—but it gave me great joy when she said, 'Why, Dave, you and I have lived on a lot less than five thousand a year, and if this appeals to you, take it.'

"So," said Dave, "I am happy to accept."

He was nominated and unanimously confirmed by the state Senate. He made a fine record on the commission. He was subsequently named a director of the Tennessee Valley Authority, and some thirteen years later he was named chairman of the Atomic Energy Commission by President Truman.

In 1931, LaFollette secured passage of a bill reorganizing the old Railroad Commission as the Public Service Commission (PSC) with wider powers to regulate privately owned public utilities. The staff of the PSC was expanded, and experts were recruited from across the country. The utilities, and ultimately the consumer, bore the expense of the commission's expanded staff and activities, and the utilities were even liable for the cost of investigations conducted into their own affairs. The Wisconsin telephone company asked for a rate increase, submitted to an investigation, and was ordered to cut its rates. Other companies reduced rates voluntarily or were told to do so. The law of 1931 initiated the regulation of public utility holding companies; thus, the commission suspended payments to an Insull holding company by a Wisconsin operating subsidiary when the effect of such payments was to weaken the subsidiary. David Lilienthal took the lead in Wisconsin in executing reforms in the regulation of public utilities, and the Wisconsin experience anticipated similar federal regulation by several years.

During the fight against his confirmation as chairman of the Atomic Energy Commission, wherein he was subjected to wholly irresponsible charges that he was a Communist sympathizer, Lilienthal wrote Phil, longhand:

February 27, 1947

My Dear Phil:

A day or so before you left the Governor's office, in late December of 1932, you wrote me a longhand letter that is one of my most treasured possessions. I have just reread it

—something I have done at tough times over the years since I left your service. I have tried my very best to live up to your confidence in me. You took a gamble on me, for I was quite untried and unproven. I would rather have anything happen to me than to destroy that faith in my integrity of purpose. And I have often repeated to myself your closing admonition: to be "Tender to the Weak, and Tough on the Strong." The present attack is one of a long succession since Wisconsin days, in which your words have given me strength and direction when I needed them so badly.

Affectionately and faithfully,
Dave

Reorganization of the Banking Department enabled us to appoint an advisory board of leading bankers. These men, with the able help of Frank Kuehl, an assistant attorney general, formed a sort of "fire brigade." They told the depositors of a bank in trouble the truth and the whole truth. All stockholders and depositors were called together. The representatives of the State Banking Department proposed that the stockholders pay voluntarily, and promptly, their then required double liability—a payment of the face value of their stock. These payments, together with the other good assets, were placed in one fund—to operate the bank. Each depositor received his pro rata share therein and signed a temporary waiver for the rest due him. All questionable assets went into another trust fund in which the depositor received a certificate for his remaining pro rata share.

Thus the bank could continue to operate as a sound institution and had time to work out the sale of questionable assets. In a high percentage of cases, the depositors lost nothing, for when the panic ended eventually the values in the questionable assets came back to normal.

In February, 1932, after the close of the special session, Frank Kent wrote this for the Baltimore Sun:

He really is an amazing little guy—this 34-year-old Governor of Wisconsin. Short, slender, alert, quick-moving as a cat and with the fighting spirit of two or three lions, he is in action all the time. The LaFollette idea is to do something. The LaFollettes may be pacifists in foreign affairs, but they certainly hate peace at home—particularly Phil. Conferences are all right, and he confers, but after a certain number of conferences, out of which nothing comes, Phil has just got to do something. It is essential to him to act.

He goes down to Chicago, New York, and Washington. He talks with all kinds of men—big bankers, big businessmen, and big politicians. He submits his ideas, asks to be checked up, inquires what's wrong, is anxious for suggestions. From some he gets worthwhile thoughts, sound warnings. Most, of course, are barren of ideas, look his schemes over, and tell him they are not certain they will work, are generally dubious, not to say bilious. But that does not deter Phil. In the absence of concrete reasons not to—and sometimes when such reasons are present—he acts. In the two years he has been Governor, he has been in action all the time. . . .

Of course, he makes mistakes. Of course, he comes a few croppers, and of course he stirs up violent opposition. But he scores some successes, too, and the Wisconsin machine under LaFollette leadership has run well for a good many years and runs well now. They have not ruined the State— these LaFollettes. They have kept it stirred up. They have embarked it upon one adventure after the other, but it is still a sound State and soundly managed.

And if he is re-elected—and that seems certain—the State is in for more adventures under Phil than ever it was under Phil's father. It is a mistake to consider him a demagogue, though that is what his enemies call him. It is also a mistake to regard him as a rabble rouser, though there is no more effective fellow in an emotional appeal—and he knows every breast-beating trick. But back of his campaign stuff is a fast-thinking brain. He has balance as well as imagination, and no man is a demagogue who has the sort of sincerity this little fellow has.

The LaFollettes feel that they are after fundamental things, not trivial things. They do not want to tear down the structure or change the system. There is no flavor of communism in their philosophy, but they want to make the big changes needed to adjust the system to the situation, and they think that can't be done without rebuilding the machine from the ground up, steering it toward a different star.

Isen describes how her family endeavored to adjust to life in the Executive Residence:

Engrossed as I was during Phil's governorship period in the problems of masses or groups of people, I never lost sight of my conviction that my most important job was our own children. We were blessed in that they had splendid health and were lusty, normal youngsters for whom life was a bowl of cherries for their choosing. When Phil and I were weary and distraught with the care of "public life," what a comfort and satisfaction it was to see that brimming enthusiasm and well-being.

But with regard to our children, we felt we had a problem in attempting to keep their environment as normal as possible. Having observed how public life weighed on Phil and Bob, Jr., I was anxious to keep Bob III and Judy as free of their father's responsibilities as possible. Phil felt the burden far less than his brother Bob, but even he always insisted that he did not enjoy living in the Executive Residence because it was so inextricably associated with heavy responsibility, both from his childhood when his father was governor and now for himself.

When, as a young man, Phil was deciding on his future work, he talked with his law school teacher E. A. Gilmore, who gave him the sage advice to choose that career which he not only liked but where the burdens were the least onerous. I felt that the burdens of political life never weighed too heavily on Phil, but I was not so sure about Bob, Jr., observing that with him there was a tremendous sense of duty that seemed to me to overshadow the joy. I was very anxious that Bob III grow up as free as possible in his attitude toward choosing his future work.

I recall how tickled I was when someone asked him at this stage what he was going to be when he grew up. When, quite normally, he replied, "A cowboy," he was then asked reproachfully, "Why, Bob, aren't you going into politics like the rest of your family?" Bob replied, "Well, I may mix a little politics with my cowpunching."

Because a governor's mansion must be more or less at the service of the public, I could not conduct it as a training establishment for the children—one of the most important functions of a home. Judy made her own bed because her room was not used for guests, but Bob slept in the Ole Bull room. Although it was filled with a motley collection of everything from autographed photographs of heroes like Tom Mix, drawing equipment, marbles, balls, guns, and the like, I did feel that the room had to be in better order than a child would, or could, keep it. We never knew what delegations of Norwegians from near or far would appear and want to see the furniture used by Ole Bull, the world-famous violinist.

I felt that the children should be carrying more home responsibilities—washing dishes, tending fires, cutting grass, shoveling walks, and the many insignificant, but necessary, details of everyday life. The machine age with all its mechanical devices has reduced a parent's opportunities in the city for this kind of education, but we seemed unable to make the most of what there was.

I was one of five girls, and mother saw to it that we learned from daily experience the many tasks of running a household. People have argued with me that this early training is not necessary—that "anyone with brains can learn to cook and sew." Maybe they can, but too often they don't. But I don't approach the problem from the standpoint of useful work alone. I am convinced that an interest—a knowledge, a devotion to the workings of a household—is a strong source of security, a real factor in happiness. Real home-making is an expression of the creative urge and gives genuine satisfaction, even with the inevitable drudgery involved, as in all work.

I thought of this on an autumn day when Phil and I drove out in the country where he was to speak. As we rode through the countryside on a brilliant sunny afternoon, homeowners were raking and burning leaves, with their children and dogs tumbling about in the sunshine. Phil has often remarked that one of the things he missed most while in the Pacific during World War II was the odor of burning leaves. Father and mother may groan at these household tasks, but they can't deny the real satisfaction of a well-tended garden or a good baking of bread. In other words, in the hazards of life there are tangible anchors of joy.

Isen found that "outsiders" often held several misconceptions about Wisconsin politics:

Our Madison community has always been an interesting place in which to live. To the firm foundation of the native Wisconsin sons and daughters are added the men and women who have been drawn here to work in the university or Capitol, the Federal Forest Products Laboratory, or in business and professional activities, who especially sought out work here because of Wisconsin's Progressive reputation.

The newcomers, however, usually go through a painful period of adjustment. From the outside, they had thought that Wisconsin was the greatest Progressive state in the Union and had never realized that it has always been nip and tuck between progressivism and the forces of reaction, which reach in and clutch power about half the time. When I went to Salt Lake City at the time of my mother's death in June, 1932, I told friends there that I must return to Wisconsin to campaign. They responded in surprise, "Why, everybody knows the LaFollettes run Wisconsin." No matter how seriously I tried to explain that it was a constant battle, it made no impression on them, and I wondered later, after our defeat in 1932, if they had even noted the fact.

In the early days of the New Deal, when all the liberal Progressive forces in the country were pressing ahead, it seemed to me that Wisconsin was attracting all sorts of politically-minded men and women, some fresh from college who apparently felt that a veteran Progressive state would furnish a desirable laboratory of apprenticeship for their endeavors. One type of individual, however, was amusing, irritating, and pathetic. A young man from Harvard seriously told us when he arrived, bolstered with letters of introduction, "I have been brought up from birth to be a leader." As I remarked to Phil, all he needed was a following. The public, unfortunately, was unaware that here was a tailor-made pilot waiting to take the helm. He did not remain with us long.

I felt sorry for those who, with the best of intentions, came to "enjoy" a Progressive atmosphere but who soon found themselves involved in the inevitable conflict that arises when one must challenge the status quo. Some develop stamina enough to "take it," but more retire into the shell of "tired" or "disillusioned" Liberal or Progressive, or leave for fairer climes.

15

DEFEAT

IT IS A HORRIBLE EXPERIENCE. . . .

I knew I was going to have a tough fight for reelection in 1932. The repeal of the dividend tax exemption meant that most of the state's wealthy industrialists would, according to the standards of 1932, be hit harder than ever. And a lot of smaller taxpayers would not like it either, although their contribution was really small. Wealthy Republican industrialists had met in Milwaukee in the fall of 1931 and had pledged a big fund to defeat me. One of the industrialists reportedly exclaimed, "I hate that_____ , and I'll get down in the gutter to get all the dirt I can lay my hands on to destroy him."

We got the first real sample of what was to come with the publication on February 11, 1932, of the weekly *Uncensored News*, as scurrilous as any political sheet published in modern times. Even if one wanted to sue for libel, it would have been futile, because it had no material capital and was published for only this one campaign. A typical smear was a front-page open letter reporting that Isen had bought goblets for one thousand dollars per dozen. There was truth as to the purchase of goblets —but she bought them at the five and ten for $1.20 per dozen!

Then came the publication of *LaFollette Socialism*, a book attacking the LaFollettes as atheists and as soft on radicalism and communism. The author, John B. Chapple, was editor of the

Ashland (Wisconsin) *Press.* He also attacked the university as having faculty members who taught atheism and softness on radical extremism; the latter charge was centered on Professor Max Otto. Republican Conservatives endorsed this campaign method by supporting Chapple for the Republican nomination for the United States Senate in 1932.

Nineteen thirty-two was a Presidential year, and it was clear that rival forces supporting Franklin Roosevelt and Al Smith were going to fight for the Wisconsin delegates to the Democratic National Convention. Although some of the pro-Smith vote in 1932 would be Conservative, the majority would be votes that normally would be Progressive, and the same would apply to most of—if not all—the votes cast for FDR.

When the votes in the April Presidential primary were counted, the Conservatives won control of the Republican delegation for the first time in thirty-two years. But what was most ominous for us was that the total Democratic vote jumped from 17,000 in the September, 1930, gubernatorial primary to more than 200,000. The increase was attributable to the spirited contest for delegates to the Democratic convention and, of course, to a sharp decline in support for the Hoover administration.

For anyone who had gone beyond political high school, the handwriting on the wall was clear. The visible shift of many progressive-minded persons to the Democratic column foreshadowed my defeat in the Republican gubernatorial primary in September. I was to be the first LaFollette to go down to defeat in more than thirty years. That night, for the first time in my life, I did not sleep a wink. I tossed and writhed in anger and humiliation.

It was stark personal, political disaster. That night, I could not see one single, solitary ray of hope for me in the gloom ahead. The morning after such a night you cannot stay in bed—or at home either. You have to get to the office a bit earlier than usual. And somehow you have got to twist your aching facial muscles to look as if you liked the whole business.

Fortunate is the politician who takes this kind of beating and testing when he is young. My father got his first, strangely, at almost the same age as I did. Mine, I think, was worse. He had

not risen so high, so fast. And he was the maker of a tradition—
I, only the inheritor.

After the April primary we went to New York. One important objective was to call on and meet for the first time Franklin
Delano Roosevelt, governor of New York, and, it seemed, the
certain nominee of the Democratic National Convention, and, if
so, the certain next President of the United States.

His town house was on East Sixty-fifth Street. Next to it, and
joining it, was his mother's home. When Isen and I called, we
were greeted by the Governor and his wife in the second-floor
drawing room. Isen talked with Mrs. Roosevelt, but both of
them had ears cocked for the talk between FDR and me. And
sitting with his back to us, apparently busy turning over papers
but actually the most eager listener in the room, was Louis
McHenry Howe, the Governor's secretary.

Louis Howe was a gnomelike man who, aside from Mrs. Roosevelt, was the most important person, politically, in FDR's life.
He looked on Roosevelt as a beautiful political instrument—an
instrument which, if properly developed and used, could lead
them to the pinnacle. He was brutally frank with FDR, as only
a great teacher can be with a greater pupil.

It struck me as significant that when Louis Howe died in 1936,
Roosevelt seemed relieved. It was significant as to FDR's inner
character. Louis Howe's death was a great loss to the nation.
After he died there was scarcely anyone around the President,
aside from Mrs. Roosevelt, who talked back to him. Even Bob,
who on occasion talked back to him, used to say: "No one, even
Churchill, approaches the man who sits in that chair flanked by
those two flags without some feeling of awe for that high office."

At this first meeting in 1932, I instantly felt Roosevelt's mag-
netism, the warmth of his smile, the jaunty tilt of his head, the
radiant spirit of a man who had faced personal disaster and who
had had the courage to pick himself up and go on.

I also noticed a habit he must have long had, of saying, after
someone else's statement: "Yep, yep." Most who heard that
"Yep, yep" thought it was "Yes, yes." It was only partially so.

It was more: "Go on, go on." But anyone who heard "Yep, yep" as "Yes, yes" later thought Roosevelt was a two-faced hypocrite when he acted differently on some issue from what his listener had led himself to expect. It is true, of course, that FDR never wanted to be a bearer of bad tidings. He never liked to say No to ears that were eager to hear Yes.

Regardless of differences between us that came in the years ahead, there was—at least on my part—no interruption in the warm, friendly feeling I formed with Roosevelt at that first meeting in 1932.

We went back to Madison to get ready for the September primary election, in which my opponent would be former Governor Kohler. Isen, with some valuable help, took over the task of preparing a campaign textbook for 1932. The result was a masterpiece of political pamphleteering.

Again may I remind you that the newspapers in Wisconsin were overwhelmingly hostile to Progressives and to LaFollettes? It was not their opposition on the editorial page that mattered. It was their unabashed coloring of the news, or their refusal to print our side of the story, that made our task so hard for some fifty years.

By a series of off-the-record dinners at the Executive Residence for the reporters covering the Capitol and for publishers as well, I had softened some of them enough to take some of the venom out of their ink—but that was all.

I am sure many of you who read these pages will be dubious about my comments on the hostility of the press. Just read the files of the Milwaukee *Journal*—now generally rated as a first-class American newspaper—for any of those months of June through September during any campaign year from 1900 through 1938.

After the stunning effect on me of the spring primary, I looked defeat in the eye. It is a horrible experience, but I went through the campaign and fought my best. All of us—Bob, Isen, Blaine, and our whole team—fought until the polls closed that September night. Our Progressive army worked with pride in our record and, if I may say so, with a fierce personal devotion to me that was surpassed in Wisconsin only by that to my father. The simple fact was that to the rank and file of the Progressives of Wisconsin, I was their undisputed leader.

But enough people, those without deep personal or political ties, were impatient for results they could see or feel in their own lives. I went down to defeat in the Republican primary of 1932 by about 100,000 votes. The margin for former Governor Kohler was so large that Senator Blaine (to his amazement— surprisingly for a veteran) was beaten too.

The primary results in Wisconsin in 1932 are of great interest because they are a living testimonial to the eternal truth that, "Where your treasure is, there will your heart be also." The total Progressive vote in the rural townships increased over that of 1930. The Progressive vote in the city districts shrunk us to defeat. The explanation was that our program did produce reduction in real estate taxes, which showed up on every farmer's tax receipt. But this reduction in property taxes was more than offset by the tax increase caused by the need for relief in the urban centers. Thousands of Progressives, like angry bees, were out to vote against Progressives in the primary because of a slight increase in their income tax.

Gordon Sinykin, a twenty-two-year-old law student, was La-Follette's driver and secretary in the 1932 campaign. Sinykin, later Phil's law partner, kept a diary of his experiences in 1932. The first excerpt, below, reveals the intensity of feeling in Wisconsin politics at that time. The second excerpt, though hardly an objective account, suggests the loyalty and admiration that Phil inspired.

July 27—8 P.M.—Rhinelander:

Phil spoke at the armory to about 1500 people. . . . Chapple had issued a challenge earlier in the week to debate with Phil at Rhinelander. Phil ignored it. However, Chapple [the Conservative Republican candidate for senator] appeared at the armory when Phil was finishing his speech.

When Phil stopped talking, Chapple jumped up on a chair and tried to address the crowd. They booed, hissed, and yelled at him. Then the crowd grabbed him and his friend, Malcolm Jeffris, and bodily threw them out of the hall and into the street where it was raining very hard. Meanwhile Phil had left the armory. Chapple stood outside in the rain with an officer next to him and tried to speak to the throng. They merely booed and honked their car horns at him. He yelled louder, and the crowd answered still louder. This kept up for almost an hour. Finally, Chapple paid the janitor $15 and hired the hall. He spoke to 60 people most of whom booed him continually. Phil spoke 1¾ hours.

September 20—Primary Election Day:

Phil was defeated for the Republican nomination for Governor. . . . The Stalwart campaign of money-spending, poison, fear, and muckraking proved effective. It seemed incredible that the people of Wisconsin would succumb to such vicious lies and malicious propaganda. Phil discussed the vital issues with a frankness and fervor that was inspiring. His night speech was a work of art. People would stand for two hours, after a full day's work, to hear Phil. They would drink in every word he would say, and as he would swing further into his speech, their eyes would glow with a light that spelled determination to stick to Phil through hell-fire.

But the Stalwart campaign, with its poison, pressure, money, newspapers, and mud-slingers, together with the depression, worked its evil. . . . Thus, the people of Wisconsin were seduced into forsaking the Progressives who have given them the greatest and most efficient government in this nation. But Phil wasn't discouraged. "The important thing is to be right, not to win, for if we're right and keep fighting, eventually we shall win."

In the hour of his defeat he was smiling broadly, his chin up and his heart resolute to fight all the harder.

Power attracts. Defeat repels. So the governor's office, for the next 3½ months, was somewhat like a funeral parlor. While outwardly I kept a good face, inwardly things looked black, and the future looked bleak. The trend against Hoover and for Roosevelt had set in throughout the country, but there was no escaping the simple fact that I had been defeated—the first LaFollette to take a licking in Wisconsin since 1898. And I can't hide from the reader that it was a deep and profound humiliation.

I volunteered my services in the Presidential campaign of 1932. I had no hesitancy in supporting Franklin D. Roosevelt against Herbert Hoover, just as I had no hesitancy in 1928 in supporting Alfred E. Smith against Hoover. At the general election in November, Progressives turned out against the reactionary Republican nominees, and elected Democrats Albert G. Schmedeman as governor and F. Ryan Duffy as United States senator.

An event of great personal importance took place that fall. We had come to know Mr. and Mrs. James Causey. Jim had made a fortune in the brokerage business, but he had the simplest tastes for himself and delighted in using his money for what he considered benevolent causes. The personal world of Phil LaFollette was looking pretty black when Jim Causey phoned us from Rockford, Illinois, to ask if we could come down to dinner.

If you bear in mind that all that I had at that time was a bad licking—no assets of any kind except a meager bank account—you will get some idea of the pleasant shock that we got that night while visiting the Causeys. After dinner, Jim said, "I think that you and Isabel ought to go to Europe." He had in mind a real exploration into the facts and minds of Europe during one of its most critical periods. Jim went on, "You could earn enough money writing articles to pay for your trip, and something over. Peg and I will be glad to advance the grubstake." It would be difficult to describe the pleasure and happiness that Isen and I felt as we drove back from Rockford that night.

16

EUROPE
1933

. . . IN THE GRIP
OF CHILLING EVENTS

After our defeat in the September primary, we rented and moved into a house on the west side of Madison. We settled Bob and Judy with Eleanor and a university student and began to prepare for our trip to Europe.

A literary agent in New York seemed optimistic about selling articles based on our trip. If he succeeded, it meant that we would return to Madison with (for us) a nice nest egg to tide us over until I could resume my law practice.

I escorted my successor, Albert Schmedeman, to the oath-taking at noon on January 4, 1933, and left immediately with Isen for New York. We sailed on the fifth on the French Line's *LaFayette*. Our comfortable cabin was filled with flowers, fruit, books, and heart-warming messages.

I brought my portable typewriter along and worked every day of the voyage on the addresses that I was scheduled to give in London at the London School of Economics, the English-Speaking Union, and the Royal Institute of International Affairs.

The British do not go in for spread-eagle oratory. As Sir Winston Churchill has pointed out, the physical size of the House of Commons has been the frame that has dominated and formed British public speaking. The members of the House of Commons meet in a room small enough to permit conversation to be plainly heard. Here, oratory of the William Jennings Bryan type would sound ridiculous. The British like carefully prepared, meticulously accurate presentations, delivered with studied informality, with wit if you have any, and with the honesty that is the foundation of all effective human communication.

Associates of Churchill have told me that his great speeches, with their priceless phrases, were memorized, but that they were often delivered from notes on the back of an envelope, to give the appearance of casualness. Prince Philip, on the other hand, has that gift of being able to write a speech and then, without a note, deliver it "off the cuff."

I did not intend to deliver any profundities in my speeches. I did understand that if I did fairly well, and if I hit the proper note, that would be my entrance fee to The Establishment. In Britain, as you doubtless know, The Establishment is the name given to the ruling class—the Royal Family, the established Church, the armed services (the navy comes first), the aristocracy, the Bank of England, the BBC, and, mark this, the best brains in any walk of life.

Jim Causey had written ahead to friends in Germany and to Seebohm Rowntree, a Quaker and one of the chocolate millionaires. I learned that Mr. Rowntree's assistant would meet us in London and have a schedule ready for me.

When we left New York, the Depression was a raging economic fire with no national governmental action to combat it until Roosevelt's inauguration on March 4. Naturally, my chief interest in Europe was what I could learn about the causes and remedies for this economic holocaust doing such frightful damage throughout the industrialized world.

We landed at Plymouth on Friday, January 13, at 5:00 A.M. in a bitterly chilling drizzle. Everything was shut, and we walked the streets shivering with cold until our train for London left at 8:25 A.M. As we left Plymouth, Isen remarked that the awful British climate might have had as strong an effect on her ancestors, who left that port in 1620, as did their religious beliefs.

We arrived at Brown's Hotel on Dover Street on Friday afternoon. Frank Stuart—Rowntree's assistant—phoned us, and we
were to meet on Sunday. Both Isen and I were so fagged out and
chilled that we wanted nothing but food, hot baths, and beds
for the next twenty-four hours. It took Isen a week to get back
on her feet.

Frank Stuart proved invaluable. He did not pretend to be a
part of The Establishment. He did not know personally all of the
leading figures in Britain, but he did know who they were and
how to get to them.

Beginning Monday morning, the sixteenth, I was seeing and
talking with people in the morning, at lunch, in the afternoon, at
tea, at dinner, and until late at night. In spite of a friendly warning that I would be pumped for information about American
political affairs, I am not bad as a pumper myself. It did not take
long to find that leaders in Britain (and elsewhere in Europe)
were deeply concerned by the danger of another world war.
This apprehension about war did not deter me in my search for
the causes and remedies for the ailing economy at home and
abroad.

I had been told that the economist Sir Josiah Stamp was about
the most difficult man in England to see. He was chairman of the
London Midland and Scottish Railway and director of the Bank
of England. But like so many really busy people he had plenty of
time, once you got to him, for an hour's unhurried visit.

In his modest office, a warm fire burned in the grate. With tea
and biscuits, we settled down to talk. We discussed the frontier
theories of Frederick Jackson Turner. Sir Josiah endeavored, as
I had in my messages to the Legislature, to apply the economic
theories of Turner to the Depression of the thirties. He said,
essentially, this:

"This horizontal expansion of the frontier performed two vital
functions: It made it possible for the dissatisfied—for whatever
reason—who had energy and daring—to 'pull up stakes' and to
make a fresh start on the frontier. And the expanding frontier
was a magnet which attracted investment capital for replanting
and for the multiplication of wealth, like seed grain. This, in turn,
increased purchasing power which again provided expanding
markets for industry.

"The frontier was thus 'a safety valve' for restless human energy and a natural means of increasing purchasing power to keep it in some balance with expanding productive capacity.

"At the early stages of this Depression, governor, I, like so many others, including President Hoover, thought that it was like others in the past and that when confidence was restored, money would come out of hiding, business would pick up, and we would be off to good times again.

"But I began to think of the frontier, and then I realized that that powerful magnet was no longer at work on investment capital. So, as you go on your travels here in Europe, you will see in every industrial country you visit this new phenomenon: Every government is struggling to open the perpendicular frontier. Communism and fascism have this in common: They propose to do the job by force—they will put people to work, but the price is loss of human freedom.

"The challenge of our time is: Can we open the perpendicular frontier? Can we find means to keep purchasing power abreast of productive capacity—creative, profitable work for all who are physically able—on the farms and in the cities—and still retain human liberty? On the answer to that question hangs the fate of our civilization."

This interview with Stamp, along with other conversations I had had with outstanding thinkers from right to left, gave me comfort in the conviction that I had not made any mistake in the message I read to the Legislature in November, 1931.

After my speech to the Royal Institute, we had a very lively question period. First-class brains like Sir Herbert (later lord) Samuel took part, and the ball was batted back and forth for nearly an hour. Then Lord Charnwood rose and turned to me and said:

"Governor LaFollette, there is one question on everyone's mind here tonight which has not been asked." (Here it comes, thought I, bracing myself for some weighty problem to be posed.) "What we really want to know is this: Actually, how old are you?" (I was thirty-five.)

This brought down the house, and the meeting adjourned.

Isen and I were asked down to Cliveden—the famous country estate of Waldorf and Nancy Astor—for the weekend. Isen was ill and could not go. She was not keen on going, for it was not her "cup of tea."

Generally, if an American husband and wife receive an invitation, and if one cannot accept, the other declines as well. This, however, was not the rule for Nancy Astor; so when I phoned to express regrets, I really tangled with her and, reluctantly, went alone.

I am glad I did. Waldorf Astor was an admirable person with no false front at all. He tried to refuse his father's title and found he could not. Nancy Astor was always a controversial figure. She was full of wit, vitality, and had brains. She could give as well as take in the rough and tumble of public life. There began for us a friendship that lasted for many years—until her death.

D'Arcy Osborne, British minister at Washington, and I had become friends. D'Arcy had given me a letter to Sir Robert Vansittart, the permanent undersecretary of state for foreign affairs. (A word here on letters of introduction—especially from Britishers who belong to The Establishment. The British—especially the upper class—are often pictured as reserved, and usually as cold. Thirty years of personal experience has proved to me that this picture is false. True, there are reserved and chilly people everywhere; but experience has taught me that if one is "passed on"—usually by a letter of introduction, and often by another private letter from the introducer to the addressee—the bars are down and you are in.)

My appointment with Robert Vansittart was for eleven o'clock in the morning. His office was a corner in the Foreign Office, in the suite overlooking the Horse Guards parade ground. From those windows, Sir Edward Grey—on August 3, 1914—had watched, as he put it, the lamps going out all over Europe and had somberly remarked, "We shall not see them lit again in our lifetime." Those of us who knew the world before World War I understand that those lamps—in Grey's meaning—have never come on again.

"Van," as I came to call him, was over six feet tall, trim, tennis-muscled under his unostentatious, perfect grooming, highly sensitive, artistic, and tough. He had one of the finest minds and clearest heads I had ever known. It has been my good fortune to meet equally well-informed and intelligent persons in every country where I have been, but as a group there are more of them per capita in the Vatican and the British Foreign Service than elsewhere—at least in my experience.

On that January day, I sat enthralled as I listened to him paint the picture of the world as he saw it from his vantage point. He saw and told me of the appalling future that lay ahead—a future that, tragically, he saw only too clearly.

These points stand out in what Van had to say:

"Time after time we have seen approaching danger. Time after time we have warned our prime ministers, and on occasion the French. Each time we arrived at the right dock. But the boat was gone. So we unwillingly edge closer and closer toward World War II.

"I understand you are going on to Germany and Russia. It looks to us in our shop [the Foreign Office] as if you will be just in time to see that horrible Hitler and his Nazis come to power with consequences, unless they are stopped in their tracks, which will terrify the world."

I had also been in London in 1929. Mr. Ramsay MacDonald's status had completely changed between 1914, when he had opposed British entry into World War I, and 1929, when he had risen to the prime ministership. In the latter year I called on his son Malcolm at the Colonial Office, and after a pleasant chat he took me to the Prime Minister's official residence at "Number 10." With the Prime Minister's son as my guide, we went directly to the cabinet room, which is to one's right as one enters on the ground floor. It is a large rectangular room with windows facing the street. A long beige-covered table with red maroon leather armchairs for the cabinet were neatly placed in it. In the center, facing the table, sat the Prime Minister, writing busily.

As Malcolm and I entered the room, he looked up, smiled, and said, a bit pompously: "Be seated. I must finish my letter to the King." It is part of the prime minister's daily task to write his sovereign about what's going on. While the Prime Minister wrote I thoroughly studied this historic room. Shortly the Prime Minister finished his letter, enveloped it, rang a bell, and handed it to a secretary.

Time changes all. And Ramsay MacDonald had lost something of the charming, warm simplicity I remembered from 1914. He began to talk. His great concern was the continued Allied occupation of the German Rhineland. This was 1929. I know firsthand what concerned him about that Allied occupation. I had just come from Germany, and there I had seen the smoldering hate that that occupation was arousing in every German.

When Germany defaulted on impossible reparations payments required by the infamous Treaty of Versailles, the French sent troops into the industrial center of the Ruhr. The French not only sent troops; they sent colored troops. We had seen how these soldiers deliberately, arrogantly walked the promenades and streets four abreast, forcing civilians—women, children, and men—to the street to let them pass.

To understand the bitter resentment in millions of Germans, one must remember that Allied occupation. One must remember the Allied blockade that starved Germans after the war was over.

Having seen the beginning of World War I from a front seat; having lived through the months that, for America, evolved from "neutrality" to "peace without victory" to a world "made safe for democracy" with its "Fourteen Points" to the infamous "Treaty of Versailles"—having lived through all this, is it any wonder that in 1933 I moved toward Germany and Russia with deep forebodings?

Isen and I arrived in Berlin late Saturday night, January 28. We stayed at a small, modern hotel off Kurfürstendamm. We were a bit tired and slept late Sunday morning. After lunch, we took a train to the center of Berlin. We saw crowds gathering on Unter den Linden. We followed. As we approached the great square by the cathedral, we saw that it was packed with thousands and thousands of people.

Bands played. Flags fluttered. Loudspeakers blared with angry words. This, we were told, was the workers' protest against a similar demonstration the previous Sunday by Hitler's Nazis. At every street corner tough, rough Nazi young men, with their khaki uniforms and swastika arm bands, were shaking red tin boxes for contributions.

The air reeked with anger and hate. Small brawls—fist fights, bloody noses—were broken up by the roving squads of police, only to break out again. Everywhere one looked there were banners, and bands, and uniforms—the police, the Nazis, and the Stalhelm, a right-wing group. Berlin was a vast human powder keg. An explosion was coming. It was only a matter of days.

In Berlin, as in London, I set out to meet a cross section of the best-informed persons I could find. Through letters of introduction I saw many people. The climate was totally different. People talked with you, but their minds were riveted on the intense and violent events going on about them.

Through friends of Jim Causey, I was booked to give a lecture at the University of Berlin. I had written it out, and I delivered it in German. The audience was polite, but the air was heavy with tension and, for many, terror. Their minds were on the upheaval—indeed, the revolution—that shook and changed their lives by the hour. I felt relief when the talk was finished. Even if it had been first class, it would not have interested that audience.

Isen made these entries in her diary while in Berlin:

January 30: Things are very exciting here, and the report is that there may be a general strike if Hitler is appointed Chancellor. However, we found out that about five o'clock this afternoon Hindenburg gave Hitler the Chancellorship. The Nazis are everywhere, very cocky and noisy in their khaki uniforms.

January 31: The whole city is buzzing. There was a demonstration of the Nazis last evening before the French Embassy, demanding war and singing songs. The intelligent people are outraged about it, but the general opinion seems to be that there will be a struggle within the Nazi Party now; that Hindenburg refuses to see Hitler alone, and Hitler and von Papen are struggling to outdo each other to get complete control. Much as intelligent people abhor Hitler's methods, some of them feel hopeful that he was made to promise certain things before he was called to the chancellorship, such as regard for the constitution, etc., but the more astute fear the worst.

Hitler's appointment was tied with legal strings: none of Hitler's official acts as chancellor were to be valid without Vice-Chancellor Franz Von Papen's countersignature—and Hitler was not to see Von Hindenberg without Von Papen being present.

Von Papen, a favorite of the old president, thought he was smarter than Hitler. He thought that while Hitler sat on the hot seat in front, Von Papen would be the real power. After a time—so Von Papen planned—Hitler's popularity would be destroyed and Von Papen would take over. It was reported that Von Papen said, "Wir haben Hitler genommen." ("We have taken Hitler.") As it turned out, Von Papen was named special minister to Austria in 1934 and was lucky to get off with his life.

You will recall that I had looked on want in the midst of plenty as a monster. Now I also saw it as a sort of economic disease. Because it had been rampant in Germany longer than elsewhere, one could actually see its deadly work.

Professor Karl Brandt, then director of the Institute of Agricultural Market Research and subsequently a distinguished professor at Stanford University, took us to see this sickness. We drove into the working-class district of Berlin, with windows on empty apartments plastered with signs reading "Zu Vermieten" ("For Rent"). Then we drove to the outskirts of Berlin. There, as far as the eye could reach, we saw thousands of shanties. Those huts housed thousands whom the Depression had driven from those empty apartments back in Berlin.

Karl told us that the Depression had driven 750,000 people out of Berlin and onto the fields, and that the same economic sickness had forced farmers to take cattle into the vacant apartments in Berlin. He showed us a small herd of milk cows in a ground-floor apartment in Berlin.

I asked the city farmer, "What gives? Why are you here?"

His explanation was simple: "The rent is cheap for cows. I keep here only cows that are good milkers. I have no delivery costs. The people come morning and night with their own pails or pitchers. I don't make much money, but enough to keep me going. I wait for better times, and then I will go back to farming as God made for us to do."

Karl told us that there were some fifty thousand milk cows in Berlin. What a picture—people in the fields and cows in the apartments.

In Berlin we talked with many people. Here, far more than in London, one saw the consequences of a great economic Depression.

Originally we had not planned to go to Russia. Wise advisers urged it strongly. One put it: "Go to Russia for five days or five years—nothing in between. If you go for five days, you get lasting, invaluable impressions—but you won't think you are an expert." Isen finally made up "our mind." Also, I got a cable that the Hearst press wanted an option on articles I might write on our return. So we left Berlin in February, bound for Moscow.

As the train moved across Poland, my mind worked on what I had seen and learned in Germany. Some of these thoughts went down on paper and became articles that I wrote immediately on our return.

We arrived at the Russian border at 5:00 P.M. The station was new and bright with huge colored maps and, of course, heroic-sized busts of Lenin and Stalin. We were treated courteously by the customs officer but with no special favors.

The sleeping car in which we rode was ancient, fairly clean, but smelly. "Detective" Isen noticed that the sheets had been cleaned with lye; hence, we figured there was a national shortage of fats if the "de luxe" sleeper could not have sheets washed with soap.

Upon reaching Moscow at 9:30 A.M., February 13, we were met by an official of the Russian-American trading association. He had reserved a special hotel suite for us. We wanted no special favors from the government, and insisted on having only what we had paid for—"second category" at ten dollars a day per person.

We went to our room—clean but gloomy—with bath. Downstairs, we met our guide, Philip Bender, who spoke excellent English. He took us on a tour of Moscow.

Our first and deepest impression was that Russia was predominantly an Oriental nation. We were struck by the startling number (to us) of Oriental faces wherever we looked. The next impression was that there were more men in military uniforms than in Berlin. In the days we spent in Moscow I observed these soldiers—their uniforms, their weapons, their bearing, and tried to take their military measure.

At the opera, a lieutenant general (at thirty-eight years, so I was told) and his wife sat next to us. Next to them was a private, a Russian GI. At the intermission, the private passed in front of the general, courteously but entirely unawed by the brass. Both accepted each other as equals, off duty.

Strangely enough, nine years later, the estimate I formed of the Russian army proved considerably closer to the mark than that of one of our Russian experts in our army intelligence. He said, in April, 1942, that the German army would cut through the Russians like a hot knife through butter. My conclusion in February, 1933, was quite the contrary.

In 1933, Stalin was enforcing his ruthless program for collectivizing Russian agriculture. The awful results were apparent everywhere in Moscow—breadlines, gaunt and hungry faces, and places where people lined up to sell some last gold trinket. Here again we were impressed by the Oriental outlook. Life is cheap. People are more plentiful than goods, and breed faster than machines and animals.

We called on Walter Duranty, the able correspondent for the New York *Times*. He was a British subject and had been in Russia for more than ten years. Isen and he liked each other the instant they met. At first he and I bristled. He had a lecture all prepared for us. He delivered it. It seemed to me that he was talking down to me—"educating the little children with the 'three R's' on Russia." As he talked, I woke up to the fact that he was crowding into an hour, or a little more, what he had learned in a decade. I unbristled.

Whatever bias he may have had, he knew an immense amount about Russia. He was doing us a great favor, and I almost missed it. I had taken his outward shell as him and disliked it thoroughly. But outward impressions given off by sensitive, intelligent people often are protective color to hide their soft spots. One who seeks to see below the surface will usually be rewarded with attachments to valued and valuable people. When I woke up and distinguished between Duranty's protective shell and the keen, observant mind and the warm person beneath, I took to him at once. We became good and lasting friends.

The experience that I have had with people over the years makes me believe that we are like chemicals: we blend, or we don't. Somewhere I remember reading that Woodrow Wilson remarked that when he was in a railway station he saw so many people that he wanted to talk to that it made him uncomfortable. It is a mistake to let this Wilson-like shyness deprive you of interesting and often rewarding relations with people.

We were invited for an evening at the apartment of the commissar for foreign trade, A. P. Rosengoltz. We were asked for ten o'clock. We did not know what that meant. Cocktails? Late supper? Or just tea and talk? So we had our supper at our hotel and arrived at the commissar's apartment at ten. Neither he nor his wife were prepared for such prompt arrivals. We waited in the beautifully appointed drawing room for our hosts. They came into the room fifteen minutes after our arrival. By ten forty-five the other guests had arrived. Then we all moved into an anteroom. There, spread out on a table, was an enormous punch bowl filled with caviar; bottles of vodka, whiskey, and champagne were also plentiful.

Isen and I both thought this was it. We relished the apparently unlimited supply of caviar, but we carefully rationed ourselves on the champagne. Then at 12:30 A.M. a door opened, and we were ushered into the dining room. All before had been merely a prelude to a sumptuous dinner. We could not take it. Not only were we full of food, but neither of us could forget the bread-lines and the hungry faces we saw everywhere in the streets of Moscow.

At two fifteen we made our apologies and left—exhausted. The other guests stayed on for the rest of the dinner, and they all seemed astounded at our "early" departure. Going back to our hotel, and the next morning, Isen and I wondered how those officials could put on such a feast in the midst of so much famine. On reflection, we recalled how people who are in financial difficulties will often seek to prove that they are well off, when their financial affairs are actually very rickety.

We were guests at a small luncheon at the German Embassy. The ambassador, Dr. Herbert von Dirksen, came from the old aristocracy and was of the civil service. Previously he had been head of the Eastern Department of the German Foreign Office. He knew the old and understood the new Russia. He said the old Russia was gone forever. He put it something like this:

"The West looks at Soviet Russia from up, down. From the vantage point of their high standard of living, they see only the poverty and hunger of the Russian people and the brutal ruthlessness of the Soviet regime.

"They should look from down, up—especially with the eyes of youth. Then they would see a different picture. They would see that the lot of the vast proportion of these people has always been hard, that their rulers have always been brutally indifferent to the masses. But that the masses have a devotion to their land—'Mother Russia'—unsurpassed by any other nation. It will take years for the West to learn that Soviet Russia is here to stay. It will never go back to the old system."

We had an appointment with Karl Radek, who had been a leader in the International and, in the late thirties, would be a target in the purge. He lived in what we were told was the only penthouse apartment in Moscow. He was a short, stocky man, with a fringe of short whiskers. He was Jewish, and he spoke excellent English, an intellectual, extremely intelligent man with a mass of knowledge and an insight into world affairs that were astounding.

His living room was banked from floor to ceiling with books. From him that night came not a vestige of the evasive double-talk that we had heard from many others in Moscow. His only companion, it seemed, was a little dog, about which he was daft.

He was then close to Stalin and hence high up the Russian ladder. He had never been to America, but he made some predictions about us that were very precise.

(As I write this, it is almost as vivid as if it had happened last night. You may well ask, How do you remember all this? My wife kept a diary and I made many notes, which were the basis for the articles that I wrote on our return. And, perhaps equally important, my memory has proved far better than I could have hoped.)

It was manifest that Radek had prepared and picked every word he was to say to me that night. The following is the essence of what he said:

"The one thing certain ahead of all of us is another world war. Sooner or later Germany is going to attack the Soviet Union. Make no mistake about that. There is no mystery about our foreign policy. It is based on the inevitability of the coming war with Germany.

"We have no fear of Japan. We can always retreat if we have to—and retreat so far that Japan would wear herself out trying to follow us.

"Germany is another story. This will be a life and death struggle.

"If you will remember this in the time ahead, you will understand our basic foreign policy: We are buying time to postpone this coming war with Germany. We will pay any price—save only surrender—*any* price to buy time. Every day, every month, every year we postpone this war makes us stronger when we have to fight it. So do not be surprised at what we may be forced to do in buying that time.

"Remember two things: We will buy time. We will never surrender.

"Now, you are getting a new President. He is going to take you into this coming war. Of course, he will tell you the opposite, but take you in he will.

"The great weakness of this new President of yours is this: He thinks he is smarter than Wilson. He thinks he knows all the mistakes of Wilson and will avoid them and accomplish all that Wilson failed to achieve.

"Of course, all this means is that your Mr. Roosevelt vastly overrates himself. He will not only not avoid Mr. Wilson's mistakes; he will make vastly bigger ones."

Radek talked at length about American and Russian relations, emphasizing what an enormous potential market Russia was for the industrialized West—especially for America.

Then I channeled the talk back to Russia. I said:

"You told the people of Russia the wonders that the Five-Year Plan would work. But today conditions are more difficult than when you began. You may have explanations such as 'World Depression' as the cause of your troubles, but the people judge by results. How can you stay in power?"

He looked out the window for a moment, thinking. Then he replied:

"I'll answer your question by telling you an incident. As I came to the office today, the elevator man stopped me. His face was dark and brooding as he complained with bitterness about his lack of food, inadequate housing, et cetera.

"After he finished, I asked him about his children. His face changed. A light came into his eyes, and a beautiful smile played across his face as he said: 'One daughter is studying at the Conservatory of Music. One son is a student at the university learning to be a chemist. And my oldest boy—he is a colonel in the Red Army.'

"That is the answer to your question. We may not have accomplished all we set out to do. We may be suffering today. But each peasant and worker in Russia is like a soldier in Napoleon's army: he carries a marshal's baton in his knapsack. The present is difficult. But they have faith in the future—if not for themselves, then for their children."

Shortly before we left Russia, we had an interesting farewell with our guide, Philip Bender. We had him up to our room and shared the last of the food and wine we had brought with us from Berlin. We had prodded him during these days about conditions in Russia, lack of freedom, hunger, and hardships. He had dodged and evaded our questions with mechanical Communist double-talk, such as:

"Think about this. If you go down in the lobby of this hotel and shout denunciations of Stalin, you will be arrested. But if a man and a woman want to sleep together, in Russia that is their business and not the government's.

"In your country it is the other way around. You can denounce your President. But it is a crime for unmarried men and women to sleep together.

"Now, it might be nice to be able to do both. But I suggest that there are millions on this earth who prefer freedom in their private lives to having it in their public affairs."

In Vienna we found a situation similar to that in Berlin: Here, the dictator was Englebert Dollfuss. Dollfuss was only a little over five feet in height. He had the firm, stocky (not fat) frame of the peasant. His eyes showed keen intelligence, his jaw and mouth, courage.

When we met, we exchanged the usual banal courtesies. After ten minutes I got up to leave. In our brief visit we took to each other. As we were parting he said:

"Governor, is there anything I can do for you?"

I replied: "Yes, Chancellor, if you have the time, I would like to have a real talk with you on what is going on in Europe."

He looked startled, his face lit up with a smile, and he said, "What are your plans for Sunday?" And I said, "I'll make my plans to suit you."

"Good," he responded, "I'll call for you at your hotel at nine o'clock Sunday morning, and we will spend the day together."

At nine o'clock that Sunday morning he called—with his wife. Unfortunately, I had not understood Isen was included. Because she had gone off for sightseeing on her own, she missed this day-long ride to a mountainside restaurant in the Austrian Alps.

We all find as we travel, at home or abroad, that strangers will often unburden themselves of intimacies to mere acquaintances that they would never dream of exposing to friends back home. So, Dollfuss unburdened himself of his troubles. The big one was the squeeze that he was in between Hitler, on the one side, and Mussolini, on the other. As you know, his impossible problem was solved for him: he was assassinated the following year.

For days we had lived in the grip of chilling events. In addition, we had begun to wonder if the sun itself had deserted us. For more than two months we had scarcely seen it. Then, we arrived in Italy, the sun came out, and we were warm again.

While in Rome we had a reunion with two intimate friends, John and Jane Gaus of the University of Wisconsin faculty.

In Berlin, I had shied away from a hint that I might meet Hitler. In Moscow there had been no hint about seeing Stalin. Had there been, I undoubtedly would have reacted in the same way. Experience in politics had long ago taught me to be allergic to having one's photograph taken with certain personages. Such pictures, like ill-considered writings, can haunt you later.

But through arrangements made by Colonel House, I was to be received in Rome by Mussolini. I had yielded to this temptation because of the experience our beloved Lincoln Steffens had had with the Italian dictator.

Steffens, an old family friend, told me how he had entered Mussolini's office and had walked those seemingly endless yards from the door to Mussolini's massive desk. Mussolini was apparently absorbed in a book and oblivious of all else. Stef walked behind him and looked. The book was upside down. Mussolini looked up with a wink. Stef decided he had a sense of humor and plied him with bull's-eye questions. To one—"Why, if you are so popular, did you use force to come to power?"—Mussolini had replied: "Sir, no one *invites* you to sit on a throne."

I had decided I would like to see this fellow. But with apologies, my appointment could not be met. Later, the Italian ambassador in Washington sent me Mussolini's autographed photograph, at the latter's direction. From my teens I had collected autographed photographs, and I had quite a gallery. Mussolini's joined the others. Five years later the mere fact that I had his photograph on the wall would be used by my detractors to try to smear me as a Fascist.

In Rome two interviews remain vivid—one, a private audience with the Pope; the other, a visit with the former Italian ambassador in Washington, Prince Caetani.

The LaFollettes have always had cordial relations with the Roman Catholic hierarchy, and on our two visits to Rome we saw the Pope. John Gaus and I, attired in evening dress and accompanied by the director of the American Academy in Rome, went to the Vatican. The ceremonies and magnificent surroundings are impressive. Temporal reminders, which detracted somewhat from the religious setting, vanished when one unaffectedly knelt before the kindly, benign, wise face of Pius XI.

Here, as before and since, I was to be impressed with the breadth and depth of the knowledge found in those highly placed in the Roman Catholic Church.

In giving his blessing, His Holiness said, as I recall: "Special commendation to you for the good works of you, your father and brother, in the field of social progress. You and your family have made lasting contributions to the welfare of your people in Wisconsin, and in your nation. Special mention must be made for Wisconsin's leadership under your governorship in adopting your country's first Unemployment Compensation Law." He then blessed rosaries John and I had brought for Catholic friends, after which he blessed us.

Anyone with public experience would know that the Pope's special words to me came from a supersecretariat. But the words, nonetheless, left a lasting warmth.

Prince Caetani headed one of the old aristocratic families of Italy. As a young man he had cowpunched in the American

West. Later he had been the Italian ambassador in Washington. Nicholas Murray Butler, president of Columbia University, had given me a fistful of letters of introduction, among them one to Caetani. Caetani phoned me at my hotel and asked me to lunch, saying: "Whom would you like to meet?" I suggested that just the two of us have lunch.

The Caetani Palace dates to the Middle Ages. It is a block-square fortress. Within it are many art treasures. The Prince was waiting for me at the entrance, and he took me to the second floor to the drawing room and from there to the dining room, where we lunched. Goggle-eyed by the splendor, I was brought back to earth by this remark: "This place is really not bad, is it? You see, we had two Popes in the family, and they did very well by us."

For two hours he talked, and I listened. He said grace, made the sign of the cross, and then said:

"We Romans always see the Church as two—the temporal and the spiritual. Many, like myself, have known the Princes of the Church as boys. We have grown up together. We know them as mortals like ourselves.

"These mortal Churchmen with their human qualities are in one compartment of our brains. In quite a separate compartment are those mortals who, upon selection, become our Popes and instantly acquire Divine power. How we keep these compartments so completely separate, I do not know, but we do."

After he had given me a sweeping, fascinating view of his family's history and of his early life on our western plains, the talk turned to the rise and fall of civilization. He pointed to a church we could see through the dining room window, saying: "That church was built on the foundations of a Roman temple. The temple, in turn, was built on an earlier one. And before that there was another that goes back into the mists of time."

He paused, looked at the church, and slowly turned his head and looked at me. Then he said:

"For many years I thought America was to be another Rome. I was convinced that your country would give the world another Pax Romana—another era of world peace.

"Now—now I am not so certain. Nations and civilizations are human. They are born. They live. They die.

"The whole processes of life are speeded up. This speed of life will be vastly accelerated in your lifetime. It may well be that this terrific speeding up may shorten your country's ascendancy—perhaps of this present civilization itself.

"I have grave wonder whether human beings can survive the appalling speeds that lie ahead."

This was the essence of what I heard that bright, sunny afternoon in Rome.

Back at the hotel I found word waiting for me that changed our plans. I had expected that we would go on to Paris. But Bob had cabled me to come home. A few days after we had sailed from New York, Bob had been told that Franklin Roosevelt wanted to see me about joining his administration. During our absence, friends—especially Senator George Norris—had been urging the President-elect to include me in his administration.

The LaFollettes cut short their European tour. Isen recalls the last leg of the return to the United States:

The less said about the voyage home the better. The first evening out we met a charming young Hungarian who liked to dance as much as I did, and I prayed for good sea legs. Such was not to be, however, and when I emerged from the bowels of the ship in New York harbor, all I longed for was terra firma. Of course the inevitable news photographer was there, but I hadn't realized we were such sights—Phil's hair ruffled by the harbor breeze made him look as if he had horns, and I was looking (as I admit I felt) like the last rose of summer. When I got off the train at Madison, Fola said, "Thank Heaven you don't look as worn as your picture!" but a less kind anonymous critic sent us a copy of said newspaper picture labeled in his or her handwriting, "Trotsky and Emma Goldman."

17

A PARTY
IS BORN

. . . THE NEED
FOR A REALIGNMENT. . . .

President Roosevelt had advised Bob that he wanted to see me on
my return, and an appointment with him had been set for March
20 at eleven o'clock. It is almost impossible to re-create now
what people in general thought of FDR in 1933 except to say
that his "nothing to fear but fear itself," and his dramatic closing
and then reopening of the banks, led most people to believe that
at long last the country was going to get leadership from Washington instead of the deadly standstillism of Herbert Hoover.

Just what the new leadership would offer was as yet unknown.
Roosevelt's record as governor of New York had demonstrated
his personal integrity, and his conquest of polio had proved his
great courage. He had likewise demonstrated not only that he
understood politics as a craft but also that he was a master of
political tactics. Did he have the needed mastery of grand
strategy that was essential in a great statesman? None of Bob's
or my friends knew the answer.

The general attitude of Progressive leaders in Congress—
especially in the Senate—was one of personal liking for Roosevelt
as a warm human being. They were all hopeful that he would

adopt progressive ideas on economics and government's responsibilities in this new economic world in which we lived. But nothing in FDR's record proved that he had deep convictions as George Norris and my father had.

Many of us, including Bob and me, remembered our disappointment over what seemed to us Theodore Roosevelt's watered-down, or at times even shabby, progressivism. Most of us, too, had lived through the two Wilson administrations—his first bright with progressive achievements, the second filled with disappointments.

The Progressive leadership in both parties wanted to help President Roosevelt and his administration but wanted to know what his program was going to be. As Bob and I drove to the White House, we again reviewed the broad outline of what I should say to the President. We were shown into his office, and he greeted us with his famous smile and his hearty handshake. After the preliminaries, he asked me about Soviet Russia: What were my general impressions? And what about Hitler and the Nazis? I sermonized on these subjects for a while. We had been talking for some thirty or forty minutes, and I thought our interview must be about over. But the President then said something like this:

"Phil, I very much want you to be a part of my administration—in just what capacity I am not sure. But there are a number of spots where I think you could render outstanding service. There is the field of public works. There is the tremendous task of heading up a relief program for the unemployed. There are several of the federal commissions—such as the Federal Power Commission, the Federal Trade Commission, etc.—but the point is I want you in a proper position where your abilities can serve the public."

At this point I expressed my appreciation for his confidence in me, and then said in effect:

"Mr. President, you have the greatest challenge and the greatest opportunity of any president since Lincoln. At this particular point you don't need me as an individual. There are hundreds of able and outstanding people eager to join your administration —Conservatives as well as Progressives. But to meet the great challenge that faces you and to utilize your great opportunity to give this country a really 'New Deal,' you face the fight of your life. Entrenched economic powers are talking meekly now because they need help, but once they catch their breath, they will fight you tooth and nail if you present a real challenge to their powers and privileges.

"If you make that fight—which I believe you will—there is no position too humble in your administration I would not accept if it would really aid you. If you do not make that fight, there is no position—no matter how high—which I would accept. May we leave it for the present that as the battle lines form in the months ahead, if I can help in a *real* fight, call on me?"

Again I expressed my appreciation to the President for his expression of confidence, and with that Bob and I left.

Unless one inherits or makes a fortune (outside of public office, we trust), one has to earn the bread for his family and himself. As is often said, "The law is a jealous mistress," and I had neglected her for the better part of three years.

During the years I was governor, I withdrew completely from the law firm of which I was a member; that is, I received no share of the firm's earnings. It takes about a year to get a law business started again when you are out of it for any considerable period. Unless you get substantial retainers at once, you have to perform services before money comes into your till.

This takes time, so in fairness to my partners, I have been a partner in name only since 1933. I pay my share of the expenses, keep my own earnings separate, and pay my partners for services they may render clients of mine.

With the cash from my articles on our European trip, we had a monetary backlog. Lecturing was a means of supplementing that income. Those weeks on the Chautauqua circuit had taught me how to deliver an exciting talk on public affairs before politically "mixed" audiences without arousing antagonism.

During the last few months of 1933 and most of 1934, my time was divided between lecturing, building back my law practice, and politics. In politics, my prime interest was in Wisconsin. When my father was active in national affairs, he never forgot that in public life one must have a political base. He never neglected his political base—Wisconsin—and I knew that if Bob and I were to regain and retain leadership, we must concentrate on Wisconsin. During 1933 and 1934 I was offered a number of posts in the Roosevelt administration. At the moment I cannot remember them all, but I find a statement by Bob in 1934 that they came to a total of eight. They were all declined, because the Roosevelt administration did not come to grips with the country's real problems. Indeed, Henry Wallace's plan to kill little pigs and plow under cotton violated my deep convictions that destroying or limiting production was a profound economic fallacy.

For better or worse, the decision not to go to Washington meant, as far as public affairs were concerned, that I was to concentrate on Wisconsin.

The independent campaign of my father and Burton K. Wheeler in 1924 had carried the hopes of many that it would lay the foundation for a new national political party. Leaders like George Norris of Nebraska, Fiorello LaGuardia of New York, Wheeler of Montana, Floyd Olson of Minnesota, Bob, and many others had long felt the need for a realignment in American politics that would put the Conservatives in one camp and the Progressives in another, but the almost insurmountable task of setting up a new party, state by state, had stalled moves in that direction.

As you will remember, the resurgence of the Democratic party in the 1932 primary had been a controlling factor in the defeat of most of our Progressive candidates. The primary had again proved the bitter lesson that when the Progressive vote, which was both Democratic and Republican, was divided, the Progressives went down to defeat. Now the Wisconsin Democrats had the governorship, one United States senator, and the patronage from Washington. And Bob was up for reelection in 1934.

Some of us were convinced that Bob's best chance for reelection would be to run on a new party ticket. We had become deeply attached to the idea of a new party.

The Socialists—centered largely in Milwaukee—had a party column in Wisconsin. Their forebears had brought with them the doctrinaire Marxian ideas from Germany. They supported Progressive legislation in the Legislature but always had a full state ticket of their own at elections. If the Socialist party dissolved in favor of the new party, their votes would help us in the state. Their ablest leader, Tom Duncan, had been my executive secretary. He did not have a vestige of the doctrinaire.

If we laid aside the idea of a new party, the next question was, Should Bob and the other Progressive incumbents run as Democrats? I think that Bob, with the open support of President Roosevelt, which I think he would have received, would have won the Democratic nomination and election. But this would not have applied to other Progressives. The result would have been a Democratic sweep. And the hard core of the Democratic party in Wisconsin was just as conservative as the Stalwart Republicans. Although Bob's personal and political relations with FDR were cordial, the Roosevelt administration, while making Progressive noises, had not committed itself to any definite Progressive program. Hence, Bob was very reluctant to entertain that idea. Perhaps a determining factor in Bob's reluctance to run as a Democrat was a meeting that he had with FDR in January, 1934. At that time, Bob wrote me that the President thought the Depression was about over and was planning to start cutting back on the civil works program.

If we were to remain in the Republican party, were Progressives in 1934 really to have no program and actually only one important candidate—namely, Bob? Was the Progressive Movement in Wisconsin to be scuttled? This went against our policy. Bob wrote me of another interesting development: "I had a long talk with Arthur Vandenberg [Republican senator from Michigan] this morning. . . . He thinks the only way the party can be saved is for it to move sharply to the Left, but he believes it should stay to the Right of the Democratic Party." Bob was very dubious about such a proposal, and so was I.

Moreover if we stayed in the Republican party and had a slate of Progressive candidates, who would lead the state ticket as our candidate for governor? The fact was that we had no one at that time who would not have been a serious drag on Bob's campaign.

All through 1933 and early 1934, Progressive leaders discussed our future course. They would drop into my office when they were in town, or would come on special trips of two or three, to "talk things over." I spoke frequently at various meetings and picnics throughout the state, and every such meeting was preceded by talks with our leaders in each community. By the end of 1933 I sensed clearly that the hard core of Progressives in Wisconsin was coming increasingly to favor a separate Progressive party.

After weeks and weeks of consultation among individuals and groups of Progressives—including, of course, Bob, Blaine, our Progressive congressmen, and Secretary of State Theodore Dammann—all these talks and discussions had not really changed many minds. Those who had weathered our defeat in 1932, that is, those who held office—including Bob—opposed a new party. The hard-core Progressives, as well as the Left led by former Congressman Thomas Amlie, were for it.

By February, most had agreed that we should call a Progressive conference. There was no provision for a legal party convention. "Delegates" at such a conference would be recognized Progressive leaders from all over the state, and the meeting would reflect a cross section of Wisconsin Progressives. Strangely enough, such informal meetings worked. Over many decades of such conferences in Wisconsin, I cannot remember a single instance when an "enemy" sought admission to a meeting.

The first meeting in Madison in March 1934 drew excellent attendance from all over the state. There was no vote on the new-party issue, because it was clear that we must first have a declaratory judgment from the state Supreme Court to clarify the Wisconsin statutes about whether and how a new party could get on the state ballot. After the LaFollette-Wheeler candidacies of 1924, nothing was done to make it easier for new parties. All seemed to agree that the move to the state Supreme

Court was the most logical step, and so such an action was begun.

On May 1, 1934, the court held that a petition asking for a place and column on the state ticket should be granted for a new party if it contained valid signatures representing one-sixth of the votes for President in the most recent election from at least ten counties.

The Supreme Court had cleared the legal obstacles to the new party, but the final decision, both on a new party and on its name, must now be made at another Progressive conference. This meeting took place in Fond du Lac on Saturday, May 19. William T. Evjue, editor of the *Capital Times*, who favored a new party, was chairman. After free discussion, the resolution to form a new party was adopted, 252 to 44.

In her memoirs, Isen set down her recollections of the controversies that accompanied the convention.

At Fond du Lac the left-wingers fought to gain control of the convention, and likewise the anti-third party group continued its opposition, but the overwhelming sentiment among the rank and file was for the new party. Next came a big scrap as to the name of the party. The left-wingers—desiring to emphasize the Marxian idea of the class struggle—insisted on the name *Farmer Labor*, as did the Socialists who were there in goodly numbers. However, the main body of the convention wanted to keep the name *Progressive*, and it was so voted. The theoreticians, aided and abetted by the malcontents, were bitterly disappointed that the convention did not adopt a declaration of principles or a platform. That was not included in the call for the convention, and of course, the experienced leaders knew that the convention had accomplished as much as it could for the time being without splitting up the entire body over specific issues. They urged that we go easy and work out our platform during the campaign.

Bob did not appear at the convention until toward the end of the program. He said he was willing to run by whatever instrumentality the group wished. I wished he had felt able to go further, but I appreciated that he was doubtless sensitive to the talk at this convention about the importance of "principles rather than individuals," with less emphasis on "electing Bob at any price." Any aware observer could see that certain elements were trying to undermine the LaFollette leadership and run away with the new party.

Phil resumes the narrative:

Now we had to get the required number of signatures. Before adjournment, we set a goal of not less than 50,000 signatures. So far as I know, no one was ever paid anything by Wisconsin Progressives to go out and secure signatures. As always in Wisconsin Progressive politics, it was a question of mixing shoe leather and brains in lieu of money, which for us was always in short supply. By June 18, 1934, these Progressive workers had done their job so well that we were able to file petitions bearing more than 120,000 signatures.

Now that we had a Progressive party, who would be our candidate for governor? There was, of course, no question about Bob's being our candidate for reelection to the United States Senate.

I had strongly favored the new party. Although I had not hesitated to talk with our leaders and express my views frankly, I did not speak publicly on that question, because Bob would, and should, give his controlling view. Bob had not expressed himself openly, although he was really against a new party. If he had spoken out at the March meeting, I think he could have squelched it. By the May meeting at Fond du Lac, he could no longer lead; he had to follow the great majority of Progressive leaders.

It was the same story on selecting the Progressive candidate for governor. Bob opposed my running—more strongly than he had opposed the new party. He felt that it would be a grave political blunder to create a new party and then have two brothers heading its ticket in its first appearance on the ballot.

I might, of course, have settled that question by refusing outright to run, but it was not so easy as that. If I made a categorical refusal, it would have opened the door for a free-for-all, in which it was more than likely that a weak plurality candidate would get the nomination and damage the party and Bob's candidacy. And I would be accused of being afraid to run because of the poor prospects for victory. Bob, Isen, Fola, and my two brothers-in-law, together with many others who expressed themselves, were all against my running. Newspapers in Wisconsin and elsewhere commented on "too much LaFollette."

On June 30, our left-wing faction, the Farmer-Labor and Progressive League, met at Fond du Lac. I feared that this conference might adopt a more "radical" platform and endorse radical candidates in the Progressive primary who would appeal only to the Left. I was asked to speak, and I wrote out my talk in order to avoid any misquotations. It was not an easy job, but apparently I did a good job. They adopted a sound platform, endorsed Bob, and adjourned.

By the middle of July, Bob finally returned to Madison from Washington and at once began arranging conferences of Progressive leaders. They met at Maple Bluff Farm. Day after day our leaders came to Madison in groups of twenty-five or more and sat out on the lawn. For the first time, but not the last, I was not included in Progressive meetings. Bob told me he would begin by stating forcefully all the arguments—and there were plenty—against my becoming a candidate. Then, one by one, the leaders spoke their views.

By the time Bob had concluded the last of these meetings it was clear that whatever the professional politicians and newsmen might think, the overwhelming sentiment of Progressives favored my candidacy. Bob reported to me that it was better than ten to one. And the ten, Bob said, were adamant.

So we began circulating my nomination papers. I took the position that I would run only if no other leading Progressive stepped in. Scarcely a day went by without conferences between leaders on the question of who might run. If any one of several who might make a creditable candidate had filed his nomination papers, I most certainly would not have run. All he had to do was make an announcement and I would be out.

No other leading Progressive filed, because the rank and file were set against it, and because it was going to be a stiff, uphill fight all the way. I waited until the deadline and then filed. Being a candidate for governor meant another go—another chance at the profession to which I had been born and bred and in which, because of the timing of my birth, it was a miracle that I ever had any chance at all.

Progressive hopes for recapturing the governorship were tied to the Schmedeman administration's lack of success in coping with the Depression. Dairy farmers, in a desperate effort to raise milk prices, dumped millions of gallons of milk and resorted to occasional acts of violence. The Democratic governor responded by sending the National Guard against the strikers, an unpopular move.

Increased political activity by farmer and labor groups helped spur support for a Progressive party by those who sought to prevent the scattering of Progressive strength. The drift of Progressives into the Democratic primary had already helped defeat Phil in 1932. The resurgence of the Democrats meant, furthermore, that the Republican nomination was no longer tantamount to election, and the Progressives could not afford to wage two all-out campaigns every other year for both the September primary and the November general election.

Bob, Jr., displayed his characteristic caution in considering a third party. On October 18, 1933, he wrote Phil: "I sense your desire for action and yet all my training leads me to want to know where we are going before we leap." Bob feared that abandoning the Republican party would jeopardize his seniority on Senate committees, and he was not certain that the Wisconsin voters would develop new patterns of voting behavior.

Barely one fourth of the planks in the new party's platform dealt with problems of exclusive concern to Wisconsin. The platform declared, "Our economic system has failed." It urged "a political realignment that will place the exploiting reactionary

*on the one side and the producer, consumer, independent busi-
ness and professional interests on the other."*

In August, President Roosevelt stopped at Green Bay during
a campaign swing. He had thought through exactly how to
handle a delicate situation. He wanted to give Bob a friendly
hand and yet not violate Democratic party regularity too brashly.
At this kind of political maneuver he was a past master.

He gave James A. Farley, postmaster general and chairman
of the Democratic National Committee, a free hand in backing
the straight Democratic ticket with all the resources of his
organization. Then he invited Bob to join him and Governor
Schmedeman, my opponent, on his special train. He gave them
each a friendly boost. And, as one correspondent put it, he gave
me "a slap on the wrist."

In the September primary, the total vote cast for the Democratic candidates was greater than that cast for the Progressives,
but the margin was narrow enough to indicate that we had a
fighting chance for the governorship in the general election.
Because the candidate who won the Democratic nomination for
the United States Senate, by a small margin, was an Al Smith
supporter and anti-Roosevelt, Bob had clear sailing for reelection.

Through most of the 1930's, the governorship—certainly in
Wisconsin—was closer and more important to the voters than
a United States senatorship. Uncle Sam did not begin to take
huge bites out of the taxpayer's pocketbooks until World War
II. And, too, the concentration of power in Washington did not
suck away the great creative opportunities for a state government—in Wisconsin, at least—until about 1938. So in 1934 the
contest for the governorship was the center of interest. The
heat of the opposition was to be on Phil, not on Bob.

The personality and political astuteness of FDR were capturing
the imagination and the support of the American people. The
vast relief programs of the Roosevelt administration were putting
billions of dollars and thousands of jobs into its hands. It was an
undreamed-of bonanza for skillful politicians, and there were
plenty of them to do the manipulating.

We all knew that the full force of the Roosevelt administration would be behind Governor Schmedeman. We knew, too, that the Republican leaders would try out their candidate, Howard Green, and then, as the campaign took shape, try to swing the rank-and-file Republicans to Schmedeman if he looked like the better bet to beat me.

This meant that our opposition had a reserve army that it could swing from Green to Schmedeman on Election Day if that seemed wise. Could our forces hold out against the impact of thousands of Conservative Republicans voting for the Democratic candidate for governor?

Early in the campaign a lifelong Progressive—but until then one who had confined his political activities to his home county—appeared on our scene. A. W. Zeratsky, "Z," as we called him, of La Crosse, had been successful in the mail order business. He proposed that we use some of his methods in politics. He suggested that we get lists of names—schoolteachers; veterans; city, town, and county officials; etc. Having the lists, he would draft letters to go out over my facsimile signature. Each letter would stress our position on specific matters of interest to the recipient.

The number of letters he proposed appalled us. It was not a few thousand; it was to be hundreds of thousands. This idea had never been tried before on this scale—at least in Wisconsin. But Z's enthusiasm overcame our doubts. We knew we would need every possible vote so we had better try it. So while Bob and I, and all the other candidates, were busy campaigning in the usual way, Z was busy at his lists, envelopes, and letters.

As we came down the home stretch, it seemed clear that Bob would win hands down. All the talk of "too much LaFollette" disappeared into thin air, and Bob concentrated his efforts on behalf of my candidacy. As if we did not have enough opposition, an accident to Governor Schmedeman added another factor. He fell and injured his leg. A few days later, infection set in. Bob phoned me one night that the Governor's leg was to be amputated. In this close fight, would natural human sympathy turn the scales in his favor? After all the effort we had put in over the past two years, it would be hard to take if the Governor's painful accident should blast all our hopes and plans.

It did not. I won, narrowly defeating Schmedeman by 373,000 to 359,000. Green, the Republican candidate, received 172,000. In the senatorial contest, Bob won in a landslide, outpolling his Democratic and Republican opponents put together. More than half my margin of victory was provided by Socialist voters, who switched from their candidate for governor, who ran a distant fourth, to vote for me.

I note from my checkbook that my bank balance on November 6, 1934, was $342.23. As usual, I had lecture dates already booked to provide quick cash. Isen and I took a brief vacation. Then came the lectures. Then back to Madison for hearings on the state budget. Now, in December, 1934, I knew this was my only certain opportunity in politics to put into action instead of words all that I had learned. By now I knew every cog, every wheel in the government of Wisconsin. Perhaps more important, the key people—the trained, dedicated people in state service— knew that I knew, and knew me. With their help we went through the budget hearings like greased lightning.

In my previous term we had gathered a team of professionals. In the Legislature and in the Executive Department we had a group of dedicated men and women. They had brains and the energy of youth. We also had that great reservoir of knowledge in the university, which we drew on with great freedom. Each made a great contribution. Yet, all of us who worked together, in turn, must acknowledge our eternal debt to the thousands of men and women of Wisconsin who made the Progressive Movement possible.

18

WISCONSIN RECOVERY PROGRAM

. . . THE APPLICATION OF MAN'S BRAINS AND LABOR. . . .

Harold Ickes, Roosevelt's Secretary of the Interior, was a lifelong Progressive. He was aptly known as Honest Harold. He abhorred graft and corruption and was determined to administer his public works program on a level above suspicion. The public works program, with its much larger per project allocation of funds, was far sounder economically than the relief program run by Harry Hopkins, head of the Civil Works Administration (CWA). However, Ickes was so afraid of wasting money that it reached the needy only in a trickle.

An overnight change took place in the United States in the fall of 1933, when Hopkins's makeshift emergency organization began hiring people by the hundreds of thousands. A tremendous sigh of relief went up all over America as millions of dollars a day began to move out of Washington and spread over the country. One could almost hear the folks saying, "At long last, these people in Washington have found out that our pocketbooks are flat!"

However, the wasteful and ill-considered way in which Hopkins's CWA was managed could be justified only for an emergency measure used to meet a desperate situation. For this reason, Bob and I urged the President to recognize that his coming recommendations to Congress for the next program should be large enough to do a really satisfactory job. The President listened to our arguments sympathetically—at least it seemed so outwardly. It may surprise you, but in the fall of 1934 FDR was troubled about the national government's unbalanced budget. We got the impression that he would probably compromise between what people like Bob and I felt was necessary for an economically sound plan and the pressure from the budget balancers.

In politics and war there are strategy and tactics. The first is the overall, long-range plan to win a war or achieve some great goal. The second involves the steps by which the goal will be achieved. Abraham Lincoln was a master strategist. He lost his campaign against Senator Stephen A. Douglas for the latter's Senate seat in 1858, but Lincoln's strategy in that campaign was aimed at 1860; and in that year his strategy defeated Douglas and elected Lincoln to the Presidency. So, too, it was Lincoln's unerring strategy that selected as the one controlling objective of the Civil War the preservation of the Union. All other issues, all other personalities, were subordinated to that one goal.

If Lincoln is an example of the supreme strategist, Franklin Roosevelt is a superb illustration of the master tactician—the master of day-to-day maneuvering—the politician who could move successfully from one failure to another. In the end he had not achieved a great over-all objective for the simple reason that he had none. I did not fully realize at first that the President had no grasp whatever of the great economic forces at work in the world and the effect that these forces have for good or evil, for peace or war. My early impression of FDR was that of a man with a supreme confidence in himself—a confidence based on his capacity to charm and delight people by the outward warmth of his personality and his mastery of the technique of American politics. He loved power, and one not only felt that he knew how to keep it but believed that he would use it for the common good.

Early in the 1935 session of Congress, the Roosevelt administration's new relief program was introduced. It proposed an expenditure of nearly five billion dollars. The amount staggered Conservatives. It disappointed us. All one needed to do was a little arithmetic. Divide that sum by the number of unemployed and it worked out to less than one thousand dollars per man. That meant one thing: You could not hire men for constructive, wealth-creating work. There just would not be money to buy materials. Their work would have to be raking leaves or manicuring the highways, which would not generate economic growth.

Before my second inauguration, our state planning board was at work on a program of our own. That program would be based on these concepts:

Wealth is created by the application of man's brains and labor to materials on useful, constructive projects.

Many such projects are in the broad field of public works, viz., highways, streets, school buildings and equipment, and hospitals.

Others are in education, health, housing, and conservation.

Every project must eventually pay for itself and produce a profit. Never must we forget that *profit* is not a dirty word. On the contrary, it is profit that provides the seed grain for multiplying wealth—now so often referred to as the "expansion of the economy."

A substantial part of the profit in public investment is diffused through the economy. It is there—definitely. But unlike private investment, it can flow back to the investor, the public, only by taxation.

Public expenditures, so far as possible, should be made with an eye to increasing the number of employers, by keeping direct public employment decentralized. Let the work be done by the states, counties, cities, and towns. Here, too, use private contractors to the fullest extent. The grave danger to be avoided, if freedom is to remain, is the concentration of employment in too few hands, whether public or private. Soviet Russia keeps all employables at work, but there is only one employer, the state. For freedom, there must be many to choose from.

Use the tax power not only for revenue but also as a stimulus and a reward. "Harness the profit motive for desirable social and economic ends." Encourage, rather than hamper, industrial progress through rapid depreciation deductions—even, where need be, by penalties—by outlawing outmoded equipment, such as unsafe automobiles. Also, employ the Wisconsin method of rewarding industrial safety and stability of employment under workmen's and unemployment compensation methods.

What these details add up to is that government—national, state, and local—takes the necessary steps—indirectly wherever possible, but directly where necessary—to direct the flow of capital to open and keep open the perpendicular frontier: the continual "planting of the seed grain." This is what produces profits and the continual expansion of the economy.

The staff of Wisconsin's state planning board was at work on a program in keeping with these ideas. No one expected the program to be perfect. We knew that the best we could do was to put together a program of worthwhile projects which, if implemented, would enable us to end the awful business of relief for the able-bodied.

Two weeks after my inauguration in January, 1935, I went to Washington to talk over our plans with Bob and to see the President. FDR was at his cordial best. He knew practical politics from the ground up. He understood far better than almost anyone else what it meant for two brothers to move out of a major political party, help form a new one, both run on the same ticket at the same time, buck the Old Guard in both old parties, and—after all that—find the patronage power of a popular national administration arrayed against them.

The warmth of his reception for us spilled over into the press. Some persons in the governor's office expressed surprise—to which knowledgeable Tom Duncan replied: "Every good politician likes a winner—and FDR loves 'em."

In this conference we talked over the President's program for 1935. Bob emphasized that although the administration's proposed relief appropriation of nearly five billion dollars was an immense sum, it was too small to put the unemployed to real work—work that creates and multiplies wealth.

At our conference with Roosevelt, he agreed to give full and careful consideration to any program that the state of Wisconsin might submit to the federal government. He said he could not commit himself until he saw such a plan in writing. And he indicated he was not averse to allotting to Wisconsin, in a lump sum, its share of the federal relief appropriation for 1934.

So now we had a chance to put our plan into operation if the Legislature would give its approval. We proposed to assemble from each township, village, city, and county specific projects of needed, useful work that each would do if we were not in "hard times." We would then lay out a statewide program of needed, valuable, and useful projects, such as rural electrification, conservation, highways, grade crossings, and public buildings. We would thus provide useful, wealth-creating jobs for every able-bodied, unemployed person in Wisconsin.

The source of wealth is the intelligent use of energy. Since the 1930's, America has lost forever, by paying people not to work, at least three times our federal government's debt. Consider these figures: 5,000,000 unemployed, actually more than that, but we will use a minimum figure, $\times$ 8 hours $\times$ 5 days $\times$ 52 weeks $\times$ 30 years $\times$ \$1 per hour. Then add the billions of dollars we have paid these people to stay idle. The result is staggering. If you owned America—all of it—what would you do with your managers who had run your affairs in this fashion and were still doing it right now?

We planned to stop this insanity by passing legislation to create the Wisconsin Finance Corporation—plainly speaking, a state bank. It would start with \$100 million capital with the relief grant from the federal government. Towns, cities, villages, and counties would issue, on their sole initiative, bonds for their appropriate and fair share of works to be financed by the corporation. Then we would impose a modest special income surtax to get back the profit—what I called the "diffused profit"—that would inevitably arise from putting people to work. With the $100 million capital, the corporation would issue warrants—so-called to salve Treasury Secretary Henry Morgenthau's conscience. The warrants would be money. When this particular, detailed work program was completed, it would produce sufficient dollar return, profit, if you like, to enable Wisconsin to pay back to the federal government not less than 30 per cent, or $30 million, of its initial grant of $100 million.

Our plan was financially sound, as any bank would be that issued its checks for a total of $200 million backed by $100 million in cash, $100 million in municipal bonds, and sweetened by a special state income tax. There is no financial institution in the world as sound as that.

Now, in January, 1935, we had the green light from the President to produce a specific program for Wisconsin. Our staff had begun work on it a few days after the November election. That day in Washington I phoned the word to Madison: "Full speed ahead!"

By the end of April we had completed planning the program. It made up a solid volume, containing in detail specific projects throughout the state. It had its own budget spelling out how much was to be spent, how it was to be financed, and how much money would flow back into the treasury of the Wisconsin Finance Authority.

With expert legal advice, we completed a specific draft of the necessary legislation to be presented to the Wisconsin Legislature. We would be ready by May to present it to the President and his advisers. For several days we intensively checked and rechecked the Wisconsin Recovery Program as we were to submit it to the President. The final task was mine—to boil it down to one typewritten page. (FDR liked to "have it all on one page.") The result showed at a glance the total picture.

As President Roosevelt examined the one-sheet synopsis and then thumbed through the survey, one could see that he was intensely interested. We knew, however, that he would be reluctant to turn power and administrative control back to a state and its municipalities.

Harry Hopkins's old relief organization was now dressed up in a new name, Works Progress Administration. Largely because of his friendly relations with Bob, Harry took a favorable attitude toward our plan, but influential people in his organization were hostile to the idea of losing any of their administrative empire. They kept raising this and that objection. In addition, the regular Democratic organization in Wisconsin bitterly opposed the whole idea.

After hours of discussion with Harry's lawyers, and with Bob's indispensable aid, we finally got FDR's approval and his assurance that if the Wisconsin Legislature adopted the proposed bill he would turn over $100 million to the state.

We were thrilled at this opportunity for Wisconsin to demonstrate ideas that Bob and I held about the cause of the Depression and the means of ending it. Our program, if put into action, would serve as a pilot plan for the nation. If it was successful—and I had no doubt that it would be—it would become an integral part of the state's life. It could be contracted or expanded according to the needs of the times.

But as we returned to Madison, we were not under any illusions about the fight ahead in the Legislature. The vital questions would be whether we could sell the program to the people of Wisconsin, and whether they would put enough pressure on a hostile Senate to secure the adoption of the Wisconsin works program.

I was fully conscious of the terrific responsibilities that I would assume in administering such a program, but I was ready to tackle it and began to formulate plans to put it across. If I had had any doubt about the soundness of our program, it was dissipated by the ferocity of the Old Guard opposition. The smart people knew at once that we had a plan that hit at the heart of our economic difficulties. Here was a piece of economic machinery that provided people with work on wealth-producing projects instead of giving them a pittance that did little more than keep body and soul together.

Our most serious handicap was time. Both the President and Hopkins had emphasized the importance of speedy approval by the Legislature. They had pointed out that the relief program in Wisconsin would be carried out as a part of the federal administration if we did not get our plan into operation. Immediately on our return from Washington, the Wisconsin Works Bill was introduced in the Legislature and I started to work with all I had. I spent hours conferring with representatives of the state's newspapers, with organized labor, farm groups, and teachers; and finally I held hours-long conferences with members of both the Senate and the Assembly. I backed all of this up with a series of radio talks over a statewide network.

My worst enemy would never accuse me of being lazy. I never worked harder or under heavier pressure than during the weeks of that fight. When a test vote in the Senate showed we were likely to be defeated in that body, I went into a few districts and held mass meetings to gain support. As the next election would prove, the people were with us, but the Old Guard was adamant and unyielding; and the powerful daily press backed them up. The Milwaukee *Journal*, in particular, carried on a daily campaign of opposition and ridicule.

At one conference with members of the Senate, an Old Guard Democrat named Harry Bolens was at least frank. When some of his less-informed colleagues raised questions about the financial soundness of the plan, Bolens said, "Hell, this program is sound all right. The trouble with it is it's too damned sound. I'll tell you why I'm against it. If we pass this bill, we will have these LaFollettes on our hands for the next hundred years!"

The bill passed the lower house but was beaten by one vote in the Senate. It was a bitter disappointment, not just personally but because of the loss of an opportunity to do a creative and constructive job.

One factor I have not emphasized. I had only FDR's verbal commitment. I do not know to this day whether he would have fulfilled it or not. I was always certain that giving up power—turning it over to a state—went against his grain. Hence, my innermost judgment was to do everything within my legitimate power to get the Wisconsin Works Bill passed, but I did not seek to get votes by "under the table" methods. If I had it to do over again, I would not be so squeamish.

With the defeat of the Wisconsin Works Bill, we made the best of the situation under Harry Hopkins's WPA. I decided to urge the appointment of Ralph M. Immell, adjutant general of the Wisconsin National Guard, as state administrator. Ralph and I had been classmates in law school. Governor Blaine had appointed Ralph, at twenty-eight, to the lifetime civil service job of adjutant general of the guard. His appointment aroused widespread criticism (he was called the Boy General), but within a short time all criticism vanished in favor of statewide acclaim for his extraordinary gifts as an administrator.

For example, in the summer of 1931, northern Wisconsin had been swept by devastating forest fires, for which I, of course, was blamed. I called in the state Conservation Commission and read them the riot act and, appointing Ralph as a member, told them that he was the director of administration. Under Ralph's guidance, Wisconsin established a system of forest-fire protection that has no superior in the nation. The secret of reforestation is simple: keep the fires out, and nature will reforest faster and more effectively than man. With fire lanes, lookout towers, and fire apparatus, a fire is put out in the protected area of more than fifteen million acres as fast as in a metropolitan area.

Bob and I went to Harry Hopkins with our recommendation that Ralph be named administrator of the state's WPA program. Harry did not feel free to name a state administrator on his own say-so. We were recommending a permanent civil servant—not a political appointee—yet Harry said, "I'll have to check with the boss [FDR]." He did, and Ralph was appointed.

Another word about Ralph: He had served as a lieutenant of combat infantry in World War I. In 1942 he held the rank of brigadier general. In order to get active duty in World War II, he consented to being "busted" to colonel. At the end of the war he was a major general. In 1946 he resigned as adjutant general to become a candidate for governor. During this campaign I met him in Madison one day. I said, "Ralph, how is it going?" Remembering the great audiences we had talked to in the 1930's, and his rank in the war, I could sympathize with him when he replied, "Well, I'll give you an illustration. I was billed to speak at Sparta [the county seat of Monroe County] at the Courthouse

at one o'clock. When I got there, there wasn't a soul to be seen
—not one damned person. Nobody! I went down to Main Street,
played some records on my loudspeaker and finally attracted
about a dozen pensioners. They sat on cracker boxes with their
hands cupped to their ears while I tried to define the issues of
the day. Some experience for a major general!" Ralph lost his
bid for governor.

On my trip to Washington in the summer of 1935, after the
defeat of the Wisconsin works program, the President asked
Bob and me for dinner. We were the only guests, and dinner
was served in the family dining room. During the meal the
President said, "You and Bob don't know it, but there has always been a guiding hand over the Presidency of the United
States. In the heights of the Himalaya Mountains there is a special
spirit that looks out for us and sends us messages, but most come
by mail. At every critical period in our history our Presidents
receive them." I looked across the table at Bob, not knowing
whether to laugh or not, but one look at FDR stifled any
laughter. He was as sober as a judge. These remarks had new
meaning when Roosevelt named his camp at Catoctin Mountain
"Shangri-La."

After dinner, we went up to the President's study, and the
three of us talked politics. Roosevelt was still under the illusion
that his New York–Harvard–Groton social friends would support him for reelection in 1936. "Why," he said, "Bob, they have
assured me they will support me." I remember that Bob said,
"Mr. President, if you crawled to New York on your belly, they
would welcome the opportunity to kick you in the teeth." The
President was visibly shocked. He replied, "Bob, this is hard to
believe, but if you say so I must believe it." He went on to say,
"You and Phil must come up to Hyde Park so we can plan the
coming campaign."

Early in August, Bob, Zeratsky, and I went to Hyde Park.
Although Z had been very successful in the mail order business,

he had never owned a dinner jacket. Now he must have one, for we were overnight guests of the President and Mrs. Roosevelt. Z was in a dither but he purchased his one and only tuxedo and wore it with aplomb.

That visit gave me a real insight into Mrs. Roosevelt. Isen and I had called on FDR in the spring of 1932 at their New York City home. We noticed that on the second, or living room, floor folding doors connected their house and that of Mrs. James Roosevelt, FDR's mother; but at Hyde Park one really saw Eleanor Roosevelt's problem. Mrs. Roosevelt, Sr., sat at the foot of the table, with the President at the head. Eleanor Roosevelt sat at my right, and I was at the right of FDR's mother. All through the dinner, that evening, and the next day Mrs. Roosevelt, Sr., kept referring to "my house," "my servants," and "my food," expressing the hope that it was "all satisfactory." Then and there I understood the terrific difficulties under which Eleanor Roosevelt had married and lived. Her husband had never made the choice between his mother and his wife.

The next morning after breakfast, the President's wife took me for a walk to see her cottage. As she pointed it out to me she said, "One must have something of one's own." The remarkable thing about her was that with her difficulties she was able to live her own useful and creative life.

After dinner the evening we arrived, FDR took us into his small study on the ground floor. Z's eyes were glowing. He was sitting with real power now. He developed for the President his ideas for a letter campaign for the 1936 election. It would resemble the one he had undertaken for the Wisconsin Progressives in 1934. He showed the President a letter I had written and sent to the Wisconsin clergy—and if I do say so, it was a good job. Roosevelt was fascinated as his agile brain saw the possibilities in reaching people directly and, so to speak, in spite of a hostile press. He then and there authorized Z to go ahead and prepare the letter for distribution to the clergy throughout the United States. Z did so, but he pulled the only big boner of his career: he liked the letter I had written so well that he used it over again for FDR. It was almost a duplicate except that it had FDR's signature instead of mine. A Wisconsin clergyman noticed the similarity and called it to the attention of the press. This created a minor furore, but Roosevelt again demonstrated his masterly understanding of news—how simply to ignore unpleasant matters and let them die from public notice through neglect.

I think the President was at his summit during the period leading to the election of 1936. He knew he was going to win by a landslide. Harry Hopkins had pumped enough dollars into the people's pocketbooks to provide enormous relief throughout the country. Bob and I had induced the President to include farmers in the WPA program to allow them to earn money to buy feed for their livestock. So everywhere he went, the President found a grateful people. He firmly believed he had licked the Depression. Neither Bob nor I agreed with him on that point, but we did support him in 1936. Whatever reservations we had could be alibied on the grounds that his first term was an emergency period and that hasty improvisations were justified by the emergency. In this campaign there was harmony between Progressives and the Roosevelt administration. We supported him, and he gave us tacit approval. We won by a landslide.

The landslide took place in the November, 1936, general election, in which Phil won a third term. He defeated his Republican and Democratic opponents by 200,000 and 300,000 votes, respectively. The entire Progressive state ticket won. The party also gained a working control of the Legislature, including the Senate, which had blocked so much of the Governor's program in 1935. The 1936 election marked the zenith of Progressive party strength in Wisconsin. President Roosevelt also won reelection overwhelmingly.

Phil and Isen LaFollette's third child, Sherry, was born in 1936.

Immediately after the 1936 election, Isen and I followed our usual rule: "If we win, it will be a short vacation; if we lose, a long one." So we left at once for Europe. I had long wanted to visit Scandinavia, so, leaving Isen in London, I flew to Norway and Sweden. During my undergraduate days at the University of

Wisconsin, a number of students from Norway had attended the university. We became friends, and we held a real reunion in Oslo, with college songs and convivial celebration. There is no city where I felt more at home than Oslo. It was like being in Stoughton, Wisconsin, because the Norwegian faces in both places were so familiar.

A call on the Norwegian premier, Johan Nygaardsvold, brought a surprise. I began our conversation by explaining where I came from. With a broad Norwegian accent the Premier interrupted to say, "Governor, you need not tell me anything about Wisconsin or your family. As a young man I went to America and worked on the maintenance-of-way crew of the Milwaukee Railroad. I heard your father speak in North Dakota."

In Sweden, I found that this great "little" country was embarked on a near duplication of the Wisconsin works program. I asked Per Hansson, the prime minister and leader of the Social Democratic party, to explain the difference between Sweden and Germany. He said, "Whatever the reasons may be, the Versailles Treaty or what have you, Germany went into the economic crisis of the thirties backward. We went in frontside, with our eyes open. We believed we were not rich enough to pay people not to work but not so poor that we could not provide useful work for our unemployed. So we provided a plan and put our people to work."

In London we had an engagement for lunch with Sir Robert and Lady Vansittart. Van was permanent undersecretary at the Foreign Office until his opposition to Chamberlain's appeasement of Hitler ended his career. At lunch, he felt free to speak his mind. He was baffled and frustrated. The British government refused to believe its own intelligence report on what Hitler was planning. He said, "I think I'll run our Secret Service reports in the agony column [the personals column] in *The Times.* Maybe the cabinet ministers will read and believe them there."

My father, Bob, and I were often called isolationists; yet my closest friends in Europe have been people in public affairs who were looked on by American internationalists as from the "top drawer" of information and perspicacity. Whatever confidence, or confidences, they gave me was because they felt that, like themselves, I was concerned with the welfare of my own country, as they were with theirs. Behind the façade of culture, aristocracy, and social gifts was the foundation of the success of the British civil service—competence and undivided loyalty to British interests.

I talked with Vansittart only a few times, interspersed with correspondence; yet he amazed me with his frankness. His confidence was never violated. Until now I have never quoted him to anyone, aside from Isen. We spent the better part of that afternoon in November, 1936, listening while he talked of the approaching holocaust. I asked him, "Van, how can you be so frank and honest?" He replied, "Phil, it's simple. I talk with people I can trust. And equally important, I never discuss a subject on which I cannot be honest."

We left London depressed. The people we had met saw World War II coming. All the intelligent ones knew it was unnecessary and would be disastrous, but as Van again put it so well, "We are always behind events. We meet at conference; we talk and talk. When we reach a decision, we find the boat has left. We never get ahead of events to guide them. Events drag us to a disaster we should—could—but won't avoid."

19

THE GLENN FRANK CASE

". . . IT DEVELOPED INEVITABLY FROM A RIGHTEOUS INDIGNATION. . . ."

The Founding Fathers understood the importance of education to the functioning of a democracy. The Northwest Ordinance of 1787 set aside for each state-to-be in the Northwest Territory vast grants of public lands as the foundation for history's greatest effort at mass education. The appreciation—the reverence—of education was, and is, profound in American life.

Wisconsin was carved out of the Northwest Territory. The state Constitution provided for a state university and specified that the site of that institution must be at the state capital. From the beginning, the buildings that have housed the state govern- ment and the university have faced each other, just one mile apart.

My mother and father, both born in log cabins, graduated from the University of Wisconsin in 1879. It is impossible, I believe, for this generation to understand the awesome respect that my parents' generation had for a college degree and the gratitude that they felt to their state, which made it possible for people of humble birth to achieve such an education.

I write of this and what is to follow because of one of the most unpleasant, unsatisfying affairs in my public life—the decision of the university regents to terminate the presidency of Glenn Frank.

The presidents who influenced the University of Wisconsin most were John Bascom (1874–87) and Charles R. Van Hise (1903–18). In his meetings with students on Sunday evenings, Bascom introduced a theme that took root and flowered in a surprisingly large number of undergraduates: the state and its citizens were providing great opportunities for the students, and it was their bounden duty to repay this debt by good citizenship and public service in their years ahead.

Van Hise and my parents were all members of the class of 1879. In 1903 my father had been instrumental in promoting the selection of Van Hise as president of the university. In his support of his friend and classmate, father was not troubled by criticism of Van Hise for his aloofness and lack of fluency as a speaker. The controlling factors, in Dad's mind, were Van Hise's integrity and his international reputation as a scholar—in geology. Van Hise, as president of the university, proved to be an outstanding administrator.

President Van Hise died in 1918, and the regents selected Dean E. A. Birge to serve only until a new president could be found, because Birge was well along in years. My father and mother had a natural interest in who would be the new president.

John Blaine had been elected governor of Wisconsin, as we have seen, in 1920, and reelected in 1922 and 1924. The governor appoints the regents. Under the law in effect in 1925, the appointments were staggered in such a manner that a governor could appoint a majority only after he had been elected to his second term. Thus, by 1924, Governor Blaine had appointed a majority of the regents. Because Blaine was a Progressive, Dad expected that he would be consulted about a new president, not because of political considerations, but because of the lifelong interest both Mother and he had taken in the university. But he was not. Like a bolt from the blue, it was announced that the regents had selected Glenn Frank for the position.

Glenn Frank was editor-in-chief of the *Century Magazine*, a newspaper columnist, and a lecturer. My father had met him once and had summed up his impression of Frank as "shallow." After long and superficially pleasant relations with Mr. Frank, I came to share that estimate of him, and I concluded further that he had no real interest in education, that he was a woefully poor administrator, and that his prime—if not sole—interest in the University of Wisconsin was to use it as a stepping-stone to the White House.

When Mr. Frank accepted the presidency, he did so under a written agreement with the regents that he was to give up lecturing and syndicated columns and other writing except as such activities were the normal part of a university president's activities. In short, he would devote full time to his job. He was given a salary more than twice that of the governor of the state, and a lump sum for official entertainment.

In 1926, Mr. Frank appeared before the Joint Committee on Finance of the state Legislature for the first time as president of the university. His smooth, facile, public relations manner impressed the committee favorably. This, plus their desire to help a new man on a vital job, made the committee members willing to provide the funds he asked. Specifically, the 1927 Legislature gave the university an extra one million dollars a year to enable the president to weed out, as he put it, "the deadwood" in the faculty and put in new vitality.

The various departments and institutions of the state submit their recommended budgets to the governor-elect before the formal public hearings. After my election in 1930, I sent the university's budget to Theodore Kronshage of Milwaukee. He was an outstanding lawyer and had served as president of the university's board of regents. I asked him to examine the budget thoroughly.

A few days before the public hearing on the university budget, Mr. Frank phoned me and asked to have a preliminary talk with me. We arranged to meet at Maple Bluff Farm the evening before the public hearing. I invited Ted Kronshage also, and the three of us began our meeting at about seven o'clock.

Kronshage had the university budget on his lap, and strips of paper seemed to stick out from nearly every page. Over the years I have heard some, and read of many, cross-examinations; however, none surpassed Kronshage's cross-examination of Glenn Frank that night. It was devastating, calm, cold, and relentless. Kronshage went through the university budget item by item. It produced a shock. He exposed Mr. Frank—not in public, but before the three of us in that room. When it was finished, he had revealed the man, his mind, his character, his spirit—everything there—naked. It was most unpleasant, almost sickening. All this without one word that was not most proper and precisely relevant to the job of president of the university.

For more than three hours Kronshage asked questions like this: "You told the regents that Professor _____ was deadwood, that you could not fire him because he had tenure. But you promised you had tied him to a salary post. Why do I now read here in your budget, page __, line __, that you have increased his pay by two thousand dollars a year?"

Questions like this by the hour, all seeking an explanation of what the president had done with an extra million dollars a year of the people's money. When it was over, a stark fact stood out: the president, out of weakness, had put a jack under the entire university payroll and boosted it willy-nilly one million dollars a year.

On the following day Mr. Frank appeared at the public hearing in the Capitol. I had invited members of the Joint Committee on Finance to attend. It was disclosed at that hearing what Mr. Frank had done with the additional four million dollars appropriated for the university by the Legislature since 1927. Aside from one new dean and the small faculty of the new experimental college, there had been no change in the teaching or administrative staffs over which Mr. Frank had any control. The changes that had occurred between 1927 and 1930 were due to normal attrition and not to administrative action. The conclusion was inevitable: Either there was no deadwood in 1927, or the dead-wood was still there in 1930.

The four million dollars that Mr. Frank had had to spend had been parceled out among individuals and departments without careful assessment of need or value. In instance after instance Mr. Frank had increased the salaries of faculty members whom he himself had singled out as incompetent, and in many cases these men received greater increases than those he had declared competent. Equally disturbing, departments and colleges the administration had strenuously maintained in 1927 to be in dire economic need were treated less considerately than others relatively better off.

There were inequalities that savored of favoritism. Salaries of administrative officers were entirely out of line with the salaries of even the most distinguished teachers and scholars. Persons in the commissary, social, and similar divisions were enjoying salaries above that of the average full professor. Whether or not it was sound educational policy to emphasize the commercial and purely administrative functions of a university, at the expense of teaching and scholarship—whether or not such an emphasis imposed by the administration must necessarily adversely affect the morale of the teacher and scholar—the Legislature never granted the increased fund for any such purpose or on any such representation.

In 1927, and again in 1929, Frank had outlined in detail the type of educational accounting that the administrator of a state university should be prepared to submit to the taxpayers and to their responsible public officers. None of this was available in 1930, five years after he became president. As late as the budget hearings of 1936 this information was still unavailable. The president could not give, at the 1936 hearings, such basic information as the teaching load carried by the several departments and colleges.

Despite the obvious maladministration of Mr. Frank, other problems demanded first consideration in 1931—principally, the crisis in our economic life arising from the Depression.

Early in 1931, however, I did ask the university's board of

regents to meet in the executive office. I presented the facts brought out at the budget hearings on the university's administration, or lack of it. I pointed out in particular the woefully bad impression that Mr. Frank had created. I urged them to begin to act—pointing out that it was not the governor's nor the Legislature's task to run the university's affairs, but theirs. And I cautioned them that both the governor and the Legislature owed a duty to the citizens of the state to see that the regents fulfilled their responsibilities.

My remarks were ill-received by some regents. Indeed, an older man—highly respected and a Progressive—complained privately that he objected to being scolded by a youngster.

In any position of responsibility, one's values are important; but in a university president, they are especially vital. And they are more conspicuous in a smaller city like Madison. The two presidents who preceded Frank—Van Hise and Birge—were scholars with values that one associates with universities. They lived comfortably and with dignity but with no trace of ostentation. (When James Bryce, then British ambassador to Washington, visited the Van Hises, he put his shoes in the hall by his bedroom door for polishing. Because the Van Hises kept no male servant, two of their daughters took the shoes to the kitchen, where they gave them a fine polishing. Later, when Lord Bryce heard of the incident, he was reportedly a bit shocked and not amused.)

Until the Depression, the Franks' lavish style of living did not cause serious criticism, even though it was out of keeping with, and grated against the values of, most of the faculty. With the Depression came enforced cuts in salaries of all state employees, including university employees. This brought real hardship, especially to instructors, assistants, and to many in the student body. Not a few were without funds even for an adequate diet and had to count every penny.

In January, 1931, two days after my first inauguration, Isen and I reluctantly accepted a dinner invitation from the Franks on the plea that this affair for the governor had become a tradition. It was white-tie-and-tails, with more than twenty guests. Bob and his wife and Senator Blaine stayed over for it. Mrs. Frank had sent to Chicago for uniforms (black trousers, blue dress coats with brass buttons, and red vests) for her "English footmen"—who were students. All this was done, of course, at state expense. The most embarrassing moment occurred when one of the footmen brought in a cake of ice lighted from the inside and hollowed out to hold an enormous pile of Russian caviar. The footman probably had never seen such a thing—let alone handled one. He managed well enough until he reached Senator Blaine. At that point he lost his balance just enough to pour what seemed like a small Niagara of ice water down John's neck, drenching him fore and aft.

The dinner did not make a favorable impression on most of the guests, some of whom were university instructors' families and graduate students who did not have enough money to eat properly.

The budget hearings in 1934 showed that the management of the university's affairs had not improved. But I could not act at that time because of continuing preoccupation with the Depression, which took all the reserve energy I possessed. Then, early in 1936, Harold Wilkie came to my office—at his request—to talk about university matters, particularly the administration of Mr. Frank. I had appointed Wilkie to the board of regents, and he was now its president.

During his visit Harold told me, in substance, that he was convinced that Frank was unsuited to his position and that a new president was essential. I asked him if any other regents felt the same way. He replied that Daniel Grady and John Callahan felt exactly the same—"only more so." We arranged for a meeting with the three of them a few days later.

John Callahan was state superintendent of public instruction and, *ex officio*, a regent. Dan Grady was a prominent lawyer who originally had been appointed to the board by Governor Blaine. Both Callahan and Grady were friendly to our family. At the meeting, Callahan and Grady did most of the talking, and both men tore Mr. Frank's administration apart. Grady was vitriolic. Callahan was calmer but extremely firm.

After they had had their say, they discussed their next move with Harold Wilkie. Callahan said that he was going to an education meeting in Saint Louis and that Frank would be there, too. He volunteered to talk the matter over with him in confidence. Actually, all that Callahan proposed to do was to tell Frank that some of the regents were dissatisfied with his services as president and suggest that he announce that he did not want to remain as president after June. One important point should be made clear: In the American educational system, professors have tenure. They cannot be removed except for serious cause. Administrative officers—presidents, deans, etc.—have none. They can be removed at any time by their superiors, and no reasons have to be given to anyone.

Somehow, the talk between Frank and Callahan went amiss. I think it was due to Callahan's weakness. I was told by Harold Wilkie that Frank asked Callahan if he had polled the other regents. When Callahan said he had not, Frank set to work at once by telephone and continued, on his return to Madison, to "tie up" the other regents. He also charged publicly that there was a political plot against him.

The 1936 election campaign was just ahead of us. My close political advisers agreed, and I concurred, that the whole matter must wait until after the November election. We did not want to drag the university into a political campaign. To have done so would have been unfortunate for the university and stupid politics as well. You cannot argue the fitness of a university president before a million voters.

Of the fifteen regents in December, 1936, ten had been appointed by Progressive governors, but the vote on the presidency of the board in June, 1936, in which Wilkie was reelected, indicated that Frank had seven sympathizers. They included—incredibly—the same Grady and Callahan who had so vehemently denounced Mr. Frank's administration and insisted he must go.

These two had run for cover once Mr. Frank had begun his propaganda campaign.

In fact, Grady was soon leading the support for Mr. Frank among the regents—and from my firsthand knowledge, he did so without scruple and with a shocking disregard for the truth. The only explanation I can give for the conduct of Callahan and Grady is that they lacked the stamina to stand by their convictions.

After the June vote on the board's presidency showed that Callahan and Grady had taken to their heels, Regent Clough Gates of Superior, Wisconsin, teamed up with Harold Wilkie to aid him in the conduct of the Frank case. Clough, a lifelong Progressive, was a graduate of the university and took a great interest in public education.

Other than what I have mentioned here, I did not discuss any aspect of the university with any regent before or after I appointed him or her to the board. After Mr. Frank made his charges of a political plot against him, one regent, Mrs. Clara Runge, asked me who might succeed him. I pointed out that the regents alone had the authority to make that decision and that there was a large field from which to make a choice. I told her that both Bob and I would be of any help, through our wide contacts around the country, that the regents might desire.

The day before the December, 1936, meeting of the regents, Harold told me that he and Clough Gates were seeing Mr. Frank, and that they were going to advise him that they were introducing a resolution the next morning to the effect that his appointment as president not be renewed at the end of the coming semester. Harold phoned that evening, and said:

"Phil, we've just talked to Frank. He begged us not to introduce that resolution. He pleaded with us that such action would ruin his career. He promised that if we would give him a month, or at the most two months, he would resign. This would give him time to make other arrangements. So I think everything is settled very satisfactorily."

"Harold, have you got that in writing?" I asked.

"Why no, Phil. We couldn't ask that of him. He gave us his word of honor."

"Well, Harold, that is an awful mistake. You and I will pay through the nose for that. I wouldn't trust that fellow if he swore to it on a stack of Bibles. But I guess the fat's in the fire. And I have complete faith in you."

Even while Harold and I were talking, the fat was in the fire. Frank was phoning his newspaper friends in New York and elsewhere. Zona Gale, the novelist and a former regent, was in New York ringing doorbells, praising Frank and denouncing me. She had been a lifelong Progressive, and her charges of political interference by the governor carried weight in the intellectual circles there.

By the next day, the Frank Case was on the front page of daily papers across America. At the meeting of the regents on December 16, Harold made a preliminary statement of the reasons why some regents were convinced that Mr. Frank's appointment should not be renewed. Grady not only defended Frank; he also twisted the conference in the governor's office between him, Callahan, Harold, and myself. The purport of Grady's statement was that from the start I had engineered the moves to oust Frank. The implication was that my motives were bad—that he supported Frank's charge that there was a political plot against him.

The meeting was adjourned, subject to the call of President Wilkie for a formal hearing to consider further the matter of the university presidency.

Mr. Frank and his supporters conducted a vicious campaign. Isen filled two scrapbooks with clippings on the Frank Case. These, of course, covered only a small part of what was written and said on the radio in Wisconsin and all over the country. So-called liberal magazines like the *Nation* jumped into the fray to support Frank and whack at me. At the same time, the Conservative press seized the opportunity to attack Progressives in general and the LaFollettes in particular.

Some time before the Frank Case came to a head, I gave a buffet supper at the Executive Residence for the newsmen who covered the Capitol. It was purely social, but it gave them an opportunity to ask questions on an off-the-record basis. During the evening I asked them a question:

"Fellows, you follow affairs around here closely. What do you think about Glenn Frank as president of the university?"

Back like a flash and in chorus from all of them: "Fire the SOB!"

Then, as one of them told me later, "We all proceeded to write the news stories on the Frank Case exactly as our bosses told us to."

From December 16 to January 6—the date for the special board meeting—Mr. Frank tried every possible delaying tactic. His aim was to postpone the decision until the coming session of the Legislature, when the matter would be kicked around like a political football. Frank and his supporters charged that academic freedom was being infringed on. They harped on this false issue so many times that I decided to settle the matter quickly.

Some time earlier I had met President James Bryant Conant of Harvard. I sent a letter to Dr. Conant asking if he would serve on a special commission with two other persons. The two were to be a distinguished scholar from a university in another state and a justice of the Wisconsin Supreme Court.

My letter to Dr. Conant was dated December 21, and his reply came back dated December 24. In substance, he wrote that any outsider would not be competent to pass judgment on the administration of a university president. He added that after the Frank matter was decided, he would be willing to review the relationship of the regents to the state government. And he pointed out clearly that there was no issue of academic freedom involved.

The board met on January 6 and 7. Harold presented a detailed and powerful arraignment of Frank's administration. Clough Gates ably seconded him. Grady spoke for Frank, and Frank read a lengthy defense. Then, by a vote of eight to seven, the regents terminated Frank's presidency. George Sellery, dean of the College of Letters and Science, was named acting president.

There was talk of a student strike. A crowd of several hundred came pounding on the governor's door demanding to see me. I talked to them in the Assembly chamber, and they quieted down.

One intimation Frank made was that he was not in the La-Follettes' good graces because he had refused to remove Dean Sellery. The latter had signed the round robin against my father in 1918, and Frank took the position that he had "saved" Dean Sellery. This was without any foundation whatever. You will recall my father's attitude toward that round robin in his letter to Senator Henry Huber in 1923. It left scars, but the attitude of my family toward the university and its faculty on that score was "let bygones be bygones." From the time I became a member of the law faculty in 1926 until Dean Sellery's death at the age of ninety, in 1962, we were intimate friends. To charge that I was "out to get the dean" was false and malicious.

One other incident epitomizes the entire issue over Frank's administration: While the Frank Case was at white heat, I received a call one Sunday morning from Dr. Charles Slichter, the distinguished dean of the Graduate School. He had known me since my childhood, and I had grown up with his brilliant sons. He began by asking me if I was weakening under the barrage of propaganda. He added:

"Phil, you must not weaken. Frank must not remain as president. He is doing the university great damage by his mismanagement of the university's finances and his grossly ill-considered allotment of its funds between faculty members, and between colleges and departments. Do you know, Phil, if I have a secret I want to keep from Frank, do you know where I put it? I put it in my budget. I know Frank will never look there."

In the February 13, 1937, issue of the *Nation*, a letter appeared above the signature "A Faculty Wife." The writer described those aspects of the Franks' conduct that antagonized many persons in Madison. The letter then concluded:

Inevitably the Franks created a feeling throughout the state that as long as they were "sitting pretty," the rest of the world could go to. Needless to say, they were unable to make of their home anything even remotely resembling a center for the cultural enrichment of the community. . . .

So you have a picture of a community in which the LaFollettes stood for one mode of life, the Franks for another—two modes of life eternally irreconcilable and epitomizing the two warring social philosophies of shared opportunity versus special privilege which are tearing the world to pieces. The newspapers have dared to say that Governor LaFollette was jealous of Glenn Frank. That is, of course, a rank absurdity. But if the term dislike can be stretched to cover a thoroughly justified disapproval of the Franks' mode of life, I suppose one might say that the LaFollettes did dislike them as did the great majority of the university faculty and the citizens of Madison and the state of Wisconsin. However, there is nothing petty in the term used in this sense nor does it require apology, for it developed inevitably from a righteous indignation that the Franks, as heads of a great educational institution that was trying to fire Wisconsin youth with a vision of what life might be at its best, should themselves appear to have only the most superficial social and intellectual standards.

Of course, the personal attitudes of the LaFollettes and of the university faculty enter the picture only as a vivid background against which is projected Glenn Frank's indecision and evasion in handling the administrative problems of the university.

This "faculty wife" was Dorothy Walton, wife of the late chemistry professor James H. Walton.

I had refused to weaken in my position regarding Glenn Frank—but not because of stubbornness. When in public life you become involved in a struggle in which your motives are called sordid, you can never disprove the charge by words. Only actions will clear the air. The air cleared later in 1937, when Clarence Dykstra, formerly a distinguished professor at the universities of Kansas and California and at the time the city manager of Cincinnati, became president of the University of Wisconsin.

It was my brother Bob who had urged me most strongly to back the move to drop Frank at whatever cost to us personally. He strongly pointed out the importance of the university and our duty toward it. "The university will be doing its great work for centuries after we are both gone" was the way he put it. Like so many other gifted people, he had an awe for academic degrees because he had none himself. When it was "intimated" to me that perhaps the university would confer an honorary degree upon me, I suggested that they give it to Bob instead—which they did.

And it was Bob who, knowing Clarence Dykstra well—as I did not at all—asked me to call his name to Harold Wilkie's attention.

With the controversy over the university presidency settled, our opposition centered its efforts on "improving" the means of selecting the regents. The 1939 Legislature repealed the old law and then lengthened the regents' terms from six to nine years and required their appointments to be confirmed by the Senate.

The effect of this change was to build an even higher wall between the university and the State government. Even a governor twice elected by the people could not appoint a majority of the regents. This has meant that the only influence the state can have on broad educational policies is in its control of the purse strings through the Legislature and governor. This gives the state sledgehammer power where what is needed is delicate surgery.

One instance of "political interference" by the state turned out well. The Legislature passed a bill establishing courses in Polish at the university. It went entirely against my grain to sign a bill affecting the curriculum of the university. But Wisconsin has a substantial Polish population, so I signed it for "political reasons." The appropriation went to the university, and Dean Sellery established a Department of Slavic Languages. Within a few years, Wisconsin's department in that field had become one of the best in the United States. (Our son Bob majored in Russian and graduated with a distinguished academic record.)

After his dismissal as president of the University of Wisconsin, Glenn Frank, with the financial support of wealthy Republican industrialists, obtained control of Rural Progress, *a monthly magazine mailed free to two million farm families. In the magazine he attacked the Roosevelt administration's farm policies, but the publication folded in 1939 after heavy financial losses. Frank retained many admirers among businessmen and Republican political leaders, and in March, 1940, he published, under party sanction, a statement of Republican principles. The document could have triggered a Frank-for-president boom in 1940, but it didn't. After the Republican convention, Frank made his first bid for elective office, running for the Republican nomination for United States senator. A victory in the primary would pit him against the Progressive incumbent, Robert LaFollette, Jr. Then, two days before the primary election, while they hurried to attend a political rally in Green Bay, Glenn Frank and his son were killed in an automobile accident.*

20

THE
NATIONAL
PROGRESSIVES

. . . THE SATISFACTION
OF AT LEAST HAVING TRIED.

I admired the tremendous job President Roosevelt had done in the emergencies of his first term. However, I had deep reservations about him. From my point of view these reservations were confirmed by his orders to Harry Hopkins after the 1936 election to lay off the people on WPA. It seemed to me to be crass and cruel. I knew from reliable reports that thousands of these people were still in dire need.

It occurred to me that a delegation of governors might have influence with FDR. I got on the phone to Herbert Lehman, then governor of New York, and half a dozen others. We met for lunch at the White House, and it was quite a session. Governor Lehman had been induced to run for reelection as governor in 1936 at the personal behest of the President. Lehman, like the rest of us, resented the abrupt attempt to dump the relief problem in the laps of the states and municipalities. I did not have to take the lead at all. Lehman was really tough. He pounded the table, and there was fire in his and FDR's eyes.

But Roosevelt, having been elected by an enormous vote, did not feel beholden to any governor or congressman. I stayed a moment after lunch to appeal personally to the President on behalf of those in distress. He had been irritated by Governor Lehman, and the genial mask dropped as he said, "Phil, there have always been poor people; there always will be. Be practical!"

If I had had doubts before, they disappeared that moment. I knew then what I had only feared before: Roosevelt had no more real interest in the common man than a Wall Street broker. He was playing the same kind of game as Big Business, only he sought, got, and intended to keep *power*, rather than money.

Whether I was correct in my analysis or not, I concluded in December, 1936, that I would never again support him politically; he was just not aiming at the ends that Bob and I had been taught from childhood were the objectives of progressive government. This meeting with the President left no doubt in my mind that I could do nothing as a governor to solve the basic economic problem. So I decided to turn my attention to reorganizing the state government.

Under my father's tenure, Wisconsin had pioneered in establishing boards and commissions that were aimed at giving the public inexpensive, speedy relief for their grievances against the railroads and other public utilities. Thirty years later it seemed to me that these boards and commissions, as well as the administration of education and taxation, had become bureaucratized and needed to be streamlined.

No one has ever been governor of Wisconsin for more than three terms. Whatever else I might hope to accomplish for Wisconsin would almost certainly have to be done in the Legislature of 1937. As a result of the 1936 election, we had a working control of both houses but the margin in the Senate was only one or two votes. Under our parliamentary system, a determined minority can use the rules of procedure to delay action. And the Conservatives in the Senate were determined! But under Wisconsin's constitution, I had the authority to call a special session and to specify and thus limit the subjects that the Legislature could consider in the special session. After the Legislature had passed the budget and other less controversial laws, it was decided to adjourn—on a motion that cannot be blocked by interminable debate—and then to call a special session in the fall.

The call for the special session was drafted with minute care, principally by Gordon Sinykin, my intimate friend and subsequently my law partner. He typifies the best in American life—the son of an immigrant junk dealer in Madison, a Phi Beta Kappa, editor-in-chief of the *Wisconsin Law Review*, and unexcelled in knowledge of the law. The call for that session was puncture-proof. Both sides girded their loins for battle.

It seemed to me that if democracy were to survive, it had to *function*. In Wisconsin there had been talk for years about our educational system. Nearly everyone who looked at the machinery agreed that it should be changed—that is, everyone agreed until it affected his own particular bailiwick. I decided to try my hand at the job, but in order to do this—as well as to overhaul the boards and commissions that I have described—we had to have legislation. But how could we get it passed over the dilatory and delaying tactics of the Conservative minority in the Senate?

To put me on the spot, the Conservatives offered resolutions "requesting the governor to amend his call" for the special session to include old-age pension increases, etc. Their plan, it was commonly said, was to keep the Legislature in special session for months and to place the blame on me. Tom Duncan, my executive secretary, came up with the answer. I sent a message to the Legislature agreeing to amend the call if they would agree to pass a resolution fixing an adjournment date two weeks hence. They so voted.

Now we settled down into a real fight. The main issue in the special session of 1937 was my request for legislation authorizing the governor to take executive action to put the administrative house in order.

The men who wrote our national and state constitutions were wise. They knew the danger of unchecked power, and they devised our system of checks and balances between the Legislative, the Executive, and the Judiciary.

Until our time, the prime function of government was to impose rules providing that "thou shalt not. . . ." People were told, by law, that this or that was forbidden. The disappearance of the frontier, and the coming of steam and electric power revolutionized our world. A negative government was made obsolete by scientists in their laboratories and by what developed from their discoveries. We had come to a time when the Executive— the leader—must help us meet our enormous problems. To simply say No was not enough. There must be leadership. But equally important, that leadership must not be unchecked or unbridled. How could we permit the Executive to act without making him a dictator?

Where the idea came from I don't know, but it occurred to me that I could retain the basic principle of checks and balances against autocratic power while reversing in certain respects the functions of the Executive and the Legislative branches. "Let the Executive propose; let the Legislative veto." Heretofore the Executive had the power of veto. If the process were reversed, the same checks and balances would be preserved.

The Wisconsin Reorganization Bill did that. It provided that the governor, with the approval of a select committee of both houses, could issue executive orders reorganizing state agencies. These orders were to be filed with the secretary of state for presentation to the next Legislature. Either house could invalidate any order.

The problem was to put this legislation through the special session before the two-week deadline for adjournment. Our program passed the Assembly, but it was stuck in the Senate— stuck not on its merits, but by the use of the rules of parliamentary procedure to block the will of the majority. The Conservatives were sure that they could kill the bill with delaying tactics. Time was passing, and it looked as if we were going to be outmaneuvered and beaten.

It just did not seem to me possible that rules of order could countenance deliberate and willful obstruction of this kind. At two o'clock one morning, while the Senate was in session, I sent to the law library for a book on parliamentary procedure. I found a ruling by the Speaker of the United States House of Representatives which held that any motion made for the sole purpose of obstruction was in itself out of order. I showed it to the president of the Senate. He ruled accordingly. The jam was broken, the legislation was passed, and I was exhausted. But I had done what seemed to me to be right. Every daily newspaper in the state disagreed. The charges that I was a dictator were broadcast by all the Conservative newspapers and politicians in the state.

Aside from the act to reorganize the state government, Phil won passage for a number of other significant measures in the regular and special sessions of the 1937 Legislature. A state department of commerce was created to promote and assist Wisconsin business and industry. The Wisconsin Development Authority, sometimes called the Little TVA, was approved to further rural electrification and public ownership of utilities. The Wisconsin Agricultural Authority was approved with the goals of opening up new outlets for markets and raising the standards for farm produce. (After the Republicans regained power, in 1939, the Legislature scrapped all of these programs, including the Reorganization Act.)

Other 1937 legislation virtually eliminated child labor and strengthened the hand of labor unions in negotiations with management.

The governor was severely criticized for the way he handled the 1937 Legislature. Even William T. Evjue, writing in the Capital Times *(but not in the* Progressive, *which he also edited) described the conclusion of the special session as "a week in which democratic processes were abandoned and an executive dictatorship was in the saddle."*

During a visit to Costa Rica after this session, I came down with a sore throat and chills. Isen and I returned by railway down through the beautiful mountains to our ship, and that night I was really ill. When the ship docked the next morning at Colón, Panama, I was carried off on a stretcher with a temperature of 103 degrees.

At the United States military hospital, the doctors decided that I had picked up a bug called *streptococcus* hemolytic B, which has an affinity for the heart and was often fatal. But sulfa drugs were just coming into use, and I happened to be the first person on whom they were tried in that hospital. My doctor—our paths were to cross again during World War II in the Southwest Pacific—said the drug in effect turned a machine gun on the infection and that it was powerful but would require a period of rest and recuperation.

I knew I had had a close call—so close that I did a lot of thinking. From the hospital bed I could see the blue Atlantic. Its restless motion gave me perspective. After the fever left, I made plans to carry out our program for reorganizing the state government. That task I thought would not be too difficult.

However, uppermost in my mind was the question of how I could help promote an honest realignment of political parties in America, one that would unify all the Progressive forces. Nearly everyone conceded the need, but no one in a position of political leadership seemed to want to risk doing something about it. I decided that come better or worse I would try.

Isen and I have always agreed that a basic lesson of life is that the bitterest regrets are for lost opportunities—lost because of fear. If one tries and fails, he has the satisfaction of at least having tried. I have been accused of being impetuous, of "going off on my own" without taking advice. I do not think that this is accurate. A better appraisal was the comment I have noted earlier when Lady Barlow exclaimed, when I was seventeen, "My word, you *are* previous." And I have been. But my advice to those interested in a political career is that if you must choose, it is better to be ahead of the procession than behind it.

In August, 1937, Bob, Senator Alben Barkley of Kentucky, and I were weekend guests of Franklin Roosevelt on the Presidential yacht. Barkley was a fine public servant and a wonderful companion. We shared a cabin, and I shall never forget the talks we had about the mechanics of politics. He was sympathetic with my ideas about realignment but cautious, and—like so many others—inclined to go slow, that is, to ride with the tide.

Bob bore down on the President to get an expert staff to work on a basic economic program, but he did not get far. (Shortly thereafter, Roosevelt made a speech saying that the Depression was over. He said that the administration had planned it that way. When the recession of 1937 started, nobody had planned anything, and FDR, like others before and after him, turned to armaments as the way out.)

While Bob talked economics, I talked about political realignment. I suggested that we should try to get a movement started in other states as had been done in Wisconsin and Minnesota. The President was enthusiastic and said, "Go ahead!" I got the impression that Roosevelt had given up hope of liberalizing the Democratic party and was ready to go along with the realignment.

I have been in enough conferences of political leaders who met, conferred, and did nothing. I knew that if I was going to raise the issue of political realignment effectively, I would have to use some other tactic. I decided to do what my father had done—to talk to the folks and not just the politicians.

To an independent in politics, nothing is more important than his lists—names of people he can reach over the heads of hostile publishers and radio commentators. Using our lists, I called a series of meetings in the governor's office to which forty or fifty men and women at a time would come. Naturally, most were from Wisconsin, but a number came from Minnesota, Iowa, and Illinois, and a few from the eastern seaboard and the West.

Before our meetings began, I had already concluded that the essential difference between the New and Fair deals and middle western progressivism was progressive determination to make America's great productive power available to all our people instead of killing pigs and plowing under cotton. Remembering Justice Oliver Wendell Holmes's statement that men live by symbols, I sought a symbol that would tell our story—abundance with freedom. One morning my eyes fell on the license plate of the governor's automobile. It read X *1*. It hit me that if one put that X in a circle, he had the answer. The X stood for multiplication of wealth instead of less; placed in a circle, it represented American equality in the ballot box—abundance in economic life, equality and freedom at the polls.

Hundreds of people came to the conferences. I had a big black-board and drew the X in the circle and talked to that theme. I asked all who came to think the question over and to write me their considered judgment. I did not propose to form a new national party; I proposed that we form a new national organiza-tion of Progressives who *wanted* a new party. I hoped thus to bridge the gap between the Progressive officeholders and Pro-gressive-minded people—between those who thought of running for office in 1938 (and who would therefore be more skeptical about a third party) and those who were personally uninterested in public office. They were extraordinary meetings. Each was a thrilling experinece. The letters that came back were almost unanimous. I tried to interest other men in public life. Bob was in favor of my going ahead, but aside from Wisconsin Congress-man Tom Amlie the rest were as scared as rabbits.

I cannot tell you why, but our meetings attracted no news at-tention at all, nor did I expect or desire it. I saw a long struggle ahead, which would not lend itself to a splash in the news for a long time to come. In mid-April, 1938, in a further attempt to get to the people, I gave four talks over the state-owned radio station. Although the station had only a limited coverage, I wanted to use every means to give an accounting to the people of Wisconsin, and especially to our Progressive leaders, of the steps I thought we should take. To my amazement, these broad-casts caught national attention. I think they happened to come during one of those "news vacuums." During my last radio talk I announced that I would speak in the university stock pavilion a few nights later.

On a bed sheet, Isen had created our symbol, the X in a circle—to be used at the meeting. After consulting some of our associates, I took the final responsibility for using it. The day before the meeting, Madison began to fill with reporters, commentators, and photographers. On April 28 we went to the stock pavilion a few minutes before 8 P.M. As we approached the building I was astounded at the crowds moving toward the place. The building was packed with four thousand persons, and thirty-five hundred more stood outside.

The meeting was colorful, with flags and the banner Isen had made. My speech was one of my best ever. On rereading it today, it is, as I see it, essentially sound. However, in spite of this beginning, the National Progressives of America, or NPA as we called it, failed to take hold, for a number of reasons. First and foremost, as with Stafford Cripps's somewhat similar attempt to get a meaningful realignment in British politics, politicians almost to a man sensed the potential power such a movement could have. They wanted it scotched before it could get going. Also, by and large, intellectuals were against it. Many gave as their reason NPA's symbolism. For some strange reason they could accept the really meaningless Republican elephant or the Democratic donkey, but a symbol of dynamic democracy like the X in a circle they ridiculed as a "circumcised swastika."

I did not want to run for reelection in 1938. I felt, and correctly, that I had done all I could in the governorship. A job like governor or President is demanding. It draws on all one has. After six or eight years one is at the bottom of the barrel. Then, too, I still hoped I could concentrate my efforts on building NPA.

However, Progressive leaders thought the water looked cold and did not want to run for governor on our Progressive ticket. They all insisted that I run, as did Bob. But I sensed that a lot of people were tired of my strenuous pace and unending innovation and would vote for anything or anybody to get calm and quiet in the Capitol again.

I became a candidate for reelection, convinced that I would be defeated; but there are things in our kind of politics that are worse than defeat. The worst crime is to run out on your cause. With us that is not done, so I took my medicine.

LaFollette had not launched the National Progressives of America without laying his plans carefully. He talked with almost twelve hundred liberals throughout the United States. He believed that the New Deal would decline in popularity and that in any case the Democrats would revert to a pre-Rooseveltian conservatism in 1940. Phil denied White House ambitions, but virtually no one believed him. In his four radio addresses early in 1938, LaFollette characterized himself as a better administrator than President Roosevelt, with a better understanding of economics.

The rally at the stock pavilion, on April 28, 1938, drew great attention nationwide, but the excitement died within a few days. No liberal of national prominence attended the rally aside from Adolf Berle, representing Mayor LaGuardia of New York. And even Berle concluded that the cross-in-a-circle symbolism would not "go down" in the East. Bob, Jr., did not attend but sent a message of support from Washington; the Senator was not enthusiastic about the project, which undermined his friendship with the President. Bob, in fact, had opposed the plan before the April 28 rally, but he could not afford to break with Phil politically.

Several factors damaged the movement from the outset. Life magazine published a large photograph picturing Phil as a lone figure, illuminated by brilliant spotlights, with arm upraised stiffly. Other published pictures showed the massed American flags and similar trappings that troubled fair-minded persons as well as critics. Charles Backstrom, in his authoritative study of the Wisconsin Progressives, concludes that Phil believed that a massive and militant political organization could be built up "only by offering people an emotional, quasi-religious experience aroused by banners, symbols, marching, and appeals to nationalism." Many liberals, displaying their chronic skittishness, fancied that Phil was revealing a fascist mentality. LaFollette had undoubtedly been impressed by the ability of totalitarian governments to mobilize human energy. But he believed fervently—as he put it in 1939—that there would be no peace and that human liberty would never be safe so long as the Nazi regime remained in power.

Phil's keynote address at the April 28 rally was vague, intentionally so, for he disdained appeals to specific interest groups. He endorsed the idea of a strong Executive, rejected fascism and communism, and deplored scarcity economics and "coddling and spoonfeeding" of the people by the federal government. But his own prescription for action was not developed sufficiently to lure labor and farm leaders from the New Deal, in which they had invested a good deal of hope and energy during the previous seven years. Many liberal journalists feared that Phil's movement would split the liberal vote with the Roosevelt forces, opening the way for a Conservative comeback nationwide.

The new movement also suffered because LaFollette had no

*single great issue—the key to success for new political move-
ments—around which the public could be expected to rally in
great numbers.*

*Finally, the Governor suffered a serious personal loss in 1938
when his executive secretary and valued political adviser, Tom
Duncan, was imprisoned for manslaughter after his car killed a
pedestrian.*

*During the summer of 1938, LaFollette traveled across the
country endeavoring to establish National Progressive organizations. Those persons who came forward were mostly political
unknowns. Simultaneously preparing for his reelection campaign,
Phil was unable to do full justice to either task.*

*Conservatives of both old parties closed ranks to end Pro-
gressive domination of Wisconsin politics. In the 1938 gubernatorial contest, tens of thousands of Democrats supported the
Republican nominee, Julius Heil, who polled 544,000 votes to
LaFollette's 353,000. The Democratic candidate received only
78,000 votes. Phil was hurt by the "dictator" issue raised in 1937
during the special session of the Legislature, by criticism of his
role in the ouster of Glenn Frank, by disenchantment among
farmers, and—ironically—the fourth-term issue, which Franklin
Roosevelt later overcame.*

*The Wisconsin Progressives also lost the United States Senate
contest (for the seat not held by Bob, Jr.) and one third of their
strength in the Legislature. In Iowa the Progressive candidate
for governor polled fewer than 1,000 votes, and in California an
independent Progressive candidate for governor obtained only
64,000 votes out of 2.6 million cast.*

*The National Progressives of America was kept alive on paper
for a couple of years, but Roosevelt's renomination and reelection
in 1940, followed by America's entry into World War II, pre-
cluded any chance for its revival.*

21

WORLD
WAR
II

. . . POLITICAL EGGS IN
GREAT BRITAIN'S BASKET.

Isen and I sailed for Europe in January, 1939, on a trip that proved to be more revealing and exciting than any we had made theretofore.

You may well ask, "Where did the money come from for all these travels?" Our trips were paid for primarily by my writing articles. My wife and I both inherited small bequests from our respective families. Unexpectedly and from great generosity, Senator Bronson Cutting of New Mexico left Bob $50,000 and me $25,000. The basic reason, however, for our comparative financial independence has been that we have followed Benjamin Franklin's advice not to spend more than you earn. For anyone who wants to be a free person in politics, this is the first rule to obey.

By early 1939, anyone could recognize the gathering clouds of war. During our trip to Europe, I wanted to hear all I possibly could. Our chargé d'affaires in France arranged an appointment with Édouard Daladier, then premier of France. M. Daladier, received me very cordially and opened the conversation by saying that he had read the NPA speech carefully and thoroughly agreed with its basic philosophy. After discussion of the danger of approaching war, I asked him point-blank, "Sir what is your understanding of America's commitments to France if war comes?" He replied like a pistol shot, "If war comes, France expects from your country money and men in great quantities and fast." In Rome we were privileged to attend Pope Pius XI's last public audience. What a wonderful, simple, but wise man he was. His mere presence was an inspiration. But unique for me was a long talk with Monsignor Montini, the future Pope Paul VI, then an assistant secretary of state in the Church.

In the quiet seclusion of his Vatican office he talked about the world crisis. I got a sense of the great number of first-rate intelligence reports that pour into the Vatican. For more than an hour Montini gave me his view, based on that intelligence, of what was happening in Germany. He was convinced that Hitler was determined to achieve his ends by war rather than by peace. He felt that Hitler was an evil man and that if he could get the same goals by peaceful negotiations or by force of arms, he would prefer the latter. Montini painted an ominous but truthful picture of the European situation.

The stir we found in Germany was frightening. By the use of his dictatorial powers, Hitler had without question put men, materials, and work together. The fact that the primary objective was armaments and preparation for war did not alter the fact that the average man had a job and felt that he was a significant member of his community.

Isen and I were in no personal danger in Germany, but we kept looking over our shoulders to see if anyone was listening to our conversation. When I entered the apartment of the British counselor, he grabbed a pillow and placed it over the telephone. "Everything is wired," he said, "but I have found that a pillow can outsmart the Gestapo." This was February, 1939. We were not intelligence officers and had no purpose in observing military affairs in particular, but one could not fail to see the troop movements and the mounting tension everywhere.

On our return from Europe in 1936 we had met on the ship a man who was to become an intimate friend—Michael Obladen. He was the head of a large chemical firm in Hamburg and was one of the half-dozen or so leading citizens of that city. He had asked us to visit him during our 1939 trip, which we did. He met us at the station and put us up as his guests at the leading hotel, because his young wife had just presented him with a son. The Obladens entertained us at an epicurean dinner in their exquisitely appointed home, and their friends did likewise.

Michael had intimated when I talked to him over the phone that he wanted me to come to Hamburg for a mysterious and important reason. People who have never lived under a dictatorship have no appreciation of the hazards one takes in opposing the regime. I found out why Michael wanted me to come to Hamburg.

A men's luncheon was given me on board one of the Hamburg-American ships in the Hamburg harbor. The food and wine were of the best, but the point of the luncheon was not to entertain me. It was to give a high-ranking admiral in the German navy the opportunity at the close of the luncheon to say, "My aide whom you have met here today is a man of the highest integrity and trustworthiness. He would like to call on you tomorrow. I hope you will see him, listen to what he has to say, and know that you can have implicit confidence in what he tells you."

Before leaving the ship, the admiral's aide asked me for an appointment for the next morning. We set the hour, and he came to our rooms in the hotel and very seriously said, "Would you mind if we took a walk in the park?" When we entered the park, he said, "The only place one can be sure of in present-day Germany that the Gestapo can't tap one's conversations is when you're in the park."

He began our conversation by saying:

"Obladen has expressed explicit confidence in you, and he told me that he had explained to you that the least infected part of our service is the navy. We have a hundred men of rank and character who are prepared to act. We all know that we are risking not only our own lives but the lives of our families and maybe of our friends as well. We know far better than people outside of Germany what Hitler is leading to—unmitigated disaster. We are ready to take the risk.

"Our group is ready, if we have certain assurances, to seize Hitler, Göring, Goebbels, and Himmler. The only thing we are apprehensive about is that if we act, there may be an internal upheaval which France might utilize as an opportunity to invade Germany and do us great harm. Few Americans realize how bitter we Germans are over what we feel was President Wilson's betrayal of us in 1918. Germany surrendered in the last war on what we believed was the solemn assurance that the peace would be written in terms of the Fourteen Points. None of us has the slightest faith in the assurance of any politician.

"What we want is to have an outstanding naval and military officer from your country and from Great Britain to give simultaneously a radio broadcast to the armed services. I suggest that an alert be given calling all of the British and American forces to hear a 'confidential' broadcast. It has occurred to us that the speakers could be someone from Britain like Field Marshal Lord Gort, chief of the Imperial General Staff, and perhaps your Admiral Leahy. It doesn't have to be either one of these two, but it must be of their stature. What they should say, in effect, is that speaking 'on my honor as an officer and a gentleman, I am thoroughly familiar with the plans and intentions of my government. I assure you we have no intention of attacking Germany. More than that, if Germany does not act aggressively, neither Britain nor the United States will permit any other power to attack Germany.'

"We are not trying to indicate the exact form of language. What we are asking for is the solemn pledge delivered, shall I put it obliquely, to these officers in the German navy who are ready to risk their necks to save Germany and the world from the holocaust for which we are headed unless something is done.

We ask you to carry this word to responsible officers in the British government and to your President. You can assure them that the moment two such responsible military officers make the broadcast, we will act."

This was certainly the hottest potato I think I ever had dumped in my lap. Frankly, I didn't know what to do with it. Because we had our plans made to go on to Copenhagen and Stockholm, I decided to do nothing until I could think it over more carefully and perhaps get some advice. On our return from Scandinavia, we started homeward via Hamburg. I wanted another talk with Obladen to reconfirm the information I had been given a week before. He reiterated emphatically that what the naval commander had told me was completely reliable. He emphasized the point about the navy in Germany being the most independent and least Nazified service in Germany. He also pointed out that Hamburg and its vicinity had never completely lost the long tradition of the free cities of the Hanseatic League. In that section of Germany there was still a degree of independence. He told me that in the nationwide attacks on Jewish stores and synagogues during the previous November, the city least affected had been Hamburg.

Recognizing that I had no official position, I concluded that it might be dangerous to pass what I had been told to anyone in a foreign government—specifically the British government. I decided to reveal what I had learned only to President Roosevelt.

We arrived in London on March 1. On this visit I was astounded to find that aside from a few people like Vansittart, the English official world seemed unaware of what Hitler was up to on the continent. When I predicted that Hitler was headed for Czechoslovakia, most of the people I talked with were incredulous.

On March 17, Obladen came to breakfast with us during a brief visit to London. The news of Hitler's march into Czechoslovakia had come. Obladen paced the floor as he contemplated what lay ahead. He said, "I went through World War I. Twenty cousins of mine were killed. And now we are going through something even worse." His forebodings proved only too correct. Obladen survived most of the war, but near the end he lost his life.

A few days later we started for America. On arrival home I went to Washington to see Bob. He felt it vital that I tell the President about the Hamburg incident. An appointment was arranged, and Bob and I had an hour with FDR.

After the usual amenities, I reported first on my impressions of France and predicted that if all-out war came, France would collapse in six months. The President reached over and patted my knee in an avuncular fashion and said, "Bob, Phil is a nice fellow, but he just doesn't know what he's talking about when he makes that kind of a prediction."

I then gave him a detailed report of my experience in Hamburg. I told him that some German naval officers were ready to strike at Hitler and his inner circle if they could have assurances from appropriate American and British service officers that those countries had no intention of attacking Germany. I emphasized that no pledge by either American or British political leaders would have the slightest effect. The President at once said, "By Jove, that's a good idea. I can speak German and could make that radio broadcast myself." Nothing ever came of it. Perhaps Roosevelt thought the idea impractical or too dangerous. In any event, it has always seemed tragic to me that no attempt was made during the late thirties to support anti-Nazi elements in Germany.

Harold C. Deutsch, author of The Conspiracy Against Hitler in the Twilight War, *very generously made inquiries in Europe concerning the preceding episode while continuing his own investigation into the anti-Nazi plots. He believes that the German admiral who spoke to LaFollette was almost certainly Wilhelm Canaris, head of counterespionage in the German armed forces but in fact an opponent of the Nazi regime. Eventually exposed, Canaris was executed in April 1945. The research of Professor Deutsch and other scholars supports the conclusion that the German army, rather than the navy, was the source of most opposition to Hitler.*

After we left the White House, Bob and I returned to his office for a long talk. Both of us were convinced that war in

Europe was imminent. We were sure that terrific pressure would be brought to bear on the United States to get into it. Both of us agreed that it was going to be more difficult to prevent America from becoming involved in the coming war than it was in 1917. During World War I, President Wilson resisted the war pressure for three years. Bob and I felt that instead of resisting war pressure FDR might well be the astute and skillful leader for American intervention.

I came back to Madison and went to work to build up my law practice. In the next three years, for the first time in my life, I began to earn substantial fees. World War II began in September, 1939. We had kept an NPA headquarters in Madison, and Isen assumed many of the day-to-day details of that operation, but we both knew that if America became involved in World War II it would end—at least for a long period—any hope of political realignment. And so it proved.

As the storm in Europe intensified, many Americans felt it would be disastrous for America to become involved. General Robert E. Wood, chairman of the board of Sears, Roebuck, and Company, with a long and distinguished career in the army and in business, had the moral courage in 1940 to accept the chairmanship of the America First Committee. In retrospect it seems strange that decent American citizens should have been vilified for the simple fact that they believed and advocated that the prime concern of the American government should be the welfare of the American people first and not secondarily. I was not a member of the committee, but I did what I could by speeches, editorials in the *Progressive,* and on radio to oppose the Roosevelt administration's program of giving aid to Britain "short of war." I felt certain that this policy would draw us into the war.

As you will recall, I saw World War I break out in England in August, 1914. Now, I kept thinking of the warnings my father had given in 1917. I remembered, too, how I had gone in doubt to him for counsel. Like so many millions I was moved and impressed with President Wilson's idealistic Fourteen Points. My father said to me, "Whatever sugarcoating anyone tries to put on this war it is still basically imperialistic. I can't prove it, but I am as sure as I sit here that our so-called Allies have made the same kind of secret deals that have dotted European history for a thousand years. And mark my words: I may not live to see it but you will. This war will be followed by one of the worst economic collapses in history. The cost in lives and money will have been stupendous, but instead of the world being 'made safe for democracy' the whole ghastly business will sow the seeds for another and perhaps worse world war to follow."

Out of these lessons I compared the misfortunes of Woodrow Wilson and Franklin Roosevelt and wrote on August 23, 1941: "Wilson and Roosevelt each strove to unseat economic tyrants here in the United States. One called his campaign 'The New Freedom'; the other, the 'New Deal.' Each achieved a substantial measure of reform. Both were dismally defeated in their attempt to restore economic freedom to the common people and ended with their administrations controlled by their former enemies. Having failed to defeat the enemies of democracy in America, each undertook to do in the world what they could not achieve at home."

After the 1937 economic recession President Roosevelt began to turn his interest and attention from the problems at home to those of world affairs. Frank Knox, the Republican Vice-Presidential candidate in 1936 and later secretary of the navy in FDR's war cabinet, once said to me, "The President told me when I saw him in Washington the other day that the only thing that absorbed his interest was international affairs."

Churchill himself is candid in his magnificent volumes on World War II. He states unequivocally that when Britain won the air battle against the Luftwaffe in September, 1940, she was free from any real danger of an invasion by the Germans. All the propaganda poured out on the American people that the United States was in effect "hiding behind the safety of the British fleet" was false. The commitments that FDR made by in effect underwriting the "unconditional surrender" by Germany, rather than just the defense of Britain, deprived him of his political maneuverability on his own domestic front. He had put all his political eggs in Great Britain's basket.

Sentiment for a negotiated peace increased in Great Britain. Understandably, many people in Britain did not relish the idea of trying to conquer Nazi Germany on their own. This put political pressure on Churchill, and with that mastery which built the British Empire, Churchill deflected the pressure to Roosevelt. Churchill was in a position to put pressure on the President because the latter had committed *his* political fortunes in American politics on the success of the Allied victory in Europe.

In the summer of 1941, when the President and Churchill met and formulated the principles known as the Atlantic Charter, I wrote, "Mr. Roosevelt and Mr. Churchill talked about peace aims. Obviously Mr. Roosevelt could not commit himself in writing as to peace aims, *without having committed himself first on war aims.* Since all of the latter were 'secret covenants, secretly arrived at,' we can only conclude we are to learn about them after they have happened. . . . Unless I am greatly mistaken the British understand better than Mr. Roosevelt the situation he is in. They know his New Deal domestic program collapsed in 1937 and that he himself abandoned it as a dead cat in 1938."

On November, 1, 1941, speaking in Washington, I explained why I so strongly opposed Mr. Roosevelt's foreign policy. I recalled a powerful speech five years previously in which he pointed out with contempt how bankrupt leadership in Europe turned toward war as a desperate and fatal release from the problems they had been unable to solve at home. In that speech Roosevelt gave America his deep determination that we should never follow that treacherous course but would go forward courageously to find real answers to the problems of our people.

As I saw our involvement in World War II coming nearer and nearer, I stated publicly a number of times that I would go back into the army if I was acceptable. I also said that I was confident that many who vociferously supported the President's policy would find convenient pretexts for themselves and their sons to stay at home. I told Isen that it seemed important for me—as well as for Bob III if his time came, as it did—to share the experience that a gigantic upheaval such as World War II would mean to our generation.

As a small child, I had spent my summers on my maternal grandparents' farm. We came from a farming background as far back as we know anything about the family. I had always been crazy to buy a farm. Isen, on the other hand, came from a family of schoolteachers who lived in the city. As I began to earn a fairly good income, Isen somewhat reluctantly agreed to our buying a farm. She laid down this condition, however: "It will be okay with me if you buy a farm, but on one understanding. You are to take full and sole responsibility for it, and I am to have none!" So we bought two hundred acres of beautiful farmland twenty miles north of Madison. Getting the machinery and livestock seemed to me like a race with an approaching tornado. I knew that with the outbreak of war, all sorts of restrictions would be on, and if we were to get the farm operating properly, we would have to move fast.

I had been out buying cattle when I came back to our Madison home on December 7. I walked into the house, and Isen told me of the attack on Pearl Harbor. Even as sure as we had been of the inevitable coming of war to America, it was nevertheless a shock when and the way it came.

With Isen's knowledge and consent, I wrote a longhand letter to the chief of staff of the army tendering my services. Because I had been a second lieutenant of infantry in World War I, I requested assignment to that branch of the service. A few days later I received a mimeographed form recommending that I apply for a local civilian defense job in my home community. A couple of weeks later I received an offer of a commission as captain in the Military Police. That was something of a jolt and quite a comedown for a fellow who was forty-four years old and who had been commander-in-chief of the Wisconsin National Guard for six years. But I decided that I was committed and so accepted.

On March 15, 1942, a War Department telegram ordered me to active duty on the twenty-eighth of that month. Isen went with me on that date when I reported for assignment. I was in uniform now, and Isen, who really hates the destructiveness and futility of war, said with the utmost seriousness, "You are now dressed fit to kill!" It was really hard on her, but we had made the decision, and there was no turning back.

Mrs. LaFollette describes how the coming of war touched her life:

We had talked the matter out, and as accurately as I can recall our reasoning then, Phil pretty well foresaw the dislocations that the war would bring and felt that he wanted to be a part of the experience rather than sit on the sidelines. Whether or not he returned to politics, he wanted to share the experience of the mass of American men and take his chances along with the rest. I had long recognized that Phil got his satisfaction in *doing* and would be miserable trying to practice law, divorced from any political activity, which was out for the period of the war.

Did you ever have the sensation that what was happening simply could not be happening to you? From the time the army called Phil, I was in a daze. I had always loathed war; had belonged to the Women's International League for Peace and Freedom, of which Belle Case LaFollette had been a pioneer; and had lobbied for various peace proposals, including the International Court. I could not bear uniforms even though they "did things" for many men's appearances, and even resented my blood's pounding at the strain of a military band.

When Phil asked me to help him pin on his insignia properly (that sort of detail has always irked him, and I was amazed to see him using a measure to get them in the exact spot required), I could hardly force myself to do it. The worst point came when I went to Washington to visit him and found that he had volunteered for overseas service and would be leaving shortly. We were staying that weekend with my sister Lois in a broiling Washington July, and I was literally nauseated, while lying wakeful in the early morning, on seeing the shadow of Phil's battle helmet hanging on the chair, his overseas equipment spread about the room, and—as he turned restlessly in bed—his "dog tags," which clinked ominously. "It simply isn't true!" I muttered fiercely, then desolately.

Phil's sister Mary later asked me, in a spirit of sympathetic understanding, if I didn't think my wartime columns in the *Progressive* revealed that I was suffering—with the implication that this was a questionable tenor for that period. I replied that of course this was true but that I was expressing the feelings of millions of women who were enduring the same agony. That my column served as a vicarious outlet for many women during the war period was testified to by the many letters I received. Women I had never seen wrote me as a dear friend and sister caught in the same trap as themselves.

My hardest personal adjustment was to settle into a prosaic routine after eighteen years of living with a human dynamo. With all the ups and downs, the trials and errors, and the poundings and lickings, there was "never a dull moment." As the years dashed by, Phil and I had often spoken of what is probably our strongest bond—the attitude that life is given us to use. Although the specialists would probably put it down to glands, I know that his father's life and death had a profound influence on Phil. Father and son shared the belief that one must use all of one's powers so that when he comes to the end he will feel like an athlete who has run his race.

LaFollette's career in the Military Police was short-lived. Through a Wisconsin acquaintance at General MacArthur's headquarters, Phil was assigned to MacArthur's staff as a public relations officer. LaFollette wrote an extensive account of his wartime experiences, much of it based on firsthand observation in the combat zones. Because this material is not germane to the main themes developed elsewhere in this memoir, it has been omitted here. However, his impressions of MacArthur are of greater interest, and some of those impressions are extracted below:

From October, 1942, until June, 1945, I served under Douglas MacArthur. In those thirty months I came to know him well. Perhaps my own long background in public affairs helped me to assess him with something of the objectivity that he himself used to evaluate individuals, situations, and problems crossing his line of vision.

Early in life he was convinced that he was destined to play a commanding role in his generation. He was the son of a distinguished general, Arthur MacArthur, and a doting and imperious mother. He was tall, lean, athletic, with great reserves of physical and nervous energy. He was endowed with a first-class mind, which he enriched with prodigious reading and study. And all was dominated by a will of iron.

But there was a serious flaw in this otherwise almost perfect combination of human qualities. He had no humility and hence no saving grace of a sense of humor. He could never laugh at himself—never admit mistakes or defeats. When these occurred they were never admitted, and he resorted to tricks—sometimes sly, childlike attempts—to cover up.

This petty but understandable trait of wanting to be perfect, to ignore his obvious warts—warts that were insignificant against his towering intellect, superb courage, and inflexible will—became important only because they were denied. That denial convinced his detractors that they could prove the whole structure itself to be only a façade. How mistaken they were!

MacArthur was before all else an intellectual. His scholastic record at West Point has never been surpassed. His chosen field was the military, where his colleagues were never his mental equals. Except for those periods when his military service brought him into contact with civilians, MacArthur never had the benefit of daily rubbing of mental elbows with his intellectual equals—let alone his superiors.

His mind was a beautiful piece of almost perfect machinery. The surprising thing was that he kept it running so perfectly, stimulated almost exclusively by reading. In books he found minds and problems that really challenged him. Rarely was he put to his mettle by other mortals. And when he was—if in his own military field—he was superb, dazzling.

Early in the war I listened to him address General Edwin F. Harding:

"Harding, you will be on your way in a matter of hours. You will make history. You command our first offense against the Japanese. Here and now I begin a campaign of movement—where speed and tactical surprise and superior strategy will demonstrate again how generalship can win with lightning strategic strokes against potentially overwhelming forces.

"The Japanese have superiority on land, sea, and in the air through all of Asia. We start this offense in New Guinea. With less than one infantry division and a handful of airplanes we are starting on the road to Tokyo. We shall redeem the disgrace of Pearl Harbor. We shall drive the Japanese to their knees, and we shall do it by master strategy. We shall turn the jungle into a weapon to fight for us. We shall hit them where they ain't and by taking key points for our ever advancing airfields we shall interdict their forces, cut their lines of supply, and leave them to rot in the jungles behind us.

"When I commanded the Forty-Second Division in World War I, I saw both sides fling millions of men to their slaughter in the stupidity of trench warfare.

"I made up my mind then that when I commanded in the next war, as I knew I would, that I would use my brains instead of the blood and guts of my men. So, on with you and your gallant men. God be with you!"

MacArthur's greatest problem was to get the manpower and the weapons for the war against the Japanese. He had to defer to the prior claims of the war against the Germans and to the powerful demands of the American navy—so much closer to President Roosevelt's elbow than MacArthur, far away in the Southwest Pacific.

The most accurate, penetrating criticism of MacArthur that I have ever heard came from some members of his staff. But during the war they spoke only among themselves. The loyalty MacArthur got from his staff was rooted in profound respect for his military capacities. One felt supremely confident that one was working for a man who knew his business. Perhaps the members of a great orchestra felt the same way toward Toscanini.

22

AN ERA
ENDS

. . . A POLITICAL BLUNDER
OF THE FIRST ORDER.

In the summer of 1945 I reported to Fort Sheridan, Illinois, for discharge, and because I had accrued so much unused leave, my terminal orders sent me home to Madison still on army pay and status until September 5, 1945. I was now to go through that excruciatingly difficult period called reconversion.

Isen and I went to a summer resort at Green Lake, Wisconsin, for the first holiday we had had together in more than three years. I remember that after a nap one afternoon I suddenly got up, and although my terminal leave was not yet over I said to Isen, "The war is over and I have to face getting back into civilian life. As soon as we get back to Madison, this uniform comes off."

I had severed connections with my old law firm in 1942 when I entered the service. My first job was literally to find a place to hang my legal shingle. While waiting for office space, I sat around the house reading newspapers. At long last I found two small offices and a waiting room in the building where I had had an office before. Then I searched for a competent secretary. Finally, I began the wait for clients.

In the professions such as law, medicine, and engineering, advertising for business is verboten. Congress attempted to preserve the reemployment rights of GIs by requiring employers to rehire returning veterans in their old jobs. No such legislation was, or could have been, enacted to restore to a returning doctor his patients or to a lawyer his clients. One had to sit and wait.

Few persons realize the difficulty in building back a law practice for one who has been fairly prominent. People hesitate to bring such a person small matters such as deeds, contracts, and mortgages. And after an absence of three years—especially at age forty-eight—one finds that the more important and lucrative practice has been weaned away and gone to those who for one reason or another stayed home from the war.

Fortunately for my family and me, two or three of my old and substantial clients came back. Enough money came in each month to pay the bills. But what was hard was not having enough to do. Nature endowed me with an abundance of energy, and during the first two years after my release from the army my biggest cross to bear was not having a constructive outlet for it. Day after day I went to the office to do the work that was at hand, but it did not absorb a third of my time. The balance of each day I filled by reading the law reports that had been printed while I was away and the daily newspapers from cover to cover. Many old friends—personal and political—called to welcome me home, but they did not bring legal business, glad as I was to see them.

A lesson that has been deeply impressed on me is that one has no control over the cards that are dealt. You do have control over how you play them. And above all, if one avenue of your life is closed, you must find a new route, even if it is not a paved highway of your own choosing. In this difficult period for me it was a blessing that my old Redpath lecture connections opened up and came back much faster than the law practice.

Reconversion problems were not unique with me. I doubt if many who had had any considerable service found civilian life easy at first. During the period of adjustment, many of us drank too much. It was not that one had any craving for alcohol. It was simply that it seemed to help ease the painful adjustments.

Shortly after I got back to Madison, Isen and I went to a cocktail party attended largely by university faculty. It hit me like a dose of cold water to hear some of these people, who had never heard a gun go off, pontificating that Emperor Hirohito should be prosecuted as a war criminal. Those who knew the situation recognized that we were pursuing a wise policy in Japan. I made the mistake of trying to argue the point. I repeated the same mistake on other occasions until I learned of the gap between those who had been a part of this tremendous upheaval and those who had been mere observers.

I do not need to emphasize the horrors or the waste of war. About the only thing of value that comes out of a holocaust like that is the lasting comradeship with men with whom one served. When you get into a combat zone, most of the undesirables have for one reason or another been left behind. Common danger brings out the best in most people. You form relationships that last through life. When I was a youngster, the Grand Army of the Republic was still holding reunions. It seemed strange to me that old men could still be reliving the Civil War fifty years afterwards. It doesn't seem strange to me now. Every time friends from the Pacific days come to Madison we get together to chin about our common experiences. At the drop of a hat I make for my collection of photographs of the Pacific War.

After 1938, the Wisconsin Progressive party declined steadily. Bob had always relied on Phil to handle state political affairs, but the latter did not assert leadership after his defeat for reelection. No one filled the vacuum, least of all Bob, who was tied down by lengthy sessions of the Senate and who was disinclined to involve himself in local politics in any case. Bob opposed measures in the Senate that he feared would lead to American involvement in World War II. Nonetheless he supported President Roosevelt for reelection in 1940, and in that same year he was elected to the Senate for the fourth time, but only by a margin of fifty thousand votes. Still only forty-five years old, Bob was now one of the senior members of the Senate, and although he was not affiliated with either major party, he was influential and effective in that body.

Bob's attitude toward wartime politics is suggested by a letter to his brother in March, 1942. He said that he would "fight a rear guard action against reactionary measures even though it is unpopular and may lick me in 1946. Being in this mood my present feeling is that if our fellows jump into the Republican or Democratic parties I shall just stay out of the 1942 campaign. I am not in the mood to try and persuade anyone against his judgement to follow any particular course at this time. . . . Life is too short and the future too obscure to put me in any frame of mind where I want to tell others what to do. I shall take whatever satisfaction can be extracted from hell on earth by trying to do what seems right for myself."

Bob disapproved of Phil's decision to enter the service and abandon the Wisconsin Progressive cause for the duration. Phil, for his part, wrote Bob in 1943 that *"year after year has gone by and you have gotten further and further away from your constituents."*

Former state Attorney General Orland Loomis, a Progressive, was elected governor in 1942. His victory was due primarily to the unpopularity of the incumbent, Julius Heil. After the election, Loomis considered himself the leader of the Wisconsin Progressives, and he planned to lead them back into the Republican party in 1944. However, he died in December, 1942, before his inauguration. In 1944 the Progressive candidate for the Senate polled only 6 per cent of the vote, and the party elected only five of one hundred members of the Assembly.

Bob was up for reelection in 1946. The Progressive party was still on the ballot in Wisconsin, but many of Bob's advisers were urging him to run for reelection as a Republican. The division in the country as a whole over American foreign policy was reflected in the Progressive party in Wisconsin. My views on MacArthur in 1946 were again "previous." Some of Bob's friends felt that my lectures praising MacArthur's work in Japan were hurting Bob.

I was deeply concerned about Bob's reelection. I wanted to do anything that lay within my power to help him succeed and above all to do nothing that would injure his prospects. Although I felt confident that my judgment about MacArthur was correct, I decided to cease accepting speaking dates in Wisconsin and to speak only outside the state.

Those of Bob's friends who felt he should run as a Republican called a meeting of Progressive leaders at Portage, Wisconsin. I found that among these leaders I was no "returned war hero." On the contrary, they looked on me as what they called a "controversial figure." They felt—I am sure sincerely—that Bob would be reelected on the basis of his outstanding record. Like my father's advisers in 1922, they urged that no controversial issues be raised.

I was never in a more difficult personal political position. This conference was called to disband the Progressive party that I had helped form in 1934. I felt deeply that what was being proposed was a political blunder of the first order. But Bob was the candidate, not I. Bob's principal advisers were sanguine that the convention at Portage would vote overwhelmingly to disband the party. I was not invited to attend; and then, I guess, to safeguard against my causing any disruption to their plans for burying the party, I was formally advised that I could attend the convention if I desired, providing it was understood that I would not participate or speak. I did not know what to do. If I appeared and spoke my convictions, I was reasonably sure the convention would not vote for disbandment. Yet I had been away from Wisconsin for more than three years. I knew there was a good chance that this long absence had deprived me of the "feel of the situation" that is essential to sound judgment.

To go against the judgment of many of Bob's close political friends and to take a course that they felt would hazard his reelection could be done only with the positive certainty that one was right.

The outcome of the convention at Portage was not a foregone conclusion. As it turned out, the rank and file knew better than some of Bob's friends. Instead of Bob's being able to sit on the sidelines while the convention took its action, he had to come out openly and forcefully in favor of returning to the Republican party. But even after he spoke, a strong minority opposed returning to the Republican fold.

After the convention voted to disband the Progressive party, Bob ran for the Republican nomination and lost. He was defeated for a number of reasons. First of all, he was caught in the same squeeze that I was in 1932. Thousands of liberal Democrats were over in the Democratic primary. (Most of these would have voted for Bob in the November general election if he had been on the Progressive ballot; they could split their ticket and vote for him.) Wisconsin has an open primary only to the extent that any voter may select the ballot of any party. So Democrats could have taken a Republican ballot and voted for Bob. No doubt some did, but many did not wish to pass up the opportunity to vote in the contested races on the Democratic primary ballot. Many of these fine and sincere liberal Democrats were horrified to find that their failure to vote in the Republican primary for Bob had defeated him and given us in Wisconsin a man known as Joe McCarthy. The day after the primary, the wife of one liberal Democratic candidate—who didn't himself have a chance of election in November—came to Isen with tears in her eyes over Bob's defeat.

Bob bore a share of the blame for his defeat. He never relished campaigning, yet ironically when he did take to the stump he always did a splendid job. A few years ago I ran into former Senator Henry Fountain Ashurst of Arizona. I said to him, "You remind me of Bob." He said, "What do you mean?" I replied, "You were both beaten for the same reason." When asked, "What was that?" I said, "You didn't come home and campaign."

A gleam of humor came over Ashurst's face as he said, "My Lord, how right you are! My opponent went up and down the state speaking to what audiences he could attract. He never said an unkind word about me, but how devastating his attack was! To his audiences he would say something like this: 'Senator Ashurst is not only a big man physically, but he's a big statesman. How many of you in this audience have ever seen him?'" Ashurst said, "You know, Phil, he didn't find a handful who had seen me. He would then go on along this line: 'If you haven't seen our able and distinguished senator, let me tell you about him. He thinks in broad international lines. When Congress adjourns, he goes to China or the Middle East, or to Europe or South America. He is a great expert on the affairs of the world. I do not want your votes under any misapprehension. I am not an authority on international affairs. If you elect me, all I can do is to come back here to Arizona when Congress adjourns and talk with you about your problems here at home.'" Then Ashurst added, with good humor, "He licked the boots off me."

Communist-infiltrated labor unions delivered the coup de grace to Bob. In a memorable speech in the Senate, on May 31, 1945, Bob had been the first outstanding American official to warn the American public about Soviet Russia's plans. He foresaw and warned against the appeasement of Soviet Russia that led to Korea. The Communist leadership sent out orders to "Get Bob LaFollette in the coming Wisconsin election."

The combination of these factors caused Bob's defeat by a mere five thousand votes. In 1892 my father was defeated for reelection to the House of Representatives by overconfidence. He learned a lesson that he never again violated in his political career. If one wants to be in public life—especially as a leader in Progressive government—he must never neglect his home fences. For an elective official the source of his strength and influence is the support of his electorate.

As affairs have taken me around the country in the past years I have been repeatedly asked, "What has become of you LaFollettes and the great Wisconsin tradition? Why aren't you and Bob in there fighting?" In justice to Bob, it should be known that in 1948 he had a severe heart attack. A similar heart affliction killed our father. It hit Bob at a comparatively young age and was probably induced by the two long illnesses that put such a terrific strain on his heart when he was a college student. It was his view that his physical condition forever barred him from further active participation in politics.

The meeting at Portage in 1946 to disband the Progressive party was sharply divided, as Phil has indicated. Bob was concerned that if Phil attended and spoke he might persuade a majority of the delegates to keep the Progressive party alive. At Bob's insistence Gordon Sinykin, Phil's longtime friend and law partner, phoned Phil from Portage and urged him not to come to the meeting. In his own address to the delegates, Bob pointed out that recent election returns indicated that the Progressive party could no longer serve as a vehicle for advancing Progressive principles. He discounted the Wisconsin Democratic party as weak and reactionary, but even after his appeal, one third of the delegates voted against returning to the Republican party.

In the summer of 1946, Bob was leading the successful fight for the Congressional Reorganization Act of 1946, which streamlined the operation of the Senate and House. He cited his work on this bill as an excuse for not returning to Wisconsin for the Republican primary contest. He campaigned for only a week. To be sure, few observers expected that his opponent, Circuit Judge (and ex-Marine) Joseph R. McCarthy, would make a good showing.

The role played by Wisconsin Communists in the primary election is still in dispute. They had been angered by Bob's speech criticizing Russia. Though few in number, they dominated the Wisconsin CIO and used the CIO newspaper to denounce LaFollette, one of the best friends labor ever had in Congress. McCarthy, whose victory with Communist support was to prove ironic indeed, defeated LaFollette by 208,000 to 202,500.

In retrospect, the voters in Wisconsin's Republican primary in 1946 may have made the worst choice ever made in any free election anywhere. They ended the LaFollette era in Wisconsin politics and simultaneously unleashed one of the most cruel demagogues that the United States has ever known.

After his defeat, Bob remained in Washington, serving as an economic consultant to private industry. He declined invitations from President Truman to serve in his administration, and he showed no interest in trying for a political comeback. In his Washington, D.C., home, on February 24, 1953, at the age of fifty-seven, Robert LaFollette, Jr., tired, discouraged, and ill, shot himself fatally.

For reasons that are somewhat complicated, I did not reenter elective politics. I have spent some fourteen years in various forms of public service. If one is honest—and our enemies concede that of the LaFollettes—one cannot accumulate much personal wealth in such employment. Our children were growing, and I think a husband should provide enough of an estate so that his wife is not dependent on others when he dies. The difficult experience that I had at age forty-eight in starting again in the law practice almost from scratch deeply impressed me with the fact that I would find it well-nigh impossible to rebuild it if I scrapped it for a fourth time. But the controlling reason for my decision not to go back into politics as a candidate for public office was the simple matter of age.

In our kind of politics the substitute for large campaign contributions and newspaper support is, as I have said before, shoe leather and brains. This requires the physical capacity to spend the time and energy to earn one's living and then on top of that to cover a state like Wisconsin, with its 55,000 square miles of territory, with speeches, conferences, and individual interviews in and out of campaigns the year round. In my twenties and thirties I could do both with what seemed like comparative ease. As one gets into his fifties, such a program becomes much more difficult.

I decided that whenever I saw an opportunity to participate in public affairs on the side that I believed right—not as a candidate but as a private citizen—I would do so.

I was sorely tempted to accept an appointment offered to me in 1948. Isen and I had driven up to a beautiful lake near Kenora, Ontario. We had been there only a few days when an urgent message came from Secretary of War Kenneth Royall to come at once to Washington.

In Washington, Royall told me that General Lucius Clay, then military governor of our zone of occupied Germany, was desperately anxious to get one or two Americans trained in civil administration to serve under him. He said, "I don't expect you to make the decision here. What General Clay and I would like is to have you go to Germany, talk with him, and see the situation for yourself."

A few days later I left by plane for Frankfurt and reported

to General Clay. He said he hoped I would accept the appointment as military governor of Bavaria, the largest and most difficult state under his authority. He suggested that if I would accept, I should first spend a few months as governor of Würtemberg-Baden, to enable me to get the feel of the situation in Germany.

General Clay's offer was, I think, the most tempting challenge I ever had. There was so much that could be done. But I was deterred by two factors. The first one was the matter of expenses. The then military governor of Würtemberg-Baden, a man of large wealth, told me that his grocery bill for feeding and wining "visiting firemen" was running to about four hundred dollars a month. The total salary for the job was only ten thousand dollars a year. But the deciding factor was the question of whether one's authority would equal his responsibility. I had no question about the full backing from General Clay, but what about the White House?

On my return, I saw Secretary of State George Marshall. He was most desirous that I accept. But having had my fingers burned a few times in politics, I thought I had better talk, before making my final decision, with President Truman. For some reason his engagement secretary failed to make an appointment for me. That settled the question. I was not going to throw away another law practice and, above all, get out on a political limb such as that type of assignment would involve in Germany at that period without the backing of the President.

In the Wisconsin Presidential preference primary of 1948, I supported delegates pledged to General MacArthur. In 1952, as a private citizen, I hired my own radio time to speak for General Eisenhower after he was nominated. He carried Wisconsin, winning more than 60 per cent of the vote. He did so because all factions in the Republican party were united behind him.

EPILOGUE

James Bryce points out in his *Modern Democracies* the important role that the states played in American development. In the past and, to a limited extent, within my time, a single state could grapple with an economic or social problem. If successful, the experiment tried in one state could set an example for the rest of the nation. No state pioneered more successfully than Wisconsin. The New Deal, with its concentration of power and administration in Washington, unquestionably limited and may possibly have destroyed this unique feature of the American political system.

It is a commentary on our age that every time that world peace appears possible, the stock market, farm prices, and business indexes drop. They do so because we have not as yet devised any financial techniques for supplying the expanding economic frontier that the free lands of the West gave our preceding generations.

Most Conservatives have forgotten that the homesteads that our forefathers took up on the expanding western frontier were *free:* they were grants of capital, land, given by the government to those willing and able to apply their native energy and intelligence to develop them. Nothing so clearly distinguished American life than the difference between the "grubstake," providing an opportunity to do something for one's self, and the "handout," living on something for nothing.

Some people who took up frontier homesteads lost them through mismanagement, laziness, or dissipation. But the high standard of living that has been built in America comes primarily from the fact that the vast percentage of men and women in this country are industrious, intelligent, and thrifty. Pessimists who think that human nature has changed in a generation do not know their anthropology. The traits of character that developed the frontier have not changed. Physical conditions have changed. There is no more free land.

It did not, and does not, shock conservative minds to think of giving the 160 acres of homestead land to pioneers, but it does shock them to think of providing a new form of homestead or grubstake for the new age in which we live. The economic difference between the grubstake and a handout is this: The first multiplies wealth and the second is just consumed, with no economic dividend.

To release the energy and creative powers of our own people, the federal government can provide a grant of capital to every able-bodied young man and woman at, say, age twenty-five, just as their ancestors were able to get a capital grant in the form of a homestead. They should get this grant as a matter of right. It should be large enough to permit industrious characters and creative minds to start the foundation for something for themselves. Each individual should pay a special income tax on the profits arising from his grant, which would provide a revolving fund for the continuous operation of the program.

Such a system would provide a continuing expansion of purchasing power to meet the expansion of American industrial and agricultural productivity, thus eliminating depressions. It would release creative ability exactly as did the homestead of pioneer days. It would rid us of the stultifying bureaucracy of the so-called welfare state, and it would restore, above all else, self-reliance and personal responsibility for one's self that typified pioneer America. It would bring back to America the truth in Douglas MacArthur's statement that there is no such thing as security; there is only opportunity.

The greatest teacher is example. The lasting influence of the United States on the rest of the world has been the power of example—demonstrating what ordinary people could do if given an opportunity to release ability dammed up by the caste system of the Old World. Not many of us appreciate today that Jefferson's doctrine of equality of opportunity is the most dynamic and revolutionary political philosophy of all time. The idea that the best, in terms of brains and character, might be in the least of us had never been effectively advanced before the American

Revolution. The strength, greatness, and might of America came from the Jeffersonian concept of opportunity for all. It was not a plan to "play down" to the common level of mediocrity. It was an effort to make it possible for persons of ability to climb to the top of the ladder.

All that is vital in life—and I use the word *vital* in its true sense—comes from the energy of the sun. All that goes to make what the philosophers call the good life comes from the proper direction and utilization of that energy. A satisfying life for men and women, whatever their occupation, comes from a sense of utilizing, of releasing productively, their creative powers. Few were shocked at the idea of President Truman's Point Four program to use American capital in the four quarters of the earth to provide increased opportunity for backward nations. The same people will view with shocked alarm an idea to afford similar opportunities for our own people.

In the last analysis, whatever influence the United States may have for the betterment of ourselves and the world must depend on our own inherent strength. Internationalists may call this isolationism. It is not. It is a realistic recognition that a nation must mobilize its own creative energies before it can effectively contribute to world economic stability and the preservation of peace.

POSTSCRIPT

After Phil left the political field in Wisconsin, he practiced law and continued his efforts at third-party action. His work in these two areas took him to various parts of the country and provided an interesting life.

Through his lifelong friend, the late electronics genius William H. Grimditch—at that time associated with the Hazeltine Electronics Corporation—Phil was brought in as counsel in Hazeltine patent cases and spent much time in New York. Through Hazeltine's president, W. A. MacDonald, Phil was asked to join the Hazeltine Corporation. He accepted, and we moved to Long Island. Phil, who became president of the corporation in 1955, said repeatedly that he "wouldn't take anything for the experience that opened up the world of electronics" to him. Even so—and notwithstanding the fact that we had made many warm friends and enjoyed the wonders of New York City—our roots were still in Wisconsin.

We returned to Madison in 1959, and Phil resumed officing with his old law firm, now headed by Gordon Sinykin. But his main interest was in writing the story of his career in politics, which he hoped would encourage young people to enter public life. After our children had left home we lived quietly, with weekends out at our farm, and periodically resumed friendships from near and far, until Phil's brief illness and his death, on August 18, 1965.

—Isabel Bacon LaFollette

BIBLIOGRAPHY

The documents and the published and unpublished works cited here have been especially helpful to me during the editing of Philip LaFollette's memoirs.

The Philip Fox LaFollette papers, comprising more than one hundred thousand items, are housed in the Division of Archives and Manuscripts of the State Historical Society of Wisconsin, in Madison. The correspondence is divided into a personal and family file and a general file. For a description—still essentially accurate—of the papers at the time they were presented to the library in 1955, see the *Wisconsin Magazine of History* 39:60. (The papers of Robert LaFollette, Sr., through about 1906 are also in the society's archives. Most of his papers after that are in the Library of Congress, as are the papers of Robert LaFollette, Jr. Access to the papers of the LaFollettes is restricted.)

Members of the LaFollette family have contributed much to the published record. *Robert M. LaFollette: June 14, 1855—June 18, 1925* (New York: The Macmillan Company, 1953), a massive two-volume chronicle of the senator's public career, was begun by Belle Case LaFollette and completed after her death by Fola LaFollette. Though of course sympathetic to its subject, the work is remarkable for its accuracy in detail and for the authors' appreciation of public affairs. *LaFollette's Autobiography*, issued in a new edition by the University of Wisconsin Press (Madison) in 1960, is a spirited and candid exposition of the senator's political philosophy, set forth originally in 1911 and 1912. Mrs. Philip LaFollette's unpublished memoirs, "If You Can Take It," written during the 1940's, reveals the author's keen understanding of politics and human nature. In *These Things Are Mine* (New York: The Macmillan Company, 1947), George Middleton offers some insights into the personal lives of his in-laws.

Only one author has written of both generations of the LaFollettes within one book, and Edward N. Doan's *The LaFollettes and the Wisconsin Idea* (New York: Rinehart & Company, Inc., 1947) is superficial and uncritical.

Published material on Wisconsin politics between 1900 and 1925 is voluminous, as one might expect considering the pioneering contributions of the state's Progressive reform movement. I will mention here only two recent contributions that may be of interest to the readers of this memoir: *The Decline of the Progressive Movement in Wisconsin, 1890–1920* (Madison: The State Historical Society of Wisconsin, 1968) by Herbert F. Margulies, and David A. Shannon's provocative article, "Was McCarthy a Political Heir of LaFollette" in the *Wisconsin Magazine of History* 45: 3-9.

To appreciate fully the more specialized works on Wisconsin politics during the Depression, one may wish to proceed first from Richard Hofstadter's *The Age of Reform* (New York: Alfred A. Knopf, 1955) through Russel B. Nye's *Midwestern Progressive Politics: A Historical Study of Its Origins and Development, 1870-1950* (East Lansing: Michigan State College Press, 1951) to Donald R. McCoy's *Angry Voices: Left-of-Center Politics in the New Deal Era* (Lawrence: University of Kansas Press, 1958). McCoy deals at length with the National Progressives of America and establishes how Governor LaFollette's movement fitted into the leftist political picture during the 1930's.

The best insight into how midwestern Progressives responded to the economic and social issues of the Great Depression era will be afforded to those who study the five hundred-odd issues of *The Progressive* published in Madison during the time William T. Evjue was editor, from 1929 to 1940.

A general—and approving—overview of Governor LaFollette's three administrations has been written by Walter Brandeis Raushenbush in "Wisconsin Under Governor Philip LaFollette: A Study in Creative State Government" (Senior honors thesis, Harvard College, 1950), which includes a useful account of the adoption of Wisconsin's unemployment compensation law. That topic is also the subject of Daniel Nelson's "The Origins of Unemployment Insurance in Wisconsin," in the *Wisconsin Magazine of History* 51: 109-121, and of Paul Raushenbush's

"Starting Unemployment Compensation in Wisconsin," in the April-May 1967 issue of *Unemployment Insurance Review*, 17-24.

Other specialized studies include L. David Carley's "The Wisconsin Governor's Legislative Role: A Case Study in the Administrations of Philip Fox LaFollette and Walter J. Kohler Jr." (Ph.D. thesis, University of Wisconsin, 1959) and Samuel Mermin's *Jurisprudence and Statecraft: The Wisconsin Development Authority and Its Implications* (Madison: The University of Wisconsin Press, 1963).

The LaFollette brothers' political careers have attracted much attention. Roger T. Johnson's *Robert M. LaFollette, Jr., and the Decline of the Progressive Party in Wisconsin* (Madison: The State Historical Society of Wisconsin, 1964) is based on extensive interviewing and on published and unpublished material. It contains a lengthy account of the 1946 election. Charles H. Backstrom's "The Progressive Party of Wisconsin, 1934–1946" (Ph.D. thesis, University of Wisconsin, 1956) is the best of the unpublished studies of the LaFollette brothers as political leaders. Karl E. Meyer's "The Politics of Loyalty: From LaFollette to McCarthy in Wisconsin, 1918–1952" (Ph.D. dissertation, Princeton University, 1956) is valuable for its analysis of the elections of 1932 and 1946 (among others).

Magazine coverage of the brothers' political activities during their heyday was extensive, usually uncritical, and repetitious. Of some value in measuring contemporary attitudes toward the brothers, and particularly Phil, are: Louis Adamic, "A Talk with Phil LaFollette," *The Nation* 140: 242-245; Mark Rhey Byers, "A New LaFollette Party," *North American Review* 237: 401-409; Elmer Davis, "The Wisconsin Brothers: A Study in Partial Eclipse," *Harper's Magazine* 178: 268-277; Max Lerner, "Phil LaFollette—an Interview," *The Nation* 146: 552-555; and Henry F. Pringle, "Youth at the Top," *World's Work* 58: 85, 156-162.

John B. Chapple's *LaFollette Socialism* and *LaFollette Road to Communism—Must We Go Further Along That Road* (privately published in Ashland, Wisconsin, in 1931 and 1936) are vitriolic examples of anti-LaFollette literature.

Philip LaFollette's opposition to Franklin Roosevelt's foreign policy in the late 1930's is touched on briefly in Wayne S. Cole's *America First: The Battle Against Intervention* (Madison: The University of Wisconsin Press, 1953). See also Alan Edmond Kent's "Portrait in Isolationism: The LaFollettes and Foreign Policy" (Ph.D. thesis, University of Wisconsin, 1956), which also contains material on the brothers' political activities, and which is based on extensive interviewing and on examination of primary sources.

Glenn Frank's downfall at the University of Wisconsin is narrated objectively and in detail by Lawrence H. Larsen in *The President Wore Spats* (Madison: The State Historical Society of Wisconsin, 1965). George C. Sellery included a restrained account of the "Frank Case" in *Some Ferments at Wisconsin, 1901–1947: Memories and Reflections* (Madison: University of Wisconsin Press, 1960). The ousting of President Frank is also reported in depth by the New York *Times* in its issues of December 1936 and January 1937.

References essential for the student of Wisconsin political history include the *Dictionary of Wisconsin Biography* (Madison: The State Historical Society of Wisconsin, 1960) and *The Wisconsin Blue Book*, published biennially by the state. Histories of the state now available will be superseded by the six-volume *History of Wisconsin* now being prepared by the State Historical Society of Wisconsin.

SOURCES

The sources for some quotations in the main text and in the editor's notes are apparent from the context in which the quotations are presented. Sources for some of the other quotations are as follows:

Foreword: Hofstadter's observations about "comfortable people" are from *The Age of Reform*, 241. Belle Case LaFollette wrote of "the very fiber of his political thought" in *Robert M. LaFollette*, 24. The specter of a "University State" was raised by Charles P. Cary, Wisconsin state superintendent of instruction; he is quoted in Margulies, 148. Phil LaFollette's interpretation of the Wisconsin Idea is from the Adamic article cited in the bibliography. John Wyngaard, manager of the Madison News Bureau, described Bob, Jr., as a *"gentle* man." Robert LaFollette warned against accepting "half a loaf" in his *Autobiography*, 166. Lilienthal's recollections were contained in a letter to the editor, February 25, 1969. Phil's characterizations of liberalism and radicalism were quoted in his obituary in the New York *Times*, August 19, 1965. Phil's remark about the legislature was quoted in the *Capital Times* of September 29, 1937, and cited by Backstrom, 451. LaFollette's assessment of Hitler is from Lerner's article cited in the bibliography.

Chapter 2: The description of Phil and Mary performing farm chores is from Belle Case LaFollette's biography, 215. The Alice Wood article appeared in the Blowing Rock, North Carolina, *Blowing Rocket*, January 7, 1966. The incident involving Bob, Jr., and Senator Aldrich's speech is from Belle Case LaFollette, 240-241; Bob, Jr.'s, letter to his family is quoted from the same biography, as continued by Fola LaFollette, 513-514.

Chapter 5: Robert LaFollette's letter to his family at Christmas, 1918, is from Fola LaFollette's biography, 908.

Chapter 20: Backstrom's thesis, 452, contains Phil's assessment of how a massive and militant political organization could be built up.

Chapter 21: Deutsch's observations on the anti-Hitler conspiracies are contained in letters to the editor dated June 20 and July 10, 1969.

INDEX